MCSA
Readiness Review

Managing a Microsoft

WINDOWS® 2000
NETWORK
ENVIRONMENT

Exam 70-218

PUBLISHED BY
Microsoft Press
A Division of Microsoft Corporation
One Microsoft Way
Redmond, Washington 98052-6399

Library of Congress Cataloging-in-Publication Data
MCSA Managing a Microsoft Windows 2000 Network Environment Readiness Review :
Exam 70-218 / Microsoft Corporation.
      p. cm.
  Includes index.
  ISBN 0-7356-1636-1
  1. Electronic data processing personnel--Certification. 2. Microsoft
software--Examinations--Study guides. 3. Microsoft Windows (Computer file) I.
Microsoft Corporation.

  QA76.3 .M32657 2002
  005.4'4769--dc21   2001059073

Printed and bound in the United States of America.

1 2 3 4 5 6 7 8 9   QWE   7 6 5 4 3 2

Distributed in Canada by Penguin Books Canada Limited.

A CIP catalogue record for this book is available from the British Library.

Microsoft Press books are available through booksellers and distributors worldwide. For further information about international editions, contact your local Microsoft Corporation office or contact Microsoft Press International directly at fax (425) 936-7329. Visit our Web site at www.microsoft.com/mspress. Send comments to *mspinput@microsoft.com*.

Acquisitions Editor: Kathy Harding
Project Editor: Kurt Stephan

Body Part No. X08-68162

Contents

Objective Domain 3: Managing, Securing, and Troubleshooting Servers and Client Computers. 103

Objective Domain 4: Configuring, Managing, Securing, and Troubleshooting Active Directory Organizational Units and Group Policy 145

Objective Domain 5: Configuring, Securing, and Troubleshooting Remote Access 199

Welcome to Managing a Microsoft Windows 2000 Network Environment

Welcome to *MCSA Readiness Review—Exam 70-218: Managing a Microsoft Windows 2000 Network Environment*. The Readiness Review series gives you a focused, timesaving way to identify the information you need to know to pass the Microsoft Certified Professional (MCP) exams. The series combines a realistic electronic assessment with a review book to help you become familiar with the types of questions that you will encounter on the MCP exam. By reviewing the objectives and sample questions, you can focus on the specific skills you need to improve before taking the exam.

This book helps you evaluate your readiness for the MCP Exam 70-218: Managing a Microsoft Windows 2000 Network Environment. When you pass this exam, you earn core credit toward Microsoft Certified System Administrator (MCSA) on Microsoft Windows 2000 certification, and elective credit toward Microsoft Certified Systems Engineer (MCSE) on Microsoft Windows 2000 certification. In addition, when you pass this exam you achieve MCP status.

Note You can find a complete list of MCP exams and their related objectives on the Microsoft Certifications Web site at *http://www.microsoft.com/traincert/mcp/default.asp*.

The Readiness Review series lets you identify any areas in which you might need additional training. To help you get the training you need to pass the certification exams, Microsoft Press publishes a complete line of self-paced training kits and other study materials. For comprehensive information about the topics covered in the Managing a Microsoft Windows 2000 Network Environment exam, see the corresponding training kit—*MCSA Training Kit: Managing a Microsoft Windows 2000 Network Environment.*

Before You Begin

This MCSA Readiness Review consists of two main parts: the Readiness Review electronic assessment program on the accompanying CD-ROM, and this Readiness Review book.

The Readiness Review Components

The electronic assessment is a practice certification test that helps you evaluate your skills. It provides instant scoring feedback, so you can determine areas in which additional study might be helpful before you take the certification exam. Although your score on the electronic assessment does not necessarily indicate what your score will be on the certification exam, it does give you the opportunity to answer questions that are similar to those on the actual certification exam.

The Readiness Review book is organized by the exam's objectives. Each chapter of the book pertains to one of the five primary groups of objectives on the actual exam, called the *Objective Domains*. Each Objective Domain lists the tested skills you need to master to adequately answer the exam questions. Because the certification exam focuses on real-world skills, the Tested Skills and Suggested Practices lists provide practices that emphasize the practical application of the exam objectives. Each Objective Domain also provides suggestions for further reading or additional resources to help you understand the objectives and increase your ability to perform the task or skills specified by the objectives.

Within each Objective Domain, you will find the related objectives that are covered on the exam. Each objective provides you with the following:

- **Key terms** you must know to understand the objective. Knowing these terms can help you answer the objective's questions correctly.

- Several sample exam questions with the correct answers. The answers are accompanied by explanations of each correct and incorrect answer. (These questions match the questions on the electronic assessment.)

You use the electronic assessment to determine the exam objectives that you need to study, and then use the Readiness Review book to learn more about those particular objectives and discover additional study materials to supplement your knowledge. You can also use the Readiness Review book to research the answers to specific sample test questions. Keep in mind that to pass the exam, you should understand not only the answer to the question, but also the concepts on which the correct answer is based.

MCP Exam Prerequisites

No exams or classes are required before you take the Managing a Microsoft Windows 2000 Network Environment exam. However, in addition to the skills tested by the exam, you should have a working knowledge of the operation and support of hardware and software on Windows 2000 computers. Microsoft recommends that candidates have at least six months of experience administering and supporting Windows 2000 server and client operating systems in medium to very large computing environments. This knowledge should include:

- Installing or upgrading computers to Windows 2000 Professional and Windows 2000 Server

- Understanding the Windows 2000 networking environment, including Transmission Control Protocol/Internet Protocol (TCP/IP) and local area network (LAN) physical components

- Connecting Windows 2000–based client computers to networks, configuring the Windows 2000 environment, and providing network access to file resources

- Creating and managing user accounts and managing access to resources by using groups

- Managing data by configuring disks, partitions, and the NT file system (NTFS)

- Implementing Windows 2000 security and disaster protection

- Monitoring and optimizing Windows 2000

Note After you use the Readiness Review and determine that you are ready for the exam, use the Get MCP Information link provided in the home page of the electronic assessment tool for information about scheduling for the exam. You can schedule exams up to six weeks in advance or as late as one working day before the exam date.

Know the Products

The Microsoft certification program relies on exams that measure your ability to perform a specific job function or set of tasks. Microsoft develops the exams by analyzing the tasks performed by people who are currently working in the field. Therefore, the specific knowledge, skills, and abilities relating to the job are reflected in the certification exam.

Because the certification exams are based on real-world tasks, you need to gain hands-on experience with the applicable technology to master the exam. Microsoft requires certification candidates to have hands-on experience in an organizational environment to pass an MCP exam. Many of the questions relate directly to Microsoft products or technology, so use opportunities at your organization or home to practice using the relevant tools.

Using the MCSA Readiness Review

Although you can use the Readiness Review in a number of ways, you might start your studies by taking the electronic assessment as a pretest. After completing the exam, review your results for each Objective Domain and focus your studies first on the Objective Domains for which you received the lowest scores. The electronic assessment allows you to print your results, and a printed report of how you fared can be useful when reviewing the exam material in this book.

After you have taken the Readiness Review electronic assessment, use the Readiness Review book to learn more about the Objective Domains you find difficult and to find listings of appropriate study materials that might supplement your knowledge. By reviewing why the answers are correct or incorrect, you can determine whether you need to study the objective topics more.

You can also use the Readiness Review book to focus on the exact objectives that you need to master. Each objective in the book contains several questions that help you determine whether you understand the information related to that particular skill. The book is also designed for you to answer each question before turning the page to review the correct answer.

The best method to prepare for the MCP exam is to use the Readiness Review book in conjunction with the electronic assessment and other study material. Thoroughly studying and practicing the material combined with substantial real-world experience can help you fully prepare for the MCP exam.

Understanding the Readiness Review Conventions

Before you start using the Readiness Review, it is important that you understand the terms and conventions used in the electronic assessment and book.

Question Numbering System

The Readiness Review electronic assessment and book contain reference numbers for each question. Understanding the numbering format will help you use the Readiness Review more effectively. When Microsoft creates the exams, the questions are grouped by job skills called *objectives*. These objectives are then organized by sections known as *Objective Domains*. Each question can be identified by the Objective Domain and the objective it covers. The question numbers follow this format:

Test Number.Objective Domain.Objective.Question Number

For example, question number 70-218.02.01.003 means this is question three (003) for the first objective (01) in the second Objective Domain (02) of the Managing a

Microsoft Windows 2000 Network Environment exam (70-218). Refer to the "Exam Objectives Summary" section later in this introduction to locate the numbers associated with particular objectives. Each question is numbered based on its presentation in the printed book. You can use this numbering system to reference questions on the electronic assessment or in the Readiness Review book. Even though the questions in the book are organized by objective, questions in the electronic assessment and actual certification exam are presented in random order.

Notational Conventions

- Characters or commands that you type appear in **bold lowercase** type.

- Variable information and URLs are *italicized*. *Italic* is also used for book titles.

- Acronyms, filenames, and utilities appear in FULL CAPITALS.

Notes

Notes appear throughout the book.

- Notes marked *Caution* contain information you will want to know before continuing with the book's material.

- Notes marked *Note* contain supplemental information.

- Notes marked *Tip* contain helpful process hints.

Using the Readiness Review Electronic Assessment

The Readiness Review electronic assessment simulates the actual MCP exam. Each iteration of the electronic assessment consists of 50 questions covering all the objectives for the Managing a Microsoft Windows 2000 Network Environment exam. (MCP certification exams generally consist of 50–70 questions.) Just like a real certification exam, you see questions from the objectives in random order during the practice test. Similar to the certification exam, the electronic assessment allows you to mark questions and review them after you finish the test.

To increase its value as a study aid, you can take the electronic assessment multiple times. Each time you are presented with a different set of questions in a revised order; however, some questions might be repeated.

If you have used one of the certification exam preparation tests available from Microsoft, the Readiness Review electronic assessment should look familiar. The difference is that this electronic assessment gives you the opportunity to learn as you take the exam.

Installing and Running the Electronic Assessment Software

Before you begin using the electronic assessment, you have to install the software. You need a computer with the following minimum configuration:

- Multimedia PC with a 75 MHz Pentium or higher processor

- 16 MB RAM for Windows 95 or Windows 98, or

- 32 MB RAM for Windows Me or Windows NT, or

- 64 MB RAM for Windows 2000 or Windows XP

- Internet Explorer 5.01 or later

- 17 MB of available hard disk space (additional 13 MB minimum of hard disk space to install Internet Explorer 6.0 from this CD-ROM)

- A double-speed CD-ROM drive or better

- Super VGA display with at least 256 colors

▶ **To install the electronic assessment**

1. Insert the Readiness Review companion CD-ROM into your CD-ROM drive.

    A starting menu appears, with links to the resources included on the CD-ROM.

Note If your system does not have Microsoft Internet Explorer 5.01 or later, you can install Internet Explorer 6.0 now by selecting the appropriate option on the menu.

---

2. Click Install Readiness Review.

    A dialog box appears, indicating that you will install the Readiness Review to your computer.

3. Click Next.

    The License Agreement dialog box appears.

4. To continue with the installation of the electronic assessment engine, you must accept the License Agreement by clicking Yes.

5. The Choose Destination Location dialog box appears showing a default installation directory. Either accept the default or change the installation directory if needed. Click Next to copy the files to your hard disk.

6. A Question dialog box appears asking whether you want Setup to create a desktop shortcut for this program. If you click Yes, an icon is placed on your desktop.

7. The Setup Complete dialog box appears. Select whether you want to view the README.TXT file after closing the Setup program, and then click Finish.

   The electronic assessment software is completely installed. If you chose to view the README.TXT file, it launches in a new window. For optimal viewing, enable word wrap.

▶ **To start the electronic assessment**

1. From the Start menu, point to Programs, point to MCSE Readiness Review, and then click MCSE RR Exam 70-218.

   The electronic assessment program starts.

2. Click Start Test.

   Information about the electronic assessment program appears.

3. Click OK.

Taking the Electronic Assessment

The Readiness Review electronic assessment consists of 50 multiple-choice questions, and as in the certification exam, you can skip questions or mark them for later review. Each exam question contains a question number that you can use to refer back to the Readiness Review book.

Before you end the electronic assessment, make sure to answer all the questions. When the exam is graded, unanswered questions are counted as incorrect and will lower your score. Similarly, on the actual certification exam you should complete all questions or they will be counted as incorrect. No trick questions appear on the exam. The correct answer is always among the list of choices. Some questions might have more than one correct answer, and this will be indicated in the question. A good strategy is to eliminate the most obvious incorrect answers first to make it easier for you to select the correct answer.

You have 75 minutes to complete the electronic assessment. During the exam, you will see a timer indicating the amount of time you have remaining. This will help you gauge the amount of time you should use to answer each question and to complete the exam. The amount of time you are given on the actual certification exam varies with each exam. Generally, certification exams take approximately 100 minutes to complete, but they can vary from 60 to 300 minutes.

Ending and Grading the Electronic Assessment

When you click the Score Test button, you have the opportunity to review the questions you marked or left incomplete. (This format is not similar to the one used on the actual certification exam, in which you can verify whether you are satisfied with your answers and then click the Grade Test button.) The electronic assessment is graded when you click the Score Test button, and the software presents your section scores and your total score.

Note You can always end a test without grading your electronic assessment by clicking the Home button.

After your electronic assessment is graded, you can view the correct and incorrect answers by clicking the Review Questions button.

Interpreting the Electronic Assessment Results

The Score screen shows you the number of questions in each Objective Domain section, the number of questions you answered correctly, and a percentage grade for each section. You can use the Score screen to determine where to spend additional time studying. On the actual certification exam, the number of questions and passing score depend on the exam you are taking. The electronic assessment records your score each time you grade an exam so you can track your progress over time.

▶   **To view your progress and exam records**

1. From the electronic assessment Main menu, click View History. Each test attempt score appears.

2. Click a test attempt date/time to view your score for each Objective Domain.

    Review these scores to determine which Objective Domains you should study further. You can also use the scores to determine your progress.

Using the Readiness Review Book

You can use the Readiness Review book as a supplement to the Readiness Review electronic assessment, or as a stand-alone study aid. If you decide to use the book as a stand-alone study aid, review the Contents or the list of objectives to find topics of interest or an appropriate starting point for you. To get the greatest benefit from the book, use the electronic assessment as a pretest to determine the Objective Domains for which you should spend the most study time. Or, if you want to research specific questions while taking the electronic assessment, you can use the question number located on the question screen to reference the question number in the Readiness Review book.

One way to determine areas in which additional study might be helpful is to carefully review your individual section scores from the electronic assessment and note objective areas where your score could be improved. The section scores correlate to the Objective Domains listed in the Readiness Review book.

Reviewing the Objectives

Each Objective Domain in the book contains an introduction and a list of practice skills. Each list of practice skills describes suggested tasks you can perform to help you understand the objectives. Some of the tasks suggest reading additional material, while others are hands-on practices with software or hardware. Pay particular attention to the hands-on practices, because the certification exam reflects real-world knowledge you can gain only by working with the software or technology. Increasing your real-world experience with the relevant products and technologies will improve your performance on the exam.

After you choose the objectives you want to study, turn to the Contents to locate the objectives in the Readiness Review book. You can study each objective separately, but you might need to understand the concepts explained in other objectives.

Make sure you understand the key terms for each objective—you will need a thorough understanding of these terms to answer the objective's questions correctly. Key term definitions are located in the Glossary of this book.

Reviewing the Questions

Each objective includes questions followed by the possible answers. After you review the question and select a probable answer, turn to the Answer section to determine whether you answered the question correctly. (For information about the question numbering format, see "Question Numbering System," earlier in this introduction.)

The Readiness Review briefly discusses each possible answer and explains why each answer is correct or incorrect. After reviewing each explanation, if you feel you need more information about a topic, question, or answer, refer to the Further Reading section of that domain for more information.

The answers to the questions in the Readiness Review are based on current industry specifications and standards. However, the information provided by the answers is subject to change as technology improves and changes.

Exam Objectives Summary

The Managing a Microsoft Windows 2000 Network Environment (70-218) exam measures your ability to administer, support, and troubleshoot information systems that incorporate Microsoft Windows 2000. Before taking the exam, you should be proficient with the job skills presented in the following sections. The sections provide the exam objectives and the corresponding objective numbers (which you can use to reference the questions in the Readiness Review electronic assessment and book) grouped by Objective Domains.

Objective Domain 1: Creating, Configuring, Managing, Securing, and Troubleshooting File, Print, and Web Resources

The objectives in Objective Domain 1 are as follows:

- Objective 1.1 (70-218.01.01)—Publish resources in Active Directory. Types of resources include printers and shared folders.

- Objective 1.2 (70-218.01.02)—Manage data storage. Considerations include file systems, permissions, and quotas.

- Objective 1.3 (70-218.01.03)—Create shared resources and configure access rights. Shared resources include printers, shared folders, and Web folders.

- Objective 1.4 (70-218.01.04)—Configure and troubleshoot Internet Information Services (IIS).

- Objective 1.5 (70-218.01.05)—Monitor and manage network security. Actions include auditing and detecting security breaches.

Objective Domain 2: Configuring, Administering, and Troubleshooting the Network Infrastructure

The objectives in Objective Domain 2 are as follows:

- Objective 2.1 (70-218.02.01)—Troubleshoot routing. Diagnostic utilities include the TRACERT command, the PING command, and the IPCONFIG command.

- Objective 2.2 (70-218.02.02)—Configure and troubleshoot TCP/IP on servers and client computers. Considerations include subnet masks, default gateways, network IDs, and broadcast addresses.

- Objective 2.3 (70-218.02.03)—Configure, administer, and troubleshoot DHCP on servers and client computers.

- Objective 2.4 (70-218.02.04)—Configure, administer, and troubleshoot DNS.

- Objective 2.5 (70-218.02.05)—Troubleshoot name resolution on client computers. Considerations include WINS, DNS, NetBIOS, the Hosts file, and the Lmhosts file.

Objective Domain 3: Managing, Securing, and Troubleshooting Servers and Client Computers

The objectives in Objective Domain 3 are as follows:

- Objective 3.1 (70-218.03.01)—Install and configure server and client computer hardware.

- Objective 3.2 (70-218.03.02)—Troubleshoot starting servers and client computers. Tools and methodologies include Safe Mode, Recovery Console, and parallel installations.

- Objective 3.3 (70-218.03.03)—Monitor and troubleshoot server health and performance. Tools include System Monitor, Event Viewer, and Task Manager.

- Objective 3.4 (70-218.03.04)—Install and manage Windows 2000 updates. Updates include service packs, hotfixes, and security hotfixes.

Objective Domain 4: Configuring, Managing, Securing, and Troubleshooting Active Directory Organizational Units and Group Policy

The objectives in Objective Domain 4 are as follows:

- Objective 4.1 (70-218.04.01)—Create, manage, and troubleshoot User and Group objects in Active Directory.

- Objective 4.2 (70-218.04.02)—Manage object and container permissions.

- Objective 4.3 (70-218.04.03)—Diagnose Active Directory replication problems.

- Objective 4.4 (70-218.04.04)—Deploy software by using Group Policy. Types of software include user applications, antivirus software, line-of-business applications, and software updates.

- Objective 4.5 (70-218.04.05)—Troubleshoot end-user Group Policy.

- Objective 4.6 (70-218.04.06)—Implement and manage security policies by using Group Policy.

Objective Domain 5: Configuring, Securing, and Troubleshooting Remote Access

The objectives in Objective Domain 5 are as follows:

- Objective 5.1 (70-218.05.01)—Configure and troubleshoot remote access and virtual private network (VPN) connections.

- Objective 5.2 (70-218.05.02)—Troubleshoot a remote access policy.

- Objective 5.3 (70-218.05.03)—Implement and troubleshoot Terminal Services for remote access.

- Objective 5.4 (70-218.05.04)—Configure and troubleshoot Network Address Translation (NAT) and Internet Connection Sharing.

Getting More Help

A variety of resources are available to help you study for the exam. Your options include instructor-led classes, seminars, self-paced kits, and other learning materials. The materials described here are created to prepare you for MCP exams. Each training resource fits a different type of learning style and budget.

Microsoft Official Curriculum (MOC)

Microsoft Official Curriculum (MOC) courses are technical training courses developed by Microsoft product groups to educate computer professionals who use Microsoft technology. The courses are developed with the same objectives used for Microsoft certification, and MOC courses are available to support most exams for the MCSE and MCSA certifications. The courses are available in instructor-led, online, and self-paced formats to fit your preferred learning style.

Self-Paced Training

Microsoft Press self-paced training kits cover a variety of Microsoft technical products. The self-paced kits are based on MOC courses, feature lessons, hands-on practices, multimedia presentations, practice files, and demonstration software. They can help you understand the concepts and get the experience you need to take the corresponding MCP exam.

To help you prepare for the Managing a Microsoft Windows 2000 Network Environment exam (70-218), Microsoft has written *MCSA Training Kit: Managing a Microsoft Windows 2000 Network Environment*. With this official self-paced training kit, you can learn the fundamentals of administering, supporting, and troubleshooting Windows 2000 networks. This kit gives you training for the real world by offering hands-on, skill-building exercises.

MCP Approved Study Guides

MCP Approved Study Guides, available through several organizations, are learning tools that help you prepare for MCP exams. The study guides are available in a variety of formats to match your learning style, including books, CD-ROMs, online content, and videos. These guides come in a wide range of prices to fit your budget.

Microsoft Seminar Series

Microsoft Solution Providers and other organizations are often a source of information to help you prepare for an MCP exam. For example, many solution providers present seminars to help industry professionals understand a particular product technology, such as networking. For information on all Microsoft-sponsored events, visit *http://www.microsoft.com/usa/events/default.asp*.

Creating, Configuring, Managing, Securing, and Troubleshooting File, Print, and Web Resources

The concepts of sharing folders, printers, and Web sites are similar, but the specific procedures to set up and maintain each network resource are unique. To successfully complete this portion of the *Managing a Microsoft Windows 2000 Network Environment* exam, you must understand the tools and processes used to establish, configure, secure, and maintain each type of shared resource. Understanding the fundamental technologies, and the theories from which they were derived, improves your chances of both passing the certification test and more effectively performing your role as a Windows 2000 network administrator.

This objective domain tests your ability to create shared network folders, shared printers, and Web sites using Windows 2000–based technologies such as the **Active Directory** service and **Internet Information Services (IIS)** 5. You must know how to use the appropriate tools to set up each type of shared resource, and how to publish those resources so users on the network can more readily locate them. You must also understand how to properly secure these resources, and how to monitor each type for unauthorized attempts to access them. Finally, you need to know how to detect and correct problems that are likely to arise with shared resources. Your ability to perform each of these tasks will be assessed. You will also face a series of case studies to verify that you understand how to use the best method to achieve stated goals most effectively.

Tested Skills and Suggested Practices

The skills that you need to master the Creating, Configuring, Managing, Securing, and Troubleshooting File, Print, and Web Resources objective domain on the *Managing a Microsoft Windows 2000 Network Environment* exam include:

- **Publishing resources in Active Directory.**

  - Practice 1: Use Active Directory Users and Computers to publish users, computers, shared network printers, and shared folders in Active Directory.

  - Practice 2: Identify the types of objects commonly found in Active Directory, and learn how to locate them using the Find dialog box. Use the Find tool in Active Directory Users and Computers to locate printers, users, shared folders, and other types of objects in Active Directory.

- **Managing data storage.**

  - Practice 1: Configure a basic disk, and create two volumes on the disk. Format the first volume with file allocation table 32 (FAT32) and the second volume with NT file system (NTFS). Convert the disk to a dynamic disk, and examine the available volume configuration options.

  - Practice 2: Enable NTFS compression on a volume. Notice how disk space utilization is affected and whether performance is noticeably impacted.

  - Practice 3: Log on as an administrator and create a new user account. Next, create a new folder with a very low disk quota for the new account. Log on as USER1, add files to the folder until the threshold is exceeded, and note the results.

  - Practice 4: Create a DFS root. If you have multiple Windows 2000 Severs in a domain environment, replicate your DFS root and DFS shared folders between multiple servers.

- **Creating shared resources and configuring access rights.**

  - Practice 1: Share a folder using both standard folder sharing and Web sharing. From another computer, connect to the folder using both methods. Access both from Windows Explorer and note which performs better.

  - Practice 2: Create a share that only members of the Administrators group can access.

  - Practice 3: Create a shared folder using the NET SHARE command.

  - Practice 4: Connect to a printer shared using the Internet Printing Protocol (IPP). Print a document, and use a browser to remove the document before it has completed printing.

- **Configuring and troubleshooting Internet Information Services (IIS).**

  - Practice 1: Add a virtual directory and a default document named DEFAULT.HTM. Modify the virtual directory's properties so authentication is required. Access the virtual directory using Microsoft Internet Explorer, and notice that you are prompted for a user name and password. Provide your authentication information, and verify that you can access the virtual directory.

  - Practice 2: Modify NTFS file permissions for a Hypertext Markup Language (HTML) file within the home directory of your default virtual server. Notice that removing Read file permissions for the IUSR_*computername* account causes your browser to prompt you for a user name and password.

  - Practice 3: Install all IIS security hotfixes.

  - Practice 4: Add a virtual File Transfer Protocol (FTP) server. Access it from Internet Explorer by providing a URL that includes both the user name and password. Next, connect to the FTP server using the FTP.EXE command-line utility.

- **Monitoring and managing network security.**

  - Practice 1: Configure success and failure auditing using the Audit Policy tool on a computer running Microsoft Windows 2000 Professional or a member server running one of the Windows 2000 Server editions. Attempt to log on to the computer by typing invalid user names and passwords. Log on to the same system with a legitimate account that has administrative privileges, and examine the security log for events relating to the failed logon attempts.

  - Practice 2: Try connecting to shared resources on that computer over the network from a computer that isn't logged on to the same domain or a trusting domain. When prompted for authentication, type invalid user names and passwords. Examine the security log for events relating to the failed logon attempts, and note how these events differ from the previous exercise.

  - Practice 3: Create and apply a security template on a Windows 2000 Professional computer using the Security Templates snap-in. Manually modify some of the security settings available in the local GPO using the Group Policy editor snap-in. Use the Security Configuration and Analysis snap-in to compare and analyze the current configuration to the one stored in the security template you created. Repeat these same procedures using the command-line tool SECEDIT.EXE.

Further Reading

This section lists supplemental readings by objective. We recommend that you study these sources thoroughly before taking exam 70-218.

Objective 1.1

Microsoft Corporation. *MCSE Training Kit: Microsoft Windows 2000 Directory Services*. Redmond, Washington: Microsoft Press, 2000. Read and complete Lessons 1 through 5 in Chapter 11, "Administering Active Directory."

Microsoft Corporation. *Microsoft Windows 2000 Server Resource Kit*. Volume: *Microsoft Windows 2000 Server Distributed Systems Guide*. Redmond, Washington: Microsoft Press, 2000. Read Chapter 5, "Service Publication in Active Directory," and Chapter 12,"Access Control."

Microsoft Corporation. *Microsoft Windows 2000 Professional Resource Kit*. Redmond, Washington: Microsoft Press, 2000. Read Chapter 23, "Windows 2000 Professional on Microsoft Networks," focusing on the section "Locating Resources on Microsoft Networks."

Objective 1.2

Microsoft Corporation. *MCSE Training Kit: Microsoft Windows 2000 Professional*. Redmond, Washington: Microsoft Press, 2000. Read and complete Lessons 1 and 2 in Chapter 6, "Managing Disks," and Lessons 1, 2, and 3 in Chapter 18, "Managing Data Storage."

Microsoft Corporation. *MCSE Training Kit: Microsoft Windows 2000 Server*. Redmond, Washington: Microsoft Press, 2000. Read and complete Lesson 1 in Chapter 2, "Installing and Configuring Microsoft Windows 2000 Server," paying particular attention to the sections on disk partitions and file systems, Read and complete Lessons 1 through 4 in Chapter 4, "Microsoft Windows 2000 File Systems," Lessons 1 and 2 in Chapter 5, "Advanced File Systems," Lesson 2 in Chapter 11, "Microsoft Windows 2000 Security," and Lesson 1 in Chapter 13, "Monitoring and Optimization."

Microsoft Corporation. *Microsoft Windows 2000 Professional Resource Kit*. Redmond, Washington: Microsoft Press, 2000. Read Chapter 17, "File Systems," and Chapter 32, "Disk Concepts and Troubleshooting."

Microsoft Corporation. *Microsoft Windows 2000 Server Administrator's Companion*. Redmond, Washington: Microsoft Press, 2000. Read Chapter 14, "Implementing Disk Management," and Chapter 16, "Configuring Storage."

Objective 1.3

Microsoft Corporation. *MCSE Training Kit: Microsoft Windows 2000 Professional.* Redmond, Washington: Microsoft Press, 2000. Read and complete Lessons 1 through 5 in Chapter 12, "Setting Up and Configuring Network Printers," Lessons 1 through 5 in Chapter 13, "Administering Network Printers," Lessons 1 through 4 in Chapter 15, "Administering Shared Folders," and Lessons 1 through 4 in Chapter 20, "Monitoring Access to Network Resources."

Microsoft Corporation. *MCSE Training Kit: Microsoft Windows 2000 Server.* Redmond, Washington: Microsoft Press, 2000. Read and complete Lessons 1 through 5 in Chapter 8, "Administering Print Services."

Microsoft Corporation. *Microsoft Windows 2000 Server Administrator's Companion.* Redmond, Washington: Microsoft Press, 2000. Read Chapter 8, "Installing and Managing Printers."

Objective 1.4

Microsoft Corporation. *Microsoft Internet Information Services 5.0 Documentation.* Redmond, Washington: Microsoft Press, 1999. Read Chapter 2, "Server Administration."

Microsoft Corporation. *Microsoft Windows 2000 TCP/IP Protocols and Services Technical Reference.* Redmond, Washington: Microsoft Press, 2000. Read Chapter 19, "Internet Information Server (IIS) and the Internet Protocols."

Microsoft Corporation. *Microsoft Windows 2000 Server Administrator's Companion.* Redmond, Washington: Microsoft Press, 2000. Read Chapter 27, "Basics of Internet Information Services" and Chapter 28, "Advanced Internet Information Services."

Objective 1.5

Microsoft Corporation. *MCSE Training Kit: Microsoft Windows 2000 Directory Services.* Redmond, Washington: Microsoft Press, 2000. Read and complete Lessons 1 through 5 in Chapter 9, "Securing Network Resources," Lessons 1 through 4 in Chapter 10, "Administering Shared Folders," Lessons 1, 2, 3, and 6 in Chapter 12, "Administering Group Policy," and Lessons 1 through 7 in Chapter 13, "Administering a Security Configuration."

Microsoft Corporation. *Microsoft Windows 2000 Server Resource Kit.* Volume: *Microsoft Windows 2000 Server Distributed Systems Guide.* Redmond, Washington: Microsoft Press, 2000. Read Chapter 12, "Access Control," and Chapter 22, "Group Policy."

Microsoft Corporation. *Microsoft Windows 2000 Server Resource Kit.*
Volume: *Microsoft Windows 2000 Server Deployment Planning Guide.* Redmond,
Washington: Microsoft Press, 2000. Read Chapter 11, "Planning Distributed Security,"
and Chapter 17, "Determining Windows 2000 Network Security Strategies."

Microsoft Corporation. *Microsoft Windows 2000 Professional Resource Kit.* Redmond,
Washington: Microsoft Press, 2000. Read Chapter 13, "Security."

Internet Security Systems. *Microsoft Windows 2000 Security Technical Reference.*
Redmond, Washington: Microsoft Press, 2000. Read the entire book but focus on
Chapter 10, "Auditing," and Chapter 11, "Network Security."

O B J E C T I V E   1 . 1

Publish resources in Active Directory.

As the administrator of a Windows 2000 network, you must know how to securely publish network resources to users so they can easily locate the information they need to do their jobs. **Active Directory** service keeps track of the locations of network resources, and Windows makes it easy for users to find that information. Active Directory service includes a security infrastructure that allows you to selectively publish resources so only authorized users can access them. The types of objects you can publish in Active Directory service include users, printers, folders, files, computers, and network services.

Information about computers and users is automatically published to Active Directory service when their accounts are created. Information that might be useful to other network users is made available to all authenticated users, while sensitive information is made available only to administrative groups such as Domain Admins and Enterprise Admins. You must deliberately publish shared folders using the **Active Directory Users and Computers Microsoft Management Console (MMC)** console. To publish a shared folder, right-click the Active Directory container, select New, and then click Shared Folder. In the New Object – Shared Folder dialog box, type the name and **Universal Naming Convention (UNC)** path to the shared folder. Publishing a printer is similar; after the printer is installed on the desired computer, open the Active Directory Users and Computers MMC console. Right-click the container where you want to publish the printer, select New, and then click Printer. In the New Object – Printer dialog box, type the name and UNC path to the shared printer.

Network-enabled services can also be published to the directory so administrators can quickly find and administer them using the **Active Directory Sites and Services** MMC console. Do not publish services focused toward the local machine to the directory; publish only services that will be accessed over the network. Other services you can consider including are those that might be useful to numerous users, are relatively steady, and have easily defined and articulated properties. For this exam, you don't need to know how to develop a program that is a network service and configure it to publish itself to Active Directory, but you should understand the concepts relating to service publication. Examples of services included with Windows 2000 Server that are published to the directory include Microsoft Certificate Services and Microsoft

Message Queuing. By opening the Active Directory Sites and Services MMC console and selecting the View menu and then Show Services Node, you can manage properties of these services across the entire domain. You can publish certificate templates for Certificate Services and perform many other administrative tasks.

In addition to these skills, you should know how to locate objects in Active Directory using Windows Explorer as well as the Active Directory Users and Computers MMC console. Windows Explorer allows you to quickly locate objects and view their properties, while you use the Active Directory Users and Computers MMC console to create new objects or modify and delete existing objects. Finally, to successfully complete this portion of the exam you should know how to troubleshoot problems with resource publication. Common errors are caused by incorrect permissions on objects, network connectivity problems, or failed Flexible Single Master Operations (FSMO) role holders.

Objective 1.1 Questions

70-218.01.01.001

You are one of many systems administrators at a medium-sized company. The company has grown quickly, and sometimes there is confusion regarding who is responsible for specific tasks. A manager in your firm's marketing department, Jim, resigned his position today. You attempt to delete his user account from the domain but find that it has already been removed. You know that auditing has been properly configured and want to verify that Jim's account has been properly removed and determine who made the deletion. What do you do?

A. Examine system events in the security log on each domain controller.

B. Examine account management events in the security log on the primary domain controller (PDC) emulator.

C. Examine warning events in the Active Directory log on each domain controller.

D. Examine account management events in the security log on each domain controller.

70-218.01.01.002

You are the administrator of a medium-sized Active Directory domain with three domain controllers. There are two other servers running DNS, DHCP, file services, print services, and certificate services. Your users connect to the network using 75 Windows 2000 Professional computers. You log on to your desktop computer and try to create a user account for a new employee but are unable to do so. You verify that no other users have the same logon name and try again, but you receive the same error message. What is the most likely cause of this problem?

A. The DNS servers are unavailable.

B. You can't create domain accounts from Windows 2000 Professional computers.

C. Your account doesn't have sufficient privileges.

D. The relative ID (RID) FSMO domain controller is unavailable.

70-218.01.01.003

Your organization consists of three Active Directory domains. You are the administrator for the Manufacturing domain and a member of the Enterprise Admins group in the root domain of your Active Directory forest, contoso.com. Users of your domain regularly access resources in the Corporate domain, as do members of the Sales domain. Today, numerous users are reporting problems connecting to servers in the Corporate domain. You are also unable to access resources in either the Corporate or Sales domains. You use PING.EXE to check for connectivity with domain controllers in the Sales and Corporate domains.

See the following figure for the output that appears.

```
C:\>ping corp-dc-02

Pinging corp-dc-02.corporate.contoso.com [192.168.22.5] with 32 bytes of data:

Reply from 192.168.22.5: bytes=32 time 70ms TTL=128
Reply from 192.168.22.5: bytes=32 time 80ms TTL=128
Reply from 192.168.22.5: bytes=32 time 75ms TTL=128
Reply from 192.168.22.5: bytes=32 time 85ms TTL=128

Ping statistics for 192.168.22.5:
    Packets: Sent = 4, Received = 4, Lost = 0 (0 loss),
Approximate round trip times in milli-seconds:
    Minimum = 70ms, Maximum = 85ms, Average = 80ms

C:\>ping sales-dc-01

Pinging sales-dc-01.sales.contoso.com [192.168.23.6] with 32 bytes of data:

Reply from 192.168.23.6: bytes=32 time 60ms TTL=128
Reply from 192.168.23.6: bytes=32 time 70ms TTL=128
Reply from 192.168.23.6: bytes=32 time 65ms TTL=128
Reply from 192.168.23.6: bytes=32 time 75ms TTL=128

Ping statistics for 192.168.23.6:
    Packets: Sent = 4, Received = 4, Lost = 0 (0 loss),
Approximate round trip times in milli-seconds:
    Minimum = 60ms, Maximum = 75ms, Average = 70ms

C:\>
```

Which of the following answers is the most likely explanation for this situation?

A. The trust between the domains has failed.

B. The DNS servers have failed.

C. One or more routers on the network are down.

D. The users do not have sufficient privileges to access resources in the other domains.

70-218.01.01.004

You want to publish a shared folder running on a Microsoft Windows NT 4 server to Active Directory. The server is a member server of the Active Directory domain. You open the Active Directory Users and Computers MMC console, and expand the tree of containers until you can view the organizational unit (OU) where you want to publish the folder. You right-click that OU and a menu appears.

See the following figure.

Which option should you select next from the menu to publish the folder?

A. You cannot publish shared folders located on Windows NT 4 servers in Active Directory service.

B. Select New.

C. Select Properties.

D. Select All Tasks.

70-218.01.01.005

You install Certificate Services on a Windows 2000 Server that is a member server in the Active Directory domain you administer. You install Certificate Services as an Enterprise Root certificate authority (CA) integrated with Active Directory service. You open the Active Directory Sites and Services MMC console to configure Certificate Services in Active Directory service, but you see only the Sites node; the Services node is not present. What is the most probable cause?

A. The Sysvol share is corrupted.

B. Your domain account does not have sufficient privileges to access that node within the Active Directory Sites and Services MMC console.

C. You have not enabled the node in the Active Directory Sites and Services MMC console.

D. The FSMO PDC emulator is unavailable.

Objective 1.1 Answers

70-218.01.01.001

▶ **Correct Answers: D**

  A. **Incorrect:** Creating, changing, and deleting user accounts generate account management events, not system events, in the security log on the domain controllers.

  B. **Incorrect:** Although creating, changing, and deleting user accounts do generate account management events, they can occur on any domain controller in the domain for the reasons outlined in answer D.

  C. **Incorrect:** Account management events are recorded in the security log, not in the Active Directory log of the domain controllers.

  D. **Correct:** Look at the security log on each domain controller in the domain where Jim's account was located. Creating, changing, and deleting user accounts generate success audits of the account management category on whatever domain controller records the change. Because Windows 2000 Active Directory domains are multimaster, the change could have occurred on any of the domain controllers.

70-218.01.01.002

▶ **Correct Answers: D**

  A. **Incorrect:** Because you are able to log on to your desktop computer normally, at least one of the DNS servers must be functioning properly.

  B. **Incorrect:** You can manage Active Directory and other Windows 2000 network services from Windows 2000 Professional computers by installing the optional Administrative Pack (ADMINPAK.MSI). This component is available on the Windows 2000 Server and Microsoft Windows 2000 Advanced Server installation media; it is automatically copied to %systemroot%\System32\ during the installation of those operating systems.

  C. **Incorrect:** The question states that you are the administrator for the domain; members of the Domain Admins group have sufficient privileges to create new user accounts by default in Windows 2000.

  D. **Correct:** Although Active Directory is based on a multimaster architecture, there are still certain roles, known as Single Master Operations roles, that can belong only to a single domain controller in the domain. One of the FSMO roles is the RID domain controller. The responsibility of this role is to generate unique identification numbers for each object added to the domain. If the RID FSMO domain controller is offline for any reason, you are unable to create new objects in the domain—including new user accounts.

70-218.01.01.003

▶ **Correct Answers: A**

A. **Correct:** This is the most likely cause of this problem. To correct this situation, use the Active Directory Domains and Trusts MMC console to reestablish the trusts between the Manufacturing domain and the two other domains. Note that the PDC emulator (another of the FSMO roles for domain controllers) must be available in each domain to establish a trust.

B. **Incorrect:** The results of the PING commands to domain controllers in the Sales and Corporate domains clearly show that name resolution through DNS is working properly.

C. **Incorrect:** The results of the PING commands to domain controllers in the Sales and Corporate domains clearly show that your computer is able to send and receive traffic to and from those computers.

D. **Incorrect:** This is a possible explanation, but it is unlikely that multiple users as well as a member of the Enterprise Admins group would all simultaneously have their permissions restricted in two other domains. Answer A provides a much more likely explanation.

70-218.01.01.004

▶ **Correct Answers: B**

A. **Incorrect:** Windows NT 4 computers can belong to Active Directory–based domains, and shared resources located on computers running that operating system can be published to Active Directory service.

B. **Correct:** After you select New from the menu, a submenu appears; selecting Shared Folder from that menu opens the New Object – Shared Folder dialog box. Type the name for the published folder and the UNC path to the shared folder in that dialog box, and then click OK.

C. **Incorrect:** Selecting Properties from the menu opens the Properties dialog box for the OU. This dialog box is used to configure many properties for the OU, but there is no way to publish objects such as shared folders to an OU using this dialog box.

D. **Incorrect:** Selecting All Tasks from the menu opens a submenu with several options: Delegate Control, Add Members To A Group, Move, and Find. None of these options can be used to publish shared folders or other objects to Active Directory service.

70-218.01.01.005

▶ **Correct Answers: C**

A. **Incorrect:** If the Sysvol share (also called the System Volume) were to become corrupted, problems with Active Directory service would appear; however, the absence of the Services node in the Active Directory Sites and Services MMC console would probably not be one of them.

B. **Incorrect:** If your account had limited access to the domain, you would not have been able to install Certificate Services within the directory.

C. **Correct:** By default, the Services node is hidden when you open Active Directory Sites and Services the first time. At any time, you can enable or disable the display of the Services node in that console by selecting the View menu and then clicking Show Services Node.

D. **Incorrect:** If the PDC emulator domain controller were unavailable, the Services node would still be visible in the Active Directory Sites and Services MMC console, provided you enabled it as described in answer C.

O B J E C T I V E   1 . 2

Manage data storage.

The most fundamental role of Windows 2000 is to provide network access to data. Managing that data, and the storage on which it resides, is a key aspect of effective systems administration. To master this objective, you must understand how Windows 2000 manages storage, including the advantages of **basic** and **dynamic disks**, the differences among file systems, the relationships between file and share permissions, and how to configure disk quotas.

The essential unit of storage in Windows 2000 is the disk, which relates directly to the physical disks connected to the computer. Windows 2000 and Microsoft Windows XP can support either basic or dynamic disks. Basic disks provide compatibility with older Microsoft operating systems, and dynamic disks provide more flexibility when configuring **volumes**.

Volumes are a layer logically above the disk and provide the flexibility that disks cannot. Any type of disk can support multiple volumes. Beyond these **simple volumes**, dynamic disks allow **spanned** and **striped volumes**, which can span multiple disks. This provides administrators with the ability to design the logical drive layout without being bound to the physical disk configuration.

Data cannot be stored directly on a volume—it must be formatted with a file system. File systems reside logically above volumes and interact directly with the operating system. Windows 2000 supports three file systems for fixed drives: **FAT (file allocation table)**, **FAT32**, and **NTFS (NT file system)**. NTFS is the preferred file system, while FAT and FAT32 exist for backward compatibility with older Windows operating systems. Other file systems are supported for use with removable media. **FAT12** is a version of FAT optimized for floppy disks. CD-ROMs are formatted with the **CD-ROM File System (CDFS)**. **Universal Disk Format (UDF)** is primarily used for digital video disc (DVD) access.

NTFS provides important features that aren't supported on other file systems, such as file permissions, Encrypting File System (EFS), file compression, and disk quotas. File permissions allow administrators to grant extremely granular privileges to users and groups. By carefully specifying file permissions, you can ensure only appropriate users can read or modify files. EFS protects data when Windows 2000 isn't running by encrypting the data as it is written to the file system. Disk quotas limit users from consuming more disk space than an administrator specifies. NTFS file compression reduces space consumed by some types of files, with minimal impact on performance.

Caution Don't confuse file permissions with share permissions. Share permissions are used to restrict users from connecting to a shared folder. File permissions restrict users from accessing a file or folder, either within a share or while logged on locally.

Disk quotas allow administrators to monitor and restrict individual users' storage. Thresholds can be configured to log an event when a user consumes a specific amount of storage. If absolutely necessary, Windows 2000 can be configured to stop users from writing to a volume once their storage threshold has been reached. This can cause problems with many applications, however, and should be used with caution.

Distributed File System (DFS) organizes shared folders on a network so that they appear to be part of a single file system. This enables users to access information stored on different servers without mapping multiple network drives. DFS also provides for replication between multiple file servers, and for fail-over between those servers. This feature provides redundancy for critical shared folders.

Objective 1.2 Questions

70-218.01.02.001

Which of the following types of file systems provide for user-level file permissions?

A. FAT

B. FAT32

C. NTFS

D. CDFS

70-218.01.02.002

Liz Keyser is a user on a Windows 2000–based network and is trying to access a file within the network share \\FILESERV\Budgets. The share permissions on the folder assign Change permissions to Everyone. Her user account, LizK, has been granted Read NTFS privileges to the shared folder and its contents. The user account LizK is a member of the domain user group Non-Managers. The Non-Managers group has been assigned No Access NTFS privileges to the folder and its contents. What are Liz's effective privileges on the file?

A. No Access

B. Read

C. Change

D. Full Control

70-218.01.02.003

Which of the following file systems supports limiting user disk space consumption using disk quotas?

A. FAT

B. FAT32

C. NTFS

D. CDFS

70-218.01.02.004

Don Funk is a user on a Windows 2000–based network and is trying to access a file within the network share \\FILESERV\Training. The share permissions on the folder assign Change permissions to Everyone. His user account, DonF, has been granted Read NTFS privileges to the shared folder and its contents. The user account DonF is a member of the domain user group Trainers. The Trainers group has been assigned Full Control NTFS privileges to the folder and its contents. What are Don's effective privileges on the file?

A. No Access

B. Read

C. Change

D. Full Control

70-218.01.02.005

You have a system in a lab environment configured to use several Microsoft operating systems: Microsoft Windows NT 4 Professional, Windows 2000 Professional, Windows 95, Windows 98, and Windows Me. While running Windows NT 4, you convert a volume from FAT to NTFS. Which operating systems will be able to access the newly converted volume? (Choose all that apply.)

A. Windows NT 4 Professional

B. Windows 2000 Professional

C. Windows 95

D. Windows 98

E. Windows Me

70-218.01.02.006

You have a system in a lab environment configured to use several Microsoft operating systems: Windows NT 4 Professional, Windows 2000 Professional, Windows XP Professional, Windows 98, and Windows Me. While running Windows 2000, you convert a disk from basic to dynamic. Which operating systems will be able to access the newly converted disk? (Choose all that apply.)

A. Windows NT 4 Professional

B. Windows 2000 Professional

C. Windows XP Professional

D. Windows 98

E. Windows Me

70-218.01.02.007

At which level do disk quotas limit a user's disk space consumption?

A. Disks

B. Volumes

C. Folders

D. Files

70-218.01.02.008

Requiring EFS on a volume would prevent which of the following attacks?

A. A hacker uses a brute-force, password-guessing tool to identify a user name and password to access a shared folder across the network.

B. An ex-employee uses a forgotten user account to access a restricted shared folder.

C. A hacker gains physical access to the system, reinstalls Windows 2000, and gains direct access to files that are normally restricted by NTFS file permissions.

D. A hacker users a network protocol analyzer, otherwise known as a sniffer, to view private information as it is transferred from a shared folder.

Objective 1.2 Answers

70-218.01.02.001

▶ **Correct Answers: C**

A. **Incorrect:** The FAT file system does not provide for user-level file permissions.

B. **Incorrect:** The FAT32 file system does not provide for user-level file permissions.

C. **Correct:** Though NTFS has gone through several versions, all versions support user-level file permissions. These permissions provide very granular control over a user's access rights to folders and files.

D. **Incorrect:** CDFS is used only on CD-ROMs. It does not provide for user-level file permissions.

70-218.01.02.002

▶ **Correct Answers: A**

A. **Correct:** Understanding a user's effective privileges for a particular file can be complicated, because there can be several access control entries (ACEs) that apply to a particular user. ACEs can be specific to the user's account, or they can specify one or more groups to which the user belongs. When multiple ACEs apply to a user, Windows 2000 calculates effective privileges by first searching for a No Access ACE. If the user, or any group to which the user belongs, has been assigned No Access, access for that user is denied. In other words, No Access always overrides any other permissions.

B. **Incorrect:** As described by the explanation for answer A, the No Access ACE associated with the Non-Managers group overrides the Read permissions associated with the LizK user account.

C. **Incorrect:** When the folder was shared, the Everyone group was assigned Change share permissions. However, both the NTFS file permissions and the share permissions must be taken into account when calculating a user's effective privileges. The more restrictive permissions always take effect. In this example, the user belongs to a group that has No Access rights to the file. So, although Liz would be able to successfully connect to the share because Everyone has Change access, restrictive NTFS permissions would prevent her from accessing any of the files within the folder.

D. **Incorrect:** As described in the explanation for answer A, the No Access ACE associated with the Non-Managers group overrides all other permissions associated with the LizK user account.

70-218.01.02.003

▶ **Correct Answers: C**

A. **Incorrect:** The FAT file system does not provide for limiting user disk space consumption using disk quotas.

B. **Incorrect:** The FAT32 file system does not provide for limiting user disk space consumption using disk quotas.

C. **Correct:** Windows 2000 provides disk quota capabilities for NTFS volumes only.

D. **Incorrect:** CDFS is used only on CD-ROMs. It does not provide for limiting user disk space consumption using disk quotas.

70-218.01.02.004

▶ **Correct Answers: C**

A. **Incorrect:** The user would have No Access privileges only if the account were explicitly assigned no access, or if the user account had no explicit ACEs at either the share or NTFS level. In this scenario, the user was explicitly assigned permissions at both the share and NTFS levels.

B. **Incorrect:** The user was assigned Read NTFS privileges. However, the user's effective NTFS privileges become Full Control because of the user's membership in the Trainers group. The NTFS permissions are overridden by the more restrictive Change permissions assigned to the shared folder.

C. **Correct:** When the folder was shared, the Everyone group was assigned Change share permissions. These Change permissions are more restrictive than the Full Control privilege assigned to the NTFS files. When share permissions are more restrictive than underlying NTFS permissions, the share permissions take precedence.

D. **Incorrect:** If Don were logged on to the system locally and accessing the file, he would have Full Control over the file because the Trainers group was assigned that level of access. However, because he is accessing the file across a network share, his effective privileges are equal to the more restrictive of the share permissions and NTFS permissions. So, the more restrictive Change permission assigned to the shared folder overrides his Full Control NTFS permissions.

70-218.01.02.005

▶ **Correct Answers: A and B**

A. **Correct:** Windows NT 4 Professional can read from and write to NTFS volumes that are created within Windows NT 4.

B. **Correct:** Windows 2000 Professional can read from and write to NTFS volumes that are created either within Windows NT 4 or Windows 2000.

C. **Incorrect:** Windows 95 cannot read to or write from any type of NTFS volume.

D. **Incorrect:** Windows 98 cannot read to or write from any type of NTFS volume.

E. **Incorrect:** Windows Me cannot read to or write from any type of NTFS volume.

70-218.01.02.006

▶ **Correct Answers: B and C**

A. **Incorrect:** This operating system can read from and write to basic disks, but it cannot access dynamic disks created in Windows 2000. It's impossible to convert a disk with an active file system from dynamic back to basic—the disk must be deleted and recreated for it to be accessible from this operating system. For this reason, create a dynamic disk only if you need the extended functionality provided by basic disks and will not be booting to an operating system older than Windows 2000.

B. **Correct:** Windows 2000 Professional can read from and write to both basic and dynamic disks.

C. **Correct:** Windows XP Professional can read from and write to both basic and dynamic disks.

D. **Incorrect:** This answer is incorrect for the reasons stated in answer A.

E. **Incorrect:** This answer is incorrect for the reasons stated in answer A.

70-218.01.02.007

▶ **Correct Answers: B**

A. **Incorrect:** Disk quotas limit a user's consumption of disk space within a single volume. If that volume spans multiple disks, or multiple volumes reside on a single disk, the user's total space is still calculated based on the files they own within that volume.

B. **Correct:** Disk quotas are calculated based on the total size of all files owned by a user on a single volume. If that volume spans multiple disks, or multiple volumes reside on a single disk, the user's total space is still calculated based on the files he or she owns within that volume.

C. **Incorrect:** Disk quotas can be enabled on a folder-by-folder basis, but a user's disk space consumption is calculated by totaling the sizes of all files owned by that user within that volume.

D. **Incorrect:** Disk quotas cannot be used to limit the size of a single file.

70-218.01.02.008

▶ **Correct Answers: C**

A. **Incorrect:** This type of attack attempts to find a valid user name and password combination by making millions of guesses. EFS does not protect against this type of attack because it does not change the way files are accessed across a network.

B. **Incorrect:** This vulnerability is caused by careless account administration, which cannot be prevented with EFS.

C. **Correct:** EFS encrypts files as they are written to a volume and unencrypts them when an authorized user accesses the files. It is entirely transparent to users while Windows 2000 is running; however, the encrypted files cannot be read if the security for Windows 2000 is bypassed.

D. **Incorrect:** EFS does not protect against this type of attack because it does not change the way files are accessed across a network.

O B J E C T I V E   1 . 3

Create shared resources
and configure access rights.

Windows 2000 does not automatically share resources on the network for other users to access. Sharing resources, and configuring the access rights, is the responsibility of the administrator. Users should understand how to connect to the resources, but administrators need to understand the different ways to create connections and know how to create batch files that automatically map drives to shared folders. To complete this domain objective, you must understand how to perform these tasks and how to troubleshoot issues that are likely to arise.

Sharing folders and printers are similar in many ways. The user interfaces for both are similar and intuitive. Both shared folders and printers rely on the same network communication protocol: **Common Internet File System (CIFS)**. Alternatively, either can be shared using Web protocols on systems that have **IIS** installed.

The most obvious difference between the shared folders and printers is the security settings. Shared printers provide different levels of access that include printing and managing the print queue, whereas shared folders allow for limiting user access to read or modify files.

Objective 1.3 Questions

70-218.01.03.001

Which of the following shares would be hidden from a user browsing network resources?

A. HIDDEN#

B. HIDDEN$

C. HIDDEN%

D. HIDDEN^

70-218.01.03.002

Which of the following built-in Windows 2000 local user groups have privileges to manage printer queues? (Choose all that apply.)

A. Account Operators

B. Administrators

C. Guests

D. Print Operators

E. Server Operators

F. Users

70-218.01.03.003

Which of the following Windows 2000 local user groups can reset account passwords? (Choose all that apply.)

A. Account Operators

B. Administrators

C. Guests

D. Print Operators

E. Server Operators

F. Users

70-218.01.03.004

Which of the following batch files would successfully map a drive to a shared folder called Backup located on a server named FILESERV, copy a file to that folder, and disconnect the shared drive?

A. `NET SHARE Z: \\FILESERV\Backup`

```
   COPY C:\boot.ini Z:\
   NET USE Z: /delete
```

B. `NET USE Z: \\FILESERV\Backup`

```
   COPY C:\boot.ini Z:\
   NET USE Z: /delete
```

C. `NET USE Z: \\FILESERV\Backup`

```
   COPY C:\boot.ini Z:\
   NET STOP Z:
```

D. `NET SESSION Z: \\FILESERV\Backup`

```
   COPY C:\boot.ini Z:\
   NET SESSION Z: /delete
```

70-218.01.03.005

Which of the following IIS subcomponents must be installed to create shared Web folders?

A. FTP Server

B. Microsoft FrontPage 2000 Server Extensions

C. Internet Services Manager (HTML)

D. World Wide Web Server

Objective 1.3 Answers

70-218.01.03.001

▶ **Correct Answers: B**

A. **Incorrect:** This is a valid share name, but the last character of the share name has no special meaning. This share would not be hidden from a user browsing network resources.

B. **Correct:** Share names that end with a $ character are not displayed to users browsing network resources. This is not a method for providing security, because users with proper privileges can still connect to the share if they explicitly type the share's full name. However, it is an effective way to stop users who casually browse the network from being aware that a share exists.

C. **Incorrect:** This answer is incorrect for the reasons stated in answer A.

D. **Incorrect:** This answer is incorrect for the reasons stated in answer A.

70-218.01.03.002

▶ **Correct Answers: B, D, and E**

A. **Incorrect:** Members of the Account Operators group are granted the rights to manage user accounts and group memberships. However, they do not have the ability to manage printer queues.

B. **Correct:** Members of the Administrators group are granted the rights to manage almost every aspect of a Windows 2000 system, including the privilege of managing printer queues.

C. **Incorrect:** The Guests group is intended for users who should have minimal access to a system. As such, this group is not granted the right to manage printer queues.

D. **Correct:** The Print Operators group does have the right to manage printer queues.

E. **Correct:** The Server Operators group does have the right to manage printer queues.

F. **Incorrect:** Members of the Users group have the right to print documents, but they do not have the right to manage printer queues.

70-218.01.03.003

▶ **Correct Answers: A and B**

A. **Correct:** Members of the Account Operators group are granted the rights to manage user accounts and group memberships, including the right to reset account passwords.

B. **Correct:** Members of the Administrators group are granted the rights to manage almost every aspect of a Windows 2000 system, including the privilege of resetting account passwords.

C. **Incorrect:** The Guests group is intended for users who should have minimal access to a system. As such, this group is not granted the right to manage user accounts.

D. **Incorrect:** The Print Operators group's administrative privileges are limited to the right to manage printer queues. The privilege of resetting user account passwords is not included.

E. **Incorrect:** The Server Operators group has the right to manage many aspects of a server but does not have the right to reset account passwords.

F. **Incorrect:** Members of the Users group have the right to change their own passwords but do not have the right to reset the passwords of other user accounts.

70-218.01.03.004

▶ **Correct Answers: B**

A. **Incorrect:** The first line of this batch file contains an error. The NET SHARE command is used to create a new share or list existing shares—it cannot be used to map a drive to a shared folder.

B. **Correct:** This batch file would successfully map the Z network drive to the \\FILESERV\Backup shared folder. After the network drive is mapped, the batch file can refer to the mapped drive just like any locally attached drive. The second line of the batch file copies a file to the network folder, without using any syntax specific to communicating with mapped drives. The last line of the batch file disconnects the mapped drive using the /delete argument of the NET USE command.

C. **Incorrect:** The first two lines of this batch file are correct and would successfully map a drive to a network folder and copy a file to the root of that mapped drive. The third line contains an error—the NET STOP command cannot be used to disconnect mapped drives. NET STOP is used to stop file sharing–related services. For example, the command NET STOP SERVER causes the Server service to stop.

D. **Incorrect:** The first and last lines of this batch file contain errors because they use the NET SESSION command instead of the NET USE command. NET SESSION is used to list the active connections on a system that hosts shared folders, and it cannot be used to map or disconnect network drives.

70-218.01.03.005

▶ **Correct Answers: D**

A. **Incorrect:** The FTP Server subcomponent of IIS is not required to create shared Web folders. FTP is a common protocol for transferring files, but shared Web folders are implemented using HTTP, which is provided by the World Wide Web Server subcomponent.

B. **Incorrect:** The FrontPage 2000 server extensions subcomponent of IIS is not required to create shared Web folders. This subcomponent provides extra functionality specifically for FrontPage users. Shared Web folders are implemented using HTTP, which is provided by the World Wide Web Server subcomponent.

C. **Incorrect:** The Internet Services Manager (HTML) subcomponent of IIS is useful for sites that will be administered remotely using a browser. However, shared Web folders are implemented using HTTP, which is provided by the World Wide Web Server subcomponent.

D. **Correct:** The World Wide Web Server subcomponent of IIS provides HTTP and HTTPS functionality. Shared Web folders are implemented using HTTP and require the World Wide Web Server subcomponent for communications. Without this subcomponent installed, Web folders cannot be used.

OBJECTIVE 1.4

Configure and troubleshoot Internet Information Services (IIS).

Internet Information Services (IIS) was originally designed to allow Windows users to share documents using common Web protocols. As the Web evolved into a critical business tool, IIS added features to meet business needs. You must understand how to configure and troubleshoot the rich set of features and protocols provided by IIS to successfully complete this objective.

Multiple Web sites can run on a single Windows 2000 system because IIS supports **virtual servers**. Each virtual server must have a unique identifying aspect—this can be an Internet Protocol (IP) address, host name, port number, or any combination thereof. **Virtual directories** allow the directory structure within a Web site to be independent of the underlying file structure. For example, the virtual directory /images can be located on a different hard disk, or even a different server, from the root Web directory.

IIS provides several mechanisms for improving security. Restricting content to specific users is as simple as modifying NTFS file permissions. When a user requests a document that the anonymous user account of IIS does not have permission to read, IIS returns a message to the user's browser indicating that a user name and password must be provided. The browser then prompts the user and provides the authentication information to IIS.

Server authentication is important to ensure that a Web site is not being maliciously impersonated. **Secure Sockets Layer (SSL) certificates** provide server authentication, and enable encryption of all network communications using **Hypertext Transfer Protocol Secure (HTTPS)**.

Hypertext Transfer Protocol (HTTP) is the most commonly used communication protocol on the Internet. However, it is not the only method of transferring files. **File Transfer Protocol (FTP)** is a common alternative and is supported by IIS. Configuring FTP virtual servers is intuitive to anyone familiar with configuring virtual Web servers with IIS.

Though Web communications are very reliable, administrators must understand how to troubleshoot problems when they appear. You must be able to identify whether the source of the problem is the client, the network, the operating system, or IIS. Windows 2000 provides many utilities to help you perform this troubleshooting, including PING.EXE, NSLOOKUP.EXE, and TRACERT.EXE. Ultimately, your best tool for troubleshooting might be Internet Explorer—however, these tools are useful only if you understand how the underlying communication mechanisms function.

Objective 1.4 Questions

70-218.01.04.001

Which of the following services must be running to share files via HTTP? (Choose all that apply.)

A. Server

B. IIS Admin Service

C. Computer Browser

D. World Wide Web Publishing Service

E. Indexing Service

70-218.01.04.002

Which of the following IIS services can have their communications encrypted using SSL? (Choose all that apply.)

A. SMTP

B. FTP

C. HTTP

D. NNTP

E. IPSec

70-218.01.04.003

Requiring SSL on a Web folder provides encrypted communications and server authentication and is useful for preventing which of the following attacks?

A. A hacker from an outside network uses a brute-force, password-guessing tool to guess a user name and password to access a protected Web folder.

B. An ex-employee uses a forgotten user account to access a password-protected Web folder.

C. A hacker initiates a distributed denial-of-service (DDOS) attack against a Web server to stop the Web server from being accessible on the network.

D. A hacker users a network protocol analyzer, otherwise known as a sniffer, to view private information as it is transferred between a Web browser and a Web server.

70-218.01.04.004

Which of the following is the default TCP port for FTP?

A. 21

B. 25

C. 80

D. 443

70-218.01.04.005

A user is attempting to browse the IIS intranet site you manage and is receiving an error indicating the server cannot be found. From the user's desk, you verify that the browser returns a server not found error when attempting to access the correct URL, *http://intranet.contoso.com*. To identify the nature of the problem, you open a command prompt and are able to successfully ping the server's host name.

Which of the following is a possible cause of the error?

A. The server is disconnected from the network.

B. The client is disconnected from the network.

C. The server's host name is not listed within DNS.

D. The server's World Wide Web Publishing Service is not started.

70-218.01.04.006

A user is attempting to browse the IIS intranet site you manage and is receiving an error indicating the server cannot be found. From the user's desk, you verify that the browser returns a server not found error when attempting to access the correct URL, *http://intranet.contoso.com*. You attempt to access the intranet server using its IP by typing **http://192.168.203.153**, and you are able to view the correct intranet Web pages.

Which of the following is a possible cause of the error?

A. The server is disconnected from the network.

B. The client is disconnected from the network.

C. The server's host name is not listed within DNS.

D. The server's World Wide Web Publishing Service is not started.

Objective 1.4 Answers

70-218.01.04.001

▶ **Correct Answers: B and D**

A. **Incorrect:** The Server service is required to share folders across a network, but it is not required for Web services such as HTTP.

B. **Correct:** The IIS Admin Service controls all of the services of IIS, including FTP, Simple Mail Transfer Protocol (SMTP), and HTTP. It must be running before any other IIS service can be started, including the World Wide Web Publishing Service, which is responsible for responding to HTTP requests.

C. **Incorrect:** The Computer Browser service helps users find resources when browsing the network. However, it does not publish Web services and is not required for the HTTP.

D. **Correct:** The World Wide Web Publishing Service is the service responsible for processing HTTP requests. Without this service, Windows 2000 cannot accept HTTP requests.

E. **Incorrect:** The Indexing Service facilitates searching IIS-based Web sites; however, it is not required for sharing files via HTTP.

70-218.01.04.002

▶ **Correct Answers: C and D**

A. **Incorrect:** SMTP cannot be encrypted using SSL. The best way to provide encryption for SMTP communications is to use Transport Layer Security (TLS) encryption—a protocol similar to SSL. Alternatively, you can use a virtual private network (VPN) technology such as IP Security (IPSec) or Point-to-Point Tunneling Protocol (PPTP).

B. **Incorrect:** FTP cannot be encrypted using SSL. The best way to provide encryption for FTP communications is to use a VPN technology, such as IPSec or PPTP.

C. **Correct:** Although in theory SSL can be used with any network protocol, in practice, SSL is commonly used only to protect HTTP communications.

D. **Correct:** The Network News Transfer Protocol (NNTP) can be encrypted using SSL by enabling a certificate for the Microsoft NNTP Service. This ensures that communications between the NNTP client and server cannot be intercepted.

E. **Incorrect:** IPSec is a set of protocols designed to improve the privacy of Internet communications. Although IPSec can be used to encrypt IIS protocols, it is not part of IIS and does not rely on SSL encryption.

70-218.01.04.003

▶ **Correct Answers: D**

A. **Incorrect:** This type of attack attempts to find a valid user name and password combination by making millions of guesses. SSL cannot prevent this type of attack because it does not provide for authenticating clients.

B. **Incorrect:** This vulnerability is caused by careless account administration, which cannot be prevented with SSL.

C. **Incorrect:** DDOS attacks flood a server with illegitimate requests so no resources are available to respond to genuine requests. SSL cannot distinguish requests that are part of an attack.

D. **Correct:** Sniffers intercept communications as they travel between a client and a server. Standard HTTP communications cross the network in clear text and can be intercepted by anyone on an intermediate network. If a sniffer intercepts SSL-encrypted communications, they cannot be decrypted without access to the server's private SSL certificate. Therefore, requiring SSL encryption prevents users from sniffing Web traffic.

70-218.01.04.004

▶ **Correct Answers: A**

A. **Correct:** FTP communications default to TCP port 21.

B. **Incorrect:** TCP port 25 is the default port for SMTP communications.

C. **Incorrect:** TCP port 80 is the default port for HTTP communications.

D. **Incorrect:** TCP port 443 is the default port for HTTPS communications.

70-218.01.04.005

▶ **Correct Answers: D**

A. **Incorrect:** You are able to eliminate the possibility that the server is disconnected from the network because the server responded to the PING command. If the server were disconnected from the network, it would not be able to respond to the PING command.

B. **Incorrect:** You are able to eliminate the possibility that the client is disconnected from the network because the server responded to the PING command. If the client were disconnected from the network, no other device would respond to PING.

C. **Incorrect:** You are able to eliminate the possibility that the server's DNS entry is not configured correctly because you issued a PING command using the server's host name as the destination. If the server's host name were not listed correctly within DNS, the PING command would have returned an error.

D. **Correct:** This is the only possible problem. The server responded to the PING command when directed at the server's host name, which indicates that both the client and server are connected to the network and that the server's DNS address is correctly configured.

70-218.01.04.006

▶ **Correct Answers: C**

A. **Incorrect:** You are able to eliminate the possibility that the server is disconnected from the network because the server responded when the IP address was used instead of the host name. If the server were disconnected from the network, it would not be able to respond to any type of request.

B. **Incorrect:** You are able to eliminate the possibility that the client is disconnected from the network because the server responded when the IP address was used instead of the host name. If the client were disconnected from the network, it would not be able to retrieve pages from any Web server.

C. **Correct:** This is the only possible problem. The server responded when Web requests were directed to the server's IP address, which indicates that the true nature of the problem is related to the host name used in the first request. Sending requests directly to a server's IP address is an excellent way to determine whether name resolution is the source of a problem.

D. **Incorrect:** You are able to eliminate the possibility that the World Wide Web Publishing Service is not started because the server did respond when requests were directed to the server's IP address. If the World Wide Web Publishing Service were not started, the server would not respond to any requests.

OBJECTIVE 1.5

Monitor and manage network security.

To effectively manage network security, you must combine the organization's computer technology with well-conceived processes and proper training for all the people who use or administer the network. After a security policy that meets the organization's overall business requirements is implemented, it must still be proactively managed. As a network administrator, one of your responsibilities is to ensure that the security policies continue to be adhered to by all who utilize the computer network. You accomplish this by **auditing** for security vulnerabilities, security breaches, and unauthorized attempts to access resources on the network. There are a number of tools available for auditing Windows 2000–based networks—become familiar with each of them and understand which one to use for auditing a particular aspect of the network.

Perhaps the most critical type of audit to perform is to verify that computers continue to meet your organization's security baseline. In other words, you need to determine whether the computer's security settings have been modified beyond an acceptable degree since deployment. You can quickly accomplish this by using the MMC snap-ins called **Security Templates** and **Security Configuration and Analysis**. You use the Security Templates snap-in to create new templates and to modify or delete existing ones. A Windows 2000 **security template** is a text file that contains security settings such as account policies, user rights, event log configuration, and file system permissions. You use the Security Configuration and Analysis snap-in to compare the current local settings with those defined in a security template; you can also use this snap-in to apply a security template. There is a command-line tool called **SECEDIT.EXE** that includes all the functionality of the Security Configuration and Analysis snap-in. This tool can be called from scripts to automate the application and monitoring of security templates. For example, you might want to use SECEDIT.EXE to apply your organization's custom security template during the unattended installation of Windows 2000 Professional.

Tip To use the Security Configuration and Analysis MMC console, or any other MMC snap-in that doesn't already have a shortcut on the Start menu, open a blank MMC console and manually add the desired snap-in. From the Start menu, select Run and type **mmc**. Select the File menu, choose Add/Remove Snap-in, and then click the Add button. Scroll down the list of available snap-ins, select the desired one, click Add, and close the dialog boxes. You can save your custom console by selecting the File menu and clicking Save.

The tools used to monitor for security breaches and attempts at unauthorized access are the auditing of logon events, auditing of object access, viewing of computer event logs, and examining of the logs generated by other network services such as IIS HTTP logs. You configure **Local Group Policy Object (LGPO) Audit Policy** using the Local Security Settings console, which is located on the Start menu. Select Programs, and then Administrative Tools, and then click Local Security Settings. You can also configure Audit Policy using security templates as described earlier, or you can manage them across multiple computers and users using Active Directory–based **Group Policy Objects (GPOs)**. Group policies are also used to configure many user and computer settings. For the purposes of this objective domain you should be thoroughly familiar with the options available for setting audit account policies such as audit account logon events, password length, and password complexity. Group policies are an effective way to manage computer startup and shutdown scripts as well as user logon and logoff scripts. Windows 2000 and Windows XP have built-in support for several script formats including shell scripts (.cmd and .bat) and Visual Basic Scripting Edition (.vbs and .wsf).

To successfully complete this portion of the exam, you should understand what categories of events each individual Audit Policy includes. For example, enabling success and failure auditing for Account Logon Events causes an event to be written to the local security log each time a user logs on or logs off the computer at the console or through a network connection. When you want to audit access to individual files, folders, registry keys, or printers, you must perform two steps: enable Audit Object Access in the Audit Policy and use Windows Explorer, the Registry Editor, or the printer's properties dialog box to configure auditing. The audit settings for an object are another part of its overall security descriptor, so you can modify the auditing settings for an object by viewing its properties and then selecting the Security tab. Click the Advanced button and configure appropriate auditing settings to allow you to monitor access to it. You should be familiar with the types of entries written to the local security logs when different events occur—you should be able to easily distinguish between a successful and failed logon event, as well as failed attempts to open restricted documents or to execute restricted programs.

Caution Auditing can negatively affect overall system performance. Be particularly careful when configuring auditing on a domain controller or other busy servers. Success auditing can be especially demanding—if you enable success auditing on all files and folders on the system drive for a Windows 2000 Professional computer, it might take several minutes to complete tasks that would normally take less than a second.

Objective 1.5 Questions

70-218.01.05.001

You manage a Windows 2000 Active Directory domain with a single site. You are frustrated that some unauthorized users have been accessing folders stored on several file servers located in the Human Resources OU. These folders contain confidential information about employees and contractors to which only a small number of people should have access. Which of the following actions do you take to determine who is accessing these files while minimizing administrative effort? (Choose all that apply.)

A. Configure an Audit Policy to monitor object access events.

B. Configure an LGPO on each server that includes an Audit Policy.

C. Configure an Audit Policy to monitor logon and logoff events.

D. Assign the Active Directory–based GPO to the domain.

E. Assign the Active Directory–based GPO to the OU containing the servers.

F. Specify the appropriate access and auditing settings in the properties dialog box for each folder to be monitored.

G. Configure an Active Directory GPO with an Audit Policy.

70-218.01.05.002

The administrator for your Windows 2000–based domain has delegated control of the Finance OU to you. The OU contains three child OUs: Servers, Workstations, and Users. These OUs contain computers and user accounts for members of your company's finance department. All these computers and users are located within the New York office of your company, and all the file servers are contained within the Servers OU. You configure auditing for all the files and folders you want to monitor on these systems. What other steps should you perform to enable auditing of file access on these servers while minimizing administrative effort?

A. Configure an Audit Policy in the LGPO for each file server.

B. Configure a GPO with the appropriate Audit Policy, and link the GPO to the Servers OU.

C. Configure a GPO with the appropriate Audit Policy, link the GPO to the Finance OU, and assign the Apply Group Policy and Read permission for the GPO to only the file servers.

D. Configure the Default Domain Policy GPO with the appropriate Audit Policy and assign the Apply Group Policy and Read permission for the GPO to only the file servers.

70-218.01.05.003

You are the administrator for a Windows 2000 Active Directory–based domain. Several members of the Help desk received Windows 2000 training and were recently promoted to your team. Since then, several users have reported problems logging on to the network even though they have made no changes to their computers or their accounts. You believe that one of the new administrators has mistakenly been improperly configuring user accounts, and you want to find out who is responsible so you can help the person better understand how to do the job effectively. What category of events do you monitor to find out who has been modifying the accounts of these users?

A. Account management events

B. System events

C. Account logon events

D. Object access events

70-218.01.05.004

Dave, a user on your network, reports that a consultant who did some work in his department the previous week might have stolen his user name and password. What should you audit to detect activity related to this incident?

A. Successful logon and logoff events

B. Failed logon and logoff events

C. Successful and failed object access events

D. Successful user rights events

70-218.01.05.005

A colleague of yours published a folder for your company's executive management team called Product Plans in Active Directory. Users in the IT, Management, and Dev OUs have access to the folder and its contents. You receive a panicked call from your company's CIO who says several files have been deleted from the folder, and she believes the contents have been sent to a competing corporation since the beginning of the week. You verify that auditing has been configured on the file server that hosts the Product Plans folder.

See the following figure.

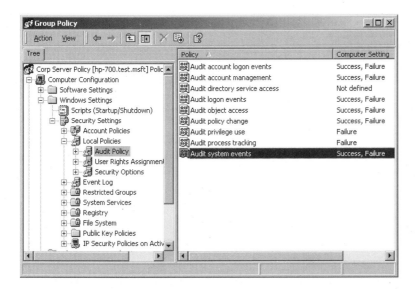

Unfortunately, the Security log on that server contains no events indicating successful or unsuccessful access to the Product Plans folder or its contents. What is the most likely reason for this situation?

A. You failed to audit the Active Directory Sysvol share.

B. You failed to configure auditing for the Product Plans folder using Windows Explorer or security templates.

C. You failed to audit for directory service access.

D. The domain controller must have been unavailable for some reason.

70-218.01.05.006

You have implemented a collection of moderately restrictive security policies on the Windows 2000 network you manage. You have used Active Directory–based GPOs for many settings. For other settings you have combined shell scripts and security templates that are applied during the unattended installation of new Windows 2000 Professional computers. Over time you've become frustrated that some of the users of your network have caused problems by changing policies on their desktop and laptop computers. What is the most efficient and effective way for you to compare the current settings with the intended settings for each computer you need to examine?

A. Configure success and failure object access auditing in an Active Directory–based GPO that applies to all the user's computers.

B. Configure failure object access auditing in an Active Directory–based GPO that applies to all the user's computers. Then use Windows Explorer to configure failure auditing for all the files and folders on the system volume for each computer.

C. Open the LGPO on each computer by selecting Run from the Start menu and typing **GPEDIT.MSC**. Compare the LGPO with the settings you previously designed.

D. Create a custom security template that contains the desired security settings for each type of computer system you need to evaluate. Use the Security Configuration and Analysis template to compare each computer to the appropriate template.

Objective 1.5 Answers

70-218.01.05.001

▶ **Correct Answers: A, E, F, and G**

    A. **Correct:** You must perform a series of steps to effectively monitor the files and folders in question—configuring the Audit Policy to monitor object access events is the second step. The first step is to create an Active Directory GPO that includes an Audit Policy. The third step is to assign the GPO to the OU containing the servers. The fourth step is to configure the appropriate access and auditing settings in the properties dialog box for each folder to be monitored.

    B. **Incorrect:** Although this would help achieve the goal of auditing access to the files and folders on the servers, it is an unnecessarily cumbersome approach. The Audit Policy for all the servers can be managed more efficiently through a single Active Directory–based GPO.

C. **Incorrect:** You are concerned with unauthorized access to specific files and folders—auditing for users logging on locally or connecting to the server over the network will not help you to monitor who is accessing the sensitive information.

D. **Incorrect:** Although this would help achieve the goal of auditing access to the files and folders on the servers, it will also apply the auditing settings to all other computers in the domain. Because auditing does affect overall system performance, this might lead to undesirable results on other computers. It would be more effective to apply the GPO to the specific OU where the servers are located, as described in answer E.

E. **Correct:** This is the third step to take; the other steps are described in answer A.

F. **Correct:** This is the fourth step to take; the previous steps are explained in answer A.

G. **Correct:** This is the first step to take; the remaining steps are described in answer A.

70-218.01.05.002

▶ **Correct Answers: B**

A. **Incorrect:** Although this will accomplish the goal of enabling auditing on the file servers, it is an unnecessarily time-consuming approach.

B. **Correct:** Monitoring file and folder accesses requires two steps: configuring Audit Policy and configuring security on each object to enable auditing. Managing Audit Policy through Active Directory–based GPOs is usually more efficient and effective than through local security settings.

C. **Incorrect:** Although this approach is effective, it is slightly more time consuming to implement than the solution described in answer B. Additionally, it is likely that this approach would make supporting the configuration more complex in the future because the GPO is linked to the parent OU and administrators might mistakenly assume that it applies to all the objects in the child OUs, not just the servers.

D. **Incorrect:** Although this approach is effective, it will take more time to implement than the solution provided in answer B. Also, for the reasons noted in answer C, it is likely that this solution would make supporting the configuration more challenging. Finally, this is a bad design decision because the Default Domain Policy is likely to contain other settings that are supposed to apply to all objects in the domain—setting security filtering on this GPO will cause those settings to no longer apply to the other objects.

70-218.01.05.003

▶ **Correct Answers: A**

A. **Correct:** To see who is making changes to user accounts, you must examine account management events in the security log on each domain controller.

B. **Incorrect:** System events indicate when computers are shut down or started.

C. **Incorrect:** Account logon events can be tracked on domain controllers to determine when a domain controller on your network received a logon request from a user.

D. **Incorrect:** Object access events can be monitored to detect access to files, folders, registry keys, and printers.

70-218.01.05.004

▶ **Correct Answers: A**

A. **Correct:** After enabling this Audit Policy, you can examine the security log for suspicious activity such as logon attempts outside the hours Dave normally works. You should take additional precautions to protect the network and Dave's data. Rename Dave's account and change his password. Create a new account with the same logon name as Dave's original one, and make it a member of the Guests group. Watch for logon attempts using the decoy account.

B. **Incorrect:** Monitoring failed logon attempts helps you detect a hacker who is attempting to gain entry by guessing passwords, but if the intruder already has a valid user name and password, you need to check for successful logon events.

C. **Incorrect:** Successful and failed object access events can be audited to track unauthorized access to printers, registry keys, files, and folders.

D. **Incorrect:** Successful user rights events can be monitored to see when users are successfully utilizing their user rights.

70-218.01.05.005

▶ **Correct Answers: B**

   A. **Incorrect:** The Sysvol share, also called the System Volume, would not provide any information about users accessing the files in the Product Plans folder.

   B. **Correct:** Setting up auditing in Windows 2000 is a two-step process; you must configure Audit Policy and configure audit settings on the objects to be monitored. In this scenario you successfully performed the first step but forgot to implement the second.

   C. **Incorrect:** Monitoring for directory service access will not reveal any information about users accessing the files in the Product Plans folder.

   D. **Incorrect:** If one domain controller becomes unresponsive to authentication requests, the computers on the network use another. Even if all the domain controllers became unavailable, only previously authorized users would be able to access properly secured files and folders. If all the domain controllers were unresponsive, the file server would be unable to allow users to establish new connections. Nevertheless, if auditing had been correctly configured and all the domain controllers failed simultaneously, the Security log of the file server would contain the desired information.

70-218.01.05.006

▶ **Correct Answers: D**

   A. **Incorrect:** This type of auditing would help you track unauthorized access to sensitive files and folders, but it's probably unnecessary for desktop and laptop systems. If you want to enable auditing of object access events, you also need to configure auditing on each file and folder to be monitored using Windows Explorer, security templates, or Active Directory–based GPOs.

   B. **Incorrect:** As explained in answer A, this type of auditing won't help resolve the problem presented in this question.

   C. **Incorrect:** This manual approach is very time consuming; using the procedures described in answer D is much more efficient.

   D. **Correct:** This is an effective way to compare local security settings with the desired settings. Security templates contain settings for account policies, auditing, user rights assignment, registry permissions, file system permissions, and many other types of security settings.

Configuring, Administering, and Troubleshooting the Network Infrastructure

The network infrastructure of any organization is the foundation for all other services and applications. As a result, if the network infrastructure is improperly configured or experiencing problems, the services and applications using the network infrastructure will experience erratic operation or complete outages. The appropriate configuration, proper administration, and expedient troubleshooting of the network infrastructure ensures that services and applications remain highly available and secure and provide optimal client computer response times.

The technologies that comprise the Microsoft Windows 2000 networking infrastructure are:

- **Transmission Control Protocol/Internet Protocol (TCP/IP)**

- **IP routing**

- **Domain Name System (DNS)**

- NetBIOS name resolution by using **Windows Internet Name Service (WINS)**

- Automatic IP configuration by using **Dynamic Host Configuration Protocol (DHCP)**

You must possess the skills necessary to perform the configuration, administration, and troubleshooting for each of the Windows 2000 network infrastructure technologies. In addition, you must be able to configure, administer, and troubleshoot the Windows 2000 network infrastructure by using Windows 2000 consoles (such as DNS) and command-line utilities (such as DNSCMD).

Tested Skills and Suggested Practices

The skills that you need to master the Configuring, Administering, and Troubleshooting the Network Infrastructure objective domain on the *Managing a Microsoft Windows 2000 Network Environment* exam include:

- **Troubleshooting routing.**

    - Practice 1: Run the Trace Route utility (TRACERT) to trace the routing path between source and destination computers. Adjust the advanced settings to list router interfaces and to not resolve IP addresses to host names.

    - Practice 2: Run the IP routing trace utility (PATHPING) to trace the route path between source and destination computers. Adjust the advanced settings to test Quality of Service (QoS) connectivity and to not resolve IP addresses to host names.

- **Configuring and troubleshooting TCP/IP on servers and client computers.**

    - Practice 1: Run the IP Configuration utility (IPCONFIG for Windows NT 4 and Windows 2000 computers; WINIPCFG for Windows 95, Windows 98, and Windows Me. View the report to determine the IP configuration. Use the /ALL option to display advanced configuration information.

    - Practice 2: Run the IP connectivity test utility (PING) to verify IP-level connectivity. View the report to determine whether IP-level connectivity exists.

    - Practice 3: Run the Address Resolution Protocol (ARP) utility to verify IP to media access control (MAC) layer addresses. View the report to verify IP to MAC address resolution and to delete incorrect ARP entries stored in the ARP cache.

    - Practice 4: Run the Network Statistics utility (NETSTAT) to view protocol statistics and current TCP/IP connections. Adjust the advanced settings to display the routing table, the owner of specific TCP and User Datagram Protocol (UDP) port numbers, and Ethernet statistics.

- **Configuring, administering, and troubleshooting DHCP on servers and client computers.**

  - Practice 1: Install the DHCP Server service. Ensure the DHCP server is not authorized in the Active Directory service. Attempt to start the DHCP Server service. View Windows 2000 event logs. Authorize the DHCP server. Configure a DHCP scope to provide automatic IP configuration. Configure client computers to use DHCP for IP configuration. Verify proper IP configuration by using DHCP.

  - Practice 2: Run the IP Configuration utility (IPCONFIG) to renew and release DHCP addresses by using the /RENEW and /RELEASE command-line options.

- **Configuring, administering, and troubleshooting DNS.**

  - Practice 1: Install the DNS Server service. Create a standard forward lookup zone. Configure a forward lookup zone to allow dynamic updates. Configure a DNS client to use the new DNS Server as the primary DNS server. Verify that the DNS client resource records are created in the zone.

  - Practice 2: Install the DNS Server service on another computer. Create a standard secondary zone. Configure the forward lookup zone on the first DNS server to be replicated to the standard secondary zone. Verify the zone resource records are replicated by using the DNS console.

  - Practice 3: Start the DNS console. Stop and start the DNS server. Verify that the DNS server responds to queries and recursive queries. View the Windows 2000 DNS server system event log by using the Event Viewer console.

  - Practice 4: Run the Name Service Lookup utility (NSLOOKUP) to determine whether DNS queries are properly resolved and to identify the DNS servers that resolved the DNS queries. Run the DNS command-line utility (DNSCMD) to configure and administer DNS.

- **Troubleshooting name resolution on client computers.**

  - Practice 1: Create entries in the hosts file. Verify that the entries in the hosts file resolve names appropriately.

  - Practice 2: Create entries in the Lmhosts file. Ensure you use the extended Lmhosts tags (such as #DOM) to create entries. Verify that the new entries in the Lmhosts file resolve names appropriately.

  - Practice 3: Run the NetBIOS over TCP/IP utility (NBTSTAT) to determine whether NetBIOS queries are properly resolved (-c option), to clear the NetBIOS cache (-R option), and to clear and refresh the NetBIOS cache (-RR option).

Further Reading

This section lists supplemental readings by objective. We recommend that you study these sources thoroughly before taking exam 70-218.

Objective 2.1

Microsoft Corporation. *Microsoft Windows 2000 Server Resource Kit*. Volume: *Windows 2000 Server TCP/IP Core Networking Guide*. Redmond, Washington: Microsoft Press, 2000. Read the "IP Routing" section of Chapter 1, "Introduction to TCP/IP," the "Internet Protocol" section of Chapter 2, "Windows 200 TCP/IP," and the "Windows 2000 TCP/IP" and "Troubleshooting IP Routing" sections of Chapter 3, "TCP/IP Troubleshooting."

Microsoft Corporation. *Microsoft Windows 2000 Professional Resource Kit*. Redmond, Washington: Microsoft Press, 2000. Read the "Configure Local IP Routing Table," "TCP/IP in Windows 2000 Professional," and "Troubleshoot Routing" sections of Chapter 22, "TCP/IP in Windows 2000 Professional."

Microsoft Corporation. *MCSA Training Kit: Managing a Microsoft Windows 2000 Network Environment*. Redmond, Washington: Microsoft Press, 2002. Read and complete the practices in Lesson 3 of Chapter 13, "TCP/IP Administration."

Objective 2.2

Microsoft Corporation. *MCSA Training Kit: Managing a Microsoft Windows 2000 Network Environment*. Redmond, Washington: Microsoft Press, 2002. Read and complete the practices in Chapter 13, "TCP/IP Administration."

Microsoft Corporation. *Microsoft Windows 2000 Server Resource Kit*. Volume: *Windows 2000 Server TCP/IP Core Networking Guide*. Redmond, Washington: Microsoft Press, 2000. Read Chapter 1, "Introduction to TCP/IP," Chapter 2, "Windows 2000 TCP/IP," and Chapter 3, "TCP/IP Troubleshooting."

Microsoft Corporation. *Microsoft Windows 2000 Professional Resource Kit*. Redmond, Washington: Microsoft Press, 2000. Read Chapter 22, "TCP/IP in Windows 2000 Professional" and the "Configure TCP/IP" section of Chapter 23, "Windows 2000 Professional on Microsoft Networks."

Objective 2.3

Microsoft Corporation. *Microsoft Windows 2000 Server Resource Kit*. Volume: *Windows 2000 Server TCP/IP Core Networking Guide*. Redmond, Washington: Microsoft Press, 2000. Read Chapter 4, "Dynamic Host Configuration Protocol."

Microsoft Corporation. *Microsoft Windows 2000 Professional Resource Kit.* Redmond, Washington: Microsoft Press, 2000. Read the "Configure DHCP" section of Chapter 22, "TCP/IP in Windows 2000 Professional."

Microsoft Corporation. *MCSA Training Kit: Managing a Microsoft Windows 2000 Network Environment.* Redmond, Washington: Microsoft Press, 2002. Read and complete the practices in Chapter 14, "Dynamic Host Configuration Protocol."

Objective 2.4

Microsoft Corporation. *Microsoft Windows 2000 Server Resource Kit.* Volume: *Windows 2000 Server TCP/IP Core Networking Guide.* Redmond, Washington: Microsoft Press, 2000. Read the "Name Resolution" section of Chapter 1, "Windows 2000 TCP/IP." Also read Chapter 5, "Introduction to DNS," and Chapter 6, "Windows 2000 DNS."

Microsoft Corporation. *Microsoft Windows 2000 Professional Resource Kit.* Redmond, Washington: Microsoft Press, 2000. Read the "Configure DNS Name Resolution" and "Configure Dynamic Update" sections of Chapter 22, "TCP/IP in Windows 2000 Professional."

Microsoft Corporation. *MCSA Training Kit: Managing a Microsoft Windows 2000 Network Environment.* Redmond, Washington: Microsoft Press, 2002. Read and complete the practices in Chapter 16, "Domain Name System."

Objective 2.5

Microsoft Corporation. *Microsoft Windows 2000 Server Resource Kit.* Volume: *Windows 2000 Server TCP/IP Core Networking Guide.* Redmond, Washington: Microsoft Press, 2000. Read the "Name Resolution" section of Chapter 1, "Windows 2000 TCP/IP," the "Unable to Reach a Host or NetBIOS Name" section of Chapter 3, "TCP/IP Troubleshooting," Chapter 6, "Windows 2000 DNS," and Chapter 7, "Windows Internet Name Service."

Microsoft Corporation. *Microsoft Windows 2000 Professional Resource Kit.* Redmond, Washington: Microsoft Press, 2000. Read the "Configure TCP/IP Name Resolution" section of Chapter 22, "TCP/IP in Windows 2000 Professional."

Microsoft Corporation. *MCSA Training Kit: Managing a Microsoft Windows 2000 Network Environment.* Redmond, Washington: Microsoft Press, 2002. Read and complete the practices in Chapter 16, "Domain Name System."

O B J E C T I V E   2 . 1

Troubleshoot routing.

Transmission Control Protocol/Internet Protocol (TCP/IP) routing is an essential part of any network infrastructure. Unless the entire network is comprised of a single network segment, routing is required. **IP routing** occurs within geographic locations between **local area network (LAN)** segments and geographic locations over **wide area network (WAN)** segments. To support these IP networks, you must be able to troubleshoot IP routing.

To answer the questions in this objective, you should be able to:

- Identify the purpose of IP routing tables.

- Identify the purpose of the ARP table.

- Troubleshoot TCP/IP-related issues.

- Run common TCP/IP connectivity command-line utilities (such as PATHPING, PING and TRACERT).

- Run common TCP/IP configuration command-line utilities (such as ARP, IPCONFIG, and ROUTE).

Objective 2.1 Questions

70-218.02.01.001

You are troubleshooting an IP routing problem in your network. Client-A is unable to access resources on Server-C. The IP configuration of Client-A, Router-A, Router-B, and Server-C are listed in the following table.

Device	IP address	Subnet mask	Default gateway
Client-A	172.16.32.101	255.255.252.0	172.16.32.1
Router-A – Segment A	172.16.32.1	255.255.252.0	
Router-A – Segment B	172.16.48.1	255.255.252.0	
Router-B – Segment B	172.16.48.2	255.255.252.0	
Router-B – Segment C	172.16.64.1	255.255.252.0	
Server-C	172.16.64.53	255.255.252.0	172.16.64.1

You run PATHPING on Client-A and the following output is displayed:

```
C:\>pathping -n Server-C
Tracing route to Server-C [172.16.64.53]
over a maximum of 30 hops:
  0  172.16.32.101
  1  172.16.32.1
  2  172.16.48.2
  3     *         *         *
Computing statistics for 75 seconds...
            Source to Here   This Node/Link
Hop  RTT    Lost/Sent = Pct  Lost/Sent = Pct  Address
  0                                            172.16.32.101
                               4/ 100 =  4%    |
  1   4ms    4/ 100 =  4%     0/ 100 =  0%   172.16.32.1
                               3/ 100 =  3%    |
  2   9ms    7/ 100 =  7%     0/ 100 =  0%   172.16.48.1
                              93/ 100 = 93%    |
  3   ---  100/ 100 =100%     0/ 100 =  0%   0.0.0.0
Trace complete.
```

What determinations can you make regarding the problem, given the information you have gathered thus far?

Examine the figure shown here.

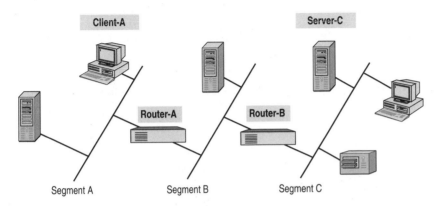

A. Client-A is incorrectly configured.

B. Router-A is incorrectly configured or a communications link is broken between Router-A and Router-B.

C. Router-B is incorrectly configured or a communications link is broken between Router-B and Server-C.

D. Server-C is incorrectly configured.

70-218.02.01.002

Your organization has two geographic locations connected through a VPN tunnel across the Internet, as illustrated in the figure. The users on Client-A are unable to connect to resources on Server-B. You want to verify TCP/IP connectivity between Client-A and Server-B. Which tool can you use to troubleshoot why Client-A is unable to connect to Server-B?

Examine the figure shown here.

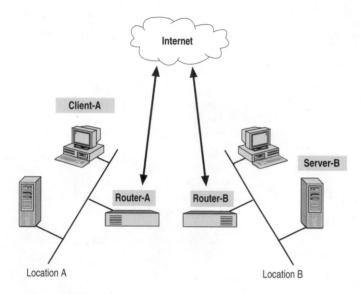

A. IPCONFIG

B. ARP

C. PATHPING

D. NETSTAT

70-218.02.01.003

You are troubleshooting the network illustrated in the figure. Users on Client-A are unable to connect to resources on Server-C. Users on Client-C are able to connect to resources on Server-C. Which tool can you use to troubleshoot why Client-A is unable to connect to Server-C?

Examine the figure shown here.

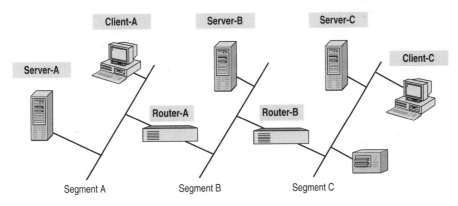

A. NBTSTAT

B. NETSTAT

C. ARP

D. TRACERT

70-218.02.01.004

You are troubleshooting a network infrastructure that relies heavily on real-time communications. As a result, all the routers in the organization respond to QoS reservation requests by using Resource Reservation Protocol (RSVP). Client computers are experiencing performance problems with applications that depend on real-time communications. How can you ensure the routers in the network infrastructure are not the source of the performance problems?

A. Use the NETSTAT command.

B. Use the NBTSTAT command.

C. Use the PATHPING command.

D. Use the TRACERT command.

70-218.02.01.005

You are troubleshooting the network illustrated in the figure. Users on Client-A are unable to connect to resources on Server-B. You run WINIPCFG on Client-A and IPCONFIG on Server-B to determine the configuration for each respective computer. The administrator responsible for managing Router-A and Router-B provides you with the configuration for each respective router. The IP configuration of Client-A, Server-B, Router-A, and Router-B are listed in the following table.

Device	IP address	Subnet mask	Default gateway
Client-A	172.16.31.101	255.255.252.0	172.16.31.1
Server-B	172.16.32.53	255.255.252.0	172.16.40.1
Router-A – Segment A	172.16.28.1	255.255.252.0	
Router-A – Internet	10.0.13.122	255.255.255.252	
Router-B – Segment B	172.16.40.1	255.255.252.0	
Router-B – Internet	10.0.13.143	255.255.255.252	

Why is Client-A unable to connect to Server-B?

Examine the figure shown here.

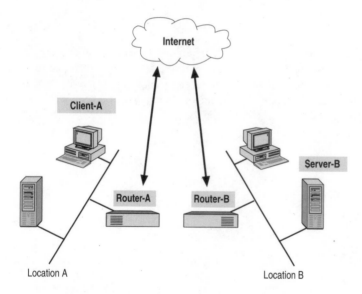

A. The default gateway setting for Client-A is incorrect.

B. The default gateway setting for Server-B is incorrect.

C. The IP address assigned to Router-B's interface on Segment-B is incorrect.

D. The IP address assigned to Server-B is incorrect.

Objective 2.1 Answers

70-218.02.01.001

► **Correct Answers: C**

A. **Incorrect:** Client-A is assigned an IP address that is valid for the network segment and is configured to use Router-A as the default gateway. Client-A can communicate with Router-B through Router-A. The configuration of Client-A is correct.

B. **Incorrect:** Router-A is forwarding packets between Segment-A and Segment-C. Client-A can communicate with Router-B. Router-A is configured correctly and the communications link between Router-A and Router-B is intact.

C. **Correct:** PATHPING is unable to communicate between Router-B and Server-C. The output confirms that Client-A is unable to talk beyond Router-B. As a result, the communications problem must be caused by Router-B or a broken communications link between Router-B and Server-C.

D. **Incorrect:** Server-C is assigned an IP address that is valid for the network segment and is configured to use Router-B as the default gateway. The configuration of Server-C is correct.

70-218.02.01.002

► **Correct Answers: C**

A. **Incorrect:** IPCONFIG can provide configuration for Client-A and Server-B, but it cannot verify the connectivity between Client-A and Server-B.

B. **Incorrect:** ARP can manage the ARP table configuration for Client-A and Server-B, but it cannot verify the connectivity between Client-A and Server-B.

C. **Correct:** PATHPING can verify the connectivity between Client-A and Server-B by verifying connectivity through intermediary routers between Client-A and Server-B.

D. **Incorrect:** NETSTAT can provide configuration for Client-A and Server-B, but it cannot verify the connectivity between Client-A and Server-B.

70-218.02.01.003

▶ **Correct Answers: D**

A. **Incorrect:** NBTSTAT can provide NetBIOS name configuration for Client-A and Server-C, but it cannot verify the connectivity between Client-A and Server-C.

B. **Incorrect:** NETSTAT can provide configuration for Client-A and Server-C, but it cannot verify the connectivity between Client-A and Server-C.

C. **Incorrect:** ARP can manage the ARP table configuration for Client-A and Server-C, but it cannot verify the connectivity between Client-A and Server-C.

D. **Correct:** TRACERT can verify the connectivity between Client-A and Server-C by verifying connectivity through intermediary routers between Client-A and Server-C.

70-218.02.01.004

▶ **Correct Answers: C**

A. **Incorrect:** This command does not report any information regarding QoS or RSVP router-awareness and cannot provide any information about the source of the performance problems.

B. **Incorrect:** This answer is incorrect for the reasons stated in answer A.

C. **Correct:** The PATHPING command can verify that each router is RSVP aware by using the -R option. The PATHPING command can test connectivity by using the -P option.

D. **Incorrect:** This answer is incorrect for the reasons stated in answer A.

70-218.02.01.005

▶ **Correct Answers: A**

A. **Correct:** The default gateway setting of Client-A points to a nonexistent router. The default gateway setting must point to the IP address of Router-A's interface connected to Segment-A.

B. **Incorrect:** The default gateway setting of Server-A contains the IP address of Router-B's interface on Segment-B. This setting is correct.

C. **Incorrect:** The IP address assigned to Router-B's interface on Segment-B falls within the IP address range assigned to Segment-B. This setting is correct and is configured as the default gateway setting of Server-A.

D. **Incorrect:** The IP address assigned to Server-B falls within the IP address range assigned to Segment-B.

O B J E C T I V E   2 . 2

Configure and troubleshoot TCP/IP on servers and client computers.

TCP/IP is the communications protocol used by the Windows 2000 network infra-structure services. **Domain Name System (DNS)**, **Dynamic Host Configuration Protocol (DHCP)**, **Windows Internet Name Service (WINS)**, **VPNs**, and other services require TCP/IP. To configure and troubleshoot the Windows 2000 network infrastructure services, you must be able to configure and troubleshoot TCP/IP.

TCP/IP is included in all versions of Windows 2000. The approach to configuring and troubleshooting TCP/IP for Microsoft Windows 2000 Professional, Windows 2000 Server, and Windows 2000 Advanced Server is identical because the user interface and TCP/IP features provided are the same across all versions of Windows 2000.

You can configure TCP/IP manually on Windows 2000, or you can automatically configure TCP/IP by using:

- DHCP servers placed within your network (for network infrastructures larger than one network segment)

- **Automatic Private IP Addressing (APIPA)** configuration provided in Windows 2000 (for networks that have only one network segment, such as home offices)

Typically, you manually configure TCP/IP on any IP device that is providing services to the network (such as file servers, print servers, and Web servers). You assign a fixed IP address to these devices so client computers can always find the device at the same IP address. In addition, some networking services generate warning messages if you use DHCP or APIPA to automatically configure TCP/IP.

Because client computers usually do not share resources with other computers on the network, you can automatically configure TCP/IP by using DHCP or APIPA.

To answer the questions in this objective, you should be able to:

- Identify the purpose of the IP routing table.

- Identify the purpose of the ARP table.

- Run common TCP/IP command-line utilities (such as PING and IPCONFIG).

- Identify how DHCP provides automatic IP configuration.

- Identify how APIPA provides automatic IP configuration.

Objective 2.2 Questions

70-218.02.02.001

You are configuring TCP/IP on a computer running Windows 2000 Server. The computer has one network adapter installed. You manually assign the following IP configuration information to the TCP/IP protocol bound to the adapter:

- IP address: 172.16.56.103

- Subnet mask: 255.255.252.0

- Default gateway: 172.16.56.1

You attempt to connect to the server from a client computer, but you are unsuccessful. However, the client computer can connect to other servers throughout your environment. At a command prompt, you run IPCONFIG /ALL and find that the server has an IP address of 0.0.0.0 with a subnet mask of 0.0.0.0. Why does the IP configuration information not reflect the setting you made?

A. The network cable is not connected to the network adapter.

B. The subnet mask specified is incorrect.

C. The IP address is within the range of private IP addresses set aside by the Internet Assigned Number Authority (IANA) and is invalid.

D. An existing IP device on the network has the same IP address.

70-218.02.02.002

You are troubleshooting the network illustrated in the figure. Users on Client-A are unable to connect to resources on Server-B. The IP configuration of Client-A, Server-B, and Router-A are listed in the following table.

Device	IP address	Subnet mask	Default gateway
Client-A	172.16.31.101	255.255.252.0	172.16.28.1
Server-B	172.16.32.53	255.255.252.0	172.16.36.1
Client-B	172.16.37.115	255.255.252.0	172.16.36.1
Router-A – Segment A	172.16.28.1	255.255.252.0	
Router-A – Segment B	172.16.36.1	255.255.252.0	
Router-A – Segment C	172.16.40.1	255.255.252.0	

Why is Client-A unable to access resources on Server-B?

Examine the figure shown here.

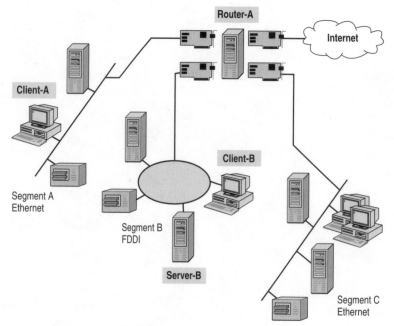

A. The IP address of the client computer is incorrect.

B. The IP address of Server-B is incorrect.

C. The IP address of the router interface connected to Segment B is incorrect.

D. The subnet mask for Client-A, Router-A, and Server-B are all the same.

70-218.02.02.003

You are troubleshooting an IP configuration problem in your network. You perform the following diagnostic procedures:

1. On Client-A, you run PING Server-C. The PING command returns the message "Request timed out."

2. On Client-A, you run ARP -a. The only entry returned by the ARP command lists the IP address of the router interface connected to Segment A.

3. On Client-C, you run PING Router-A. The PING command returns a successful status.

4. On Client-A, you run PING Client-C. The PING command returns a successful status.

5. On Client-C, you run PING Router-A. The PING command returns a successful status.

6. On Client-C, you run PING Client-A. The PING command returns a successful status.

7. On Client-C, you run PING Server-C. The PING command returns the message "Request timed out."

What determinations can you make regarding the problem, given the information you have gathered thus far?

Examine the figure shown here.

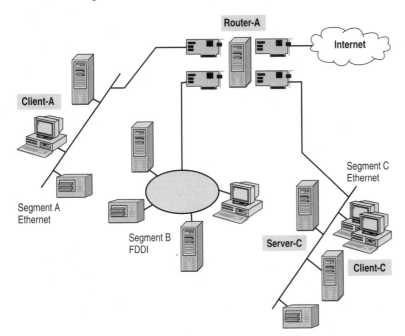

A. Client-A is the source of the problem.

B. Client-C is the source of the problem.

C. Server-C is the source of the problem.

D. Router-A is the source of the problem.

70-218.02.02.004

You are troubleshooting the network illustrated in the figure. Users on Client-A and Client-C are unable to connect to resources on Server-B. The IP configuration of the client computers, servers, and routers are listed in the following table.

Device	IP address	Subnet mask	Default gateway
Client-A	172.16.32.101	255.255.252.0	172.16.32.1
Server-A	172.16.34.51	255.255.252.0	172.16.32.1
Server-B	172.16.16.51	255.255.240.0	172.16.32.1
Client-C	172.16.48.101	255.255.252.0	172.16.48.1
Server-C	172.16.50.51	255.255.252.0	172.16.48.1
Router-A – Segment A	172.16.32.1	255.255.252.0	
Router-A – Segment B	172.16.16.1	255.255.240.0	
Router-B – Segment B	172.16.17.1	255.255.240.0	
Router-B – Segment C	172.16.48.1	255.255.252.0	

Why are Client-A and Client-C unable to access resources on Server-B?

Examine the figure shown here.

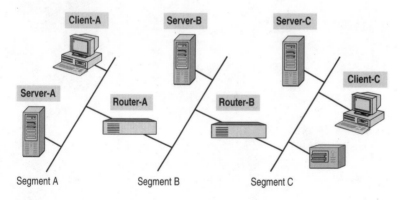

A. The default gateway of Server-B is incorrect.

B. The IP address of Router-B's interface that is connected to Segment B is incorrect.

C. The subnet mask for all interfaces connected to Segment A (Router-A, Client-A, and Server-A) and for all the interfaces connected to Segment C (Router-B, Client-C, and Server-C) are incorrect.

D. The subnet mask for all interfaces connected to Segment B (Router-A, Router-B, and Server-B) are incorrect.

70-218.02.02.005

You are configuring TCP/IP on a new Web server on your organization's network. Windows 2000 Server has been installed with the default options. The Web server has one network adapter installed. The new Web server responds only to Hypertext Transfer Protocol (HTTP) requests. The existing client computers and servers are appropriately configured to use DNS to resolve names.

You want to achieve the following goals:

- Clients must be able to retrieve Web content from the Web server.

- The Web server will not initiate any communications.

Which of the following IP configuration settings must be set on the Web server to achieve these goals? (Choose all that apply.)

A. The IP address

B. The primary DNS suffix

C. The primary DNS server

D. The subnet mask

E. The primary WINS server

F. The default gateway

70-218.02.02.006

You are troubleshooting connectivity problems with a new server running Windows 2000 Server. The new server resides in the perimeter network of your private network, and provides HTTP, File Transfer Protocol (FTP), and streaming audio to Internet users. The Internet users are able to access the HTTP and FTP information, but they cannot access the streaming audio. You suspect that the firewall protecting the perimeter network is not allowing the appropriate IP port traffic to the server. You consult the streaming audio software documentation and identify the IP port numbers used by the streaming audio server. After consulting with the firewall administrator, you discover that the firewall is configured to allow communication with the server by using the streaming audio server's IP port numbers. How can you determine whether the IP port numbers are active on the server?

A. Run NETSTAT -a at a command prompt.

B. View the contents of the SERVICES file in the WINNT\SYSTEM32\DRIVERS\ETC folder.

C. View the contents of the PROTOCOL file in the WINNT\SYSTEM32\DRIVERS\ETC folder.

D. Run IPCONFIG /SHOWCLASSID at a command prompt.

Objective 2.2 Answers

70-218.02.02.001

▶ **Correct Answers: D**

A. **Incorrect:** When the network cable is disconnected, IPCONFIG /ALL reports a "Cable Disconnected" message. However, the IP configuration information remains unchanged.

B. **Incorrect:** An incorrect subnet mask can prevent the communication between the client computer and the server. However, IPCONFIG /ALL reports the IP configuration information as specified.

C. **Incorrect:** The IP address is valid within a private network and can be used by any organization that either has no connection to the Internet or uses network address translation (NAT) to translate between private and public IP addresses. IPCONFIG /ALL would report the specified configuration information, not 0.0.0.0 for the IP address and subnet mask.

D. **Correct:** Because duplicate IP addresses can cause unpredictable results, the Windows 2000 TCP/IP protocol checks for duplicate IP address as the protocol initializes. When the Windows 2000 TCP/IP protocol finds that another device already is configured with the same IP address, Windows 2000 disables the local TCP/IP protocol stack. When the Windows 2000 TCP/IP protocol is disabled, the IP address and subnet mask are reported as 0.0.0.0 by IPCONFIG /ALL.

70-218.02.02.002

▶ **Correct Answers: B**

A. **Incorrect:** According to the diagram, Client-A exists on the same network segment as the router interface connected to Segment A. Client-A's IP address (172.16.31.101) and subnet mask (255.255.252.0) are within the same IP subnet as the router interface's IP address (172.16.28.1) and subnet mask (255.255.252.0). Because Client-A's IP address is not duplicated elsewhere in the network and falls within the IP subnet for Segment A, the IP address of the client computer is correct.

B. **Correct:** The IP address currently assigned to Server-B does not reside within the same IP subnet as the router interface connected to Segment B. The combination of the IP address (172.16.32.53) and subnet mask (255.255.252.0) for Server-B results in an IP network ID of 172.16.32.0. The combination of the IP address (172.16.36.1) and subnet mask (255.255.252.0) for the router interface connected to Segment B results in an IP network ID of 172.16.36.0. Because Server-B and the router interface connected to Segment B have different IP network IDs, they are on separate IP subnets. Each subnet in a routed IP network must have at least one router interface that resides on the same subnet. Performing the same calculations on Client-B and the router interface connected to Segment B results in Client-B and the router interface residing on the same IP subnet (with an IP network ID of 172.16.37.0). Because Server-B doesn't match the IP network ID for Client-B or for the corresponding router interface, the IP address for Server-B is incorrect.

C. **Incorrect:** According to the diagram and the table, the IP address assigned to the router interface connected to Segment A is not duplicated elsewhere in the network. The IP address (172.16.33.1) and subnet mask (255.255.252.0) assigned to the router interface connected to Segment A and Server-B's IP address (172.16.32.53) and subnet mask (255.255.252.0) fall within the same IP subnet. Because the IP addresses and subnet masks assigned to the router interface and to Server-B are within the same IP subnet range, the IP address of the router interface is correct.

D. **Incorrect:** A subnet mask is valid if the combination (logical ANDing) of the IP address and subnet mask produces the same network ID for all devices connected to the same subnet. For example, Client-A's IP address and subnet mask produce a network ID of 172.16.28.0. The IP address (172.16.28.1) and subnet mask (255.255.252.0) also produce a network ID of 172.16.28.0. Because the IP network ID is the same for Client-A and the router interface connected to Segment A, Client-A and the router interface are on the same subnet because they have the same IP network ID. Unless Variable Length Subnet Mask (VLSM) or Classless Interdomain Routing (CIDR) is used in the network (both of which implement a hierarchical subnet mask), the most common configuration is for all devices within the same private network to have the same IP subnet mask.

70-218.02.02.003

▶ **Correct Answers: C**

A. **Incorrect:** Client-A can successfully communicate with Client-C. That implies that Client-A, Router-A, and Client-C are configured correctly. The single ARP table entry, containing the IP address of the Router-A interface connected to Segment A, is correct. ARP uses broadcasts to perform IP to MAC, or hardware, address resolution. Broadcasts are not propagated across routers, so the ARP table can contain entries only from the local subnet. When communicating with IP devices on other subnets, the ARP table contains an ARP entry for the router used to communicate with the other subnet.

B. **Incorrect:** Because Client-C can successfully communicate with Client-A, that means Client-A, Router-A, and Client-C must be configured and operating correctly. Because Client-C can communicate with Client-A, Client-C is not the source of the problem.

C. **Correct:** Because Client-A can communicate with Client-C (and vice versa), that means Client-A, Client-C, and Router-A are working correctly. However, because both Client-A (on a remote network segment) and Client-C (on a local network segment) cannot communicate with Server-C, the problem resides with Server-C.

D. **Incorrect:** Because Client-A can successfully communicate with Client-C, Router-A must be configured and operating correctly. If Client-A and Client-C were not able to communicate, Router-A would be the likely source of the problem.

70-218.02.02.004

▶ **Correct Answers: A**

A. **Correct:** The default gateway setting must contain the IP address of a router interface directly connected to the same network segment. The default gateway setting for Server-B contains the IP address of the router interface connected to Segment A instead of Segment B. All other devices on the network would be able to communicate with one another.

B. **Incorrect:** According to the diagram, both Router-B and Router-A have interfaces that connect to Segment B. The IP address range for Segment B (based on the IP addresses and subnet masks assigned to Router-A, Router-B, and Server-B) result in the same IP network ID (172.16.16.0). Although the third octet for Router-B's interface on Segment B is different from Router-A and Server-B, the IP address and subnet mask result in the same IP network ID as Router-A and Server-B.

C. **Incorrect:** Although the subnet mask for all devices connected to Segment A and Segment C is different from the subnet mask for all the devices on Segment B, the difference in subnet masks is not the problem. The existing subnet masks produce IP network IDs that are the same for all devices on each respective subnet and unique across the private network. The IP network ID for Segment A (172.16.32.0), Segment B (172.16.16.0), and Segment C (172.16.48.0) are unique within the organization's private network.

D. **Incorrect:** Although the subnet mask for all devices connected to Segment B is different from the subnet mask for all the devices on Segment A and Segment C, the difference in subnet masks is not the problem. The IP network IDs for Segment A (172.16.32.0), Segment B (172.16.16.0), and Segment C (172.16.48.0) are unique within the organization's private network. In addition, all the devices on each respective subnet have the same IP network ID. This configuration of subnet masks is typical when VLSM is used in the network to implement a hierarchical subnet mask.

70-218.02.02.005

▶ **Correct Answers: A, D, and F**

A. **Correct:** The IP address must be configured to allow the Web server to communicate with the client computers. You must select an IP address that is unique to the private network and within the range of the network segment to which the Web server is connected.

B. **Incorrect:** The primary DNS suffix setting sets the fully qualified domain name (FQDN) for the computer. The client uses the primary DNS suffix setting to identify the DNS domain to which the computer belongs. When the client performs a DNS query that includes only a host name, the primary DNS suffix setting is appended to the host name. Because the Web server is not initiating any traffic, the primary DNS suffix setting is not required.

C. **Incorrect:** Because the Web server is not initiating any communication, the Web server does not require any DNS server settings. The DNS server settings allow an IP client to resolve names to IP addresses. Only computers that are initiating traffic or validating requests need to perform name resolution.

D. **Correct:** The subnet mask must be configured to allow the Web server to determine local and remote subnets. You must configure the subnet mask so the Web server will be able to communicate with local and remote subnets. The subnet mask must match the subnet mask of other IP devices connected to the same network segment.

E. **Incorrect:** Because no NetBIOS names are used in the deployment, the primary WINS server settings are not required. The primary WINS setting allows an IP client to resolve NetBIOS names to IP addresses.

F. **Correct:** The default gateway must be configured to allow the Web server to connect to network segments other than the network segment to which the Web server is directly connected. The default gateway must be configured to use a router that is directly connected to the same network segment as the Web server.

70-218.02.02.006

▶ **Correct Answers: A**

A. **Correct:** NETSTAT -a reports all active IP ports on a computer. You can compare the list of active IP ports with the IP port numbers you obtained from the streaming audio software documentation. If the IP ports are listed in the NETSTAT -a output, the ports are active on the server.

B. **Incorrect:** The SERVICES file provides translation from IP port numbers to symbolic names, and it is used by applications and utilities to provide user-friendly names for IP port numbers. However, the SERVICES file does not contain the status of the IP port numbers.

C. **Incorrect:** The PROTOCOL file provides translation from IP protocol numbers to symbolic names, and it is used by applications and utilities to provide user-friendly names for IP protocol numbers. The PROTOCOL file contains no information regarding IP port numbers.

D. **Incorrect:** IPCONFIG /SHOWCLASSID displays the DHCP class IDs allowed for a specific adapter. IPCONFIG /SHOWCLASSID does not provide any information regarding active IP port numbers.

O B J E C T I V E   2 . 3

Configure, administer, and troubleshoot DHCP on servers and client computers.

As the number of computers in your network increases, the amount of time required to configure, administer, and troubleshoot **TCP/IP** increases. **DHCP** was created to provide automatic IP configuration. DHCP centralizes the administration and the configuration of TCP/IP, and reduces the number of TCP/IP configuration errors (such as duplicate IP addresses).

DHCP is a request for comments (RFC)–compliant protocol that utilizes broadcast packets to communicate between the DHCP client and the DHCP server. Because broadcast packets are typically not forwarded through **routers**, DHCP messages must be forwarded across routers in your network by using **DHCP/BOOTP forwarding**. The majority of modern routers support some form of DHCP/BOOTP forwarding. The **Routing and Remote Access** feature in Windows 2000 includes the **DHCP Relay Agent** to provide DHCP/BOOTP forwarding.

For computers running Windows 2000 Professional, you can configure TCP/IP by using DHCP. When you configure TCP/IP to use DHCP for automatic IP configuration, **APIPA** is included by default. You can disable APIPA by creating the following registry entry in the following registry key:

```
IPAutoconfigurationEnabled: REG_DWORD = 0
HKEY_LOCAL_MACHINE\SYSTEM\CurrentControlSet\
Services\Tcpip\Parameters
```

To answer the questions in this objective, you should be able to:

- Troubleshoot TCP/IP-related issues.

- Run common TCP/IP command-line utilities (such as PING).

- Run common DHCP command-line utilities (such as IPCONFIG and NETSH).

- Perform common tasks in the DHCP console.

- Identify how DHCP provides automatic IP configuration.

- Identify how APIPA provides automatic IP configuration.

Objective 2.3 Questions

70-218.02.03.001

A computer running Windows 2000 Professional on your network is unable to connect to other devices on the network. TCP/IP is configured to automatically configure IP. On the client computer, you run IPCONFIG /ALL from a command prompt. The output from IPCONFIG /ALL is shown in the following figure. Why is the client computer unable to connect to other devices on the network?

Examine the figure shown here.

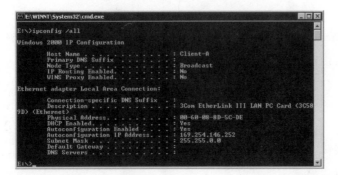

A. The client computer is assigned an incorrect IP address by the DHCP server.

B. The client computer is assigned an incorrect default gateway by the DHCP server.

C. The client computer is assigned an incorrect subnet mask by the DHCP server.

D. The client computer is unable to contact a DHCP server.

70-218.02.03.002

After your organization deploys Active Directory, you restructure your existing DHCP infrastructure as you migrate the DHCP servers to Windows 2000. The existing DHCP servers are running Microsoft Windows NT 4 Server. The existing DHCP servers lack the system resources to run Windows 2000. As a result, you are deploying new DHCP servers. The existing DHCP servers will be phased out as the new DHCP servers are able to take on the responsibilities of an existing DHCP server. As you restructure your DHCP infrastructure, you want to ensure that all DHPC servers are authorized in Active Directory.

You install Windows 2000 Server on the new DHCP servers by:

- Using the default options

- Assigning a static IP address, subnet mask, and default gateway

- Making the DHCP server a member server in an Active Directory domain

What remaining installation steps must you complete to authorize the DHCP server? (Choose all that apply.)

A. Log on as a user that is a member of the Domain Admins group in the domain where the DHCP servers are members.

B. Log on as a user that is a member of the Enterprise Administrators group in the forest root domain.

C. Log on as a user that is a member of the DHCP Administrators group in the domain where the DHCP servers are members.

D. Use the Active Directory Users and Computers console to authorize the DHCP servers.

E. Use the Active Directory Sites and Services console to authorize the DHCP servers.

F. Use the DHCP console to authorize the DHCP servers.

70-218.02.03.003

A number of client computers on your network are unable to connect to any network resources. From a command prompt on one of the client computers, you run IPCONFIG /ALL and determine that the client computers have not been assigned a DHCP IP address. At the same client computer, you run IPCONFIG /RENEW. The IPCONFIG /RENEW command reports that the DHCP server cannot be reached. From a Windows 2000 Server on the same network segment as the client computer, you are able to ping the DHCP server successfully. You examine the DHCP server and discover that the DHCP Server service is stopped. The DHCP server is a member server in an Active Directory domain. You attempt to start the DHCP Server service but are unable to do so. What is the most likely reason you are unable to start the DHCP Server service?

A. The DHCP server has been assigned a dynamic IP address.

B. The DHCP server has not been authorized in Active Directory service.

C. The DHCP server is unable to perform dynamic updates to an Active Directory integrated DNS zone.

D. The DHCP server has no valid DHCP scope defined.

70-218.02.03.004

All the client computers on a specific network segment are unable to connect to any network resources. From a command prompt on a number of the client computers you run IPCONFIG /ALL and determine that the client computers have not been assigned an IP address. From a Windows 2000 Server on the same network segment as the client computers, you are able to ping the DHCP server successfully. You examine the DHCP server and discover that the DHCP Server service is running. The DHCP server is a member server in an Active Directory domain. What is the most likely reason that the DHCP server is not assigning IP addresses to the client computers?

A. The DHCP server has been assigned a dynamic IP address.

B. The DHCP server has not been authorized in Active Directory.

C. The DHCP server is unable to perform dynamic updates to an Active Directory integrated DNS zone.

D. The DHCP server has no valid DHCP scope defined for the network segment.

70-218.02.03.005

In your organization a significant number of users work on laptop computers running Microsoft Windows XP Professional. Your organization's Help desk team uses the remote desktop feature in Windows XP Professional to assist users when they encounter problems. As part of a migration strategy, completed last year, your organization has eliminated all NetBIOS over TCP/IP (NetBT) traffic. The laptop computers are assigned IP configuration by DHCP. As the users attend meetings, the laptops are frequently disconnected from one network segment and reconnected to another network segment. Based on the sequence the users follow for disconnecting and reconnecting the network segments involved, the users cannot connect to network resources. Because the users cannot connect to the network resources, the Help desk team is unable to connect to the laptop to assist the users. What command can you provide to the users that would allow them to connect to network resources and allow the Help desk team to connect to the laptop?

A. At a command prompt on the laptop, run IPCONFIG /RENEW.

B. At a command prompt on the laptop, run IPCONFIG /SETCLASSID.

C. At a command prompt on the laptop, run IPCONFIG /REGISTERDNS.

D. At a command prompt on the laptop, run IPCONFIG /RELEASE.

70-218.02.03.006

You have recently deployed new DNS servers in your organization. Now that the deployment is complete, you want to accomplish the following:

- Update the list of DNS servers on all client computers that obtain IP configuration by DHCP.

- Ensure that the updates to the corresponding DHCP scope options for DNS servers are consistent across the 50 DHCP servers located throughout the world.

- Minimize any administration costs associated with the updates to DHCP.

How do you update the DHCP servers to achieve these objectives?

A. Write a NETSH script to update the DNS servers' IP addresses in the appropriate DHCP scope options. Test the script on one DHCP server in the network. Verify that the scopes are updated appropriately and then run the script on the 50 DHCP servers.

B. On one of the DHCP servers, update the appropriate DHCP scope options with the new DNS server IP addresses. After the updates are complete, back up the DHCP database and restore the DHCP database to the other 49 DHCP servers.

C. On one of the DHCP servers in your organization, run the DHCP console. Using the DHCP console, create a DHCP superscope that includes all the scopes from the 50 DHCP servers. In the superscope, create a DHCP scope option that includes the new DNS servers' IP addresses.

D. On each of the DHCP servers in your organization, create a new DHCP scope. In the new DHCP scope, create a scope option that includes the new DNS servers' IP addresses. Migrate users from the existing DHCP scopes to the new DHCP scopes. When all users are migrated to the new DHCP scopes, delete the old DHCP scopes.

70-218.02.03.007

Client computers within your private network are unable to receive IP configuration from the new DHCP server you recently installed. You installed and configured the new DHCP server by completing the following steps:

1. Install Windows 2000 Server by using the default options.

2. Assign an appropriate fixed IP address, subnet mask, and default gateway to the IP stack bound to the server's only network adapter.

3. Install DHCP on the new server.

4. Authorize the new DHCP server in Active Directory.

5. Create a DHCP scope for Segment A, Segment B, and Segment C.

6. Create the appropriate DHCP scope options for each scope you created.

7. Activate the DHCP scopes you created.

8. Configure client computers for automatic IP configuration.

How do you resolve the problem?

Examine the figure shown here.

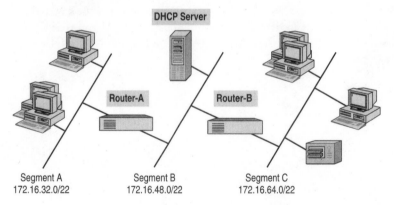

```
DHCP Server


                Router-A              Router-B



Segment A             Segment B             Segment C
172.16.32.0/22        172.16.48.0/22        172.16.64.0/22
```

A. Install and configure the DHCP Relay Agent on the new DHCP server.

B. Enable DHCP/BOOTP forwarding on Router-A and Router-B.

C. Install and configure the DHCP Relay Agent on the client computers.

D. Create a DHCP superscope that contains all the existing DHCP scopes.

Objective 2.3 Answers

70-218.02.03.001

▶ **Correct Answers: D**

A. **Incorrect:** IPCONFIG /ALL returned an IP address of 169.254.146.252 with a subnet mask of 255.255.0.0. The IP address is set to an IP address in the IP range between 169.254.0.1 and 169.254.255.254 by APIPA. When TCP/IP is configured by APIPA, the IP address of 169.254.0.132 is normal.

B. **Incorrect:** IPCONFIG /ALL returned an IP address of 169.254.146.252 with a subnet mask of 255.255.0.0. The default gateway is empty because when TCP/IP is configured by APIPA, the IP gateway setting is left empty. Because APIPA is used to configure TCP/IP, the blank IP gateway setting is normal.

C. **Incorrect:** IPCONFIG /ALL returned an IP address of 169.254.146.252 with a subnet mask of 255.255.0.0. The subnet mask is set to 255.255.0.0 by APIPA. When TCP/IP is configured by APIPA, a subnet mask of 255.255.0.0 is normal.

D. **Correct:** IPCONFIG /ALL returned an IP address of 169.254.146.252 with a subnet mask of 255.255.0.0. The IP address returned is an APIPA address that was assigned to the client computer when a DHCP server is not contacted. When Windows 2000 Professional is configured to configure IP, TCP/IP attempts to contact a DHCP server for IP configuration information. If no DHCP server can be contacted, TCP/IP assigns an APIPA address to the local adapter.

70-218.02.03.002

▶ **Correct Answers: B and F**

A. **Incorrect:** Members of the Domain Admins group are unable to authorize DHCP servers.

B. **Correct:** You must log on as a user account that is a member of the Enterprise Administrators group to authorize DHCP servers.

C. **Incorrect:** There is no built-in DHCP Administrators group in Active Directory.

D. **Incorrect:** The Active Directory Users and Computers console cannot authorize DHCP servers.

E. **Incorrect:** The Active Directory Sites and Services console cannot authorize DHCP servers.

F. **Correct:** You authorize DHCP servers by using the DHCP console. Start the DHCP console. In the console tree, click DHCP. On the Action menu, click Manage Authorized Servers. Click Authorize and when prompted, type the name or IP address of the DHCP servers to be authorized.

70-218.02.03.003

▶ **Correct Answers: B**

A. **Incorrect:** Because you are able to successfully ping the DHCP server, the DHCP server has a valid IP address. Although not recommended, the DHCP Server service can work with a dynamically assigned address.

B. **Correct:** Because the DHCP server is a member of an Active Directory domain, the DHCP server must be authorized in Active Directory. If the DHCP server is unauthorized, the DHCP Server service will not start. The system event log on the DHCP server will contain a log entry that says the DHCP Server services failed to start because the DHCP server is not authorized in Active Directory.

C. **Incorrect:** DHCP can perform dynamic updates in an Active Directory integrated DNS zone. However, the DHCP Server service is not dependent on the ability to make dynamic updates to an Active Directory integrated DNS zone.

D. **Incorrect:** The DHCP server must have a valid DHCP scope defined to provide configuration to DHCP clients. The DHCP Server service will start without any DHCP scopes. The lack of DHCP scopes is not the reason the DHCP Server service will not start.

70-218.02.03.004

▶ **Correct Answers: D**

A. **Incorrect:** Because you are able to successfully ping the DHCP server, the DHCP server has a valid IP address. Although not recommended, the DHCP Server service can work with a dynamically assigned address and should not prevent the DHCP server from assigning IP addresses to the client computers.

B. **Incorrect:** Because the DHCP server is a member of an Active Directory domain, the DHCP server must be authorized in Active Directory to run the DHCP Server service. If the DHCP server is unauthorized, the DHCP Server service will not start. Because the DHCP server is a member of an Active Directory domain and the DHCP Server service is running, the DHCP server must be authorized in Active Directory.

C. **Incorrect:** DHCP can perform dynamic updates in an Active Directory integrated DNS zone. However, the DHCP server is not dependent on the ability to make dynamic updates to an Active Directory integrated DNS zone to provide configuration for client computers.

D. **Correct:** When a DHCP server has no valid DHCP scope defined for a network segment, no IP addresses can be assigned to the computer on that network segment. You must create a DHCP scope for each network segment in your network that includes client computers that are configured by DHCP.

70-218.02.03.005

▶ **Correct Answers: C**

A. **Incorrect:** IPCONFIG /RENEW allows the user to release the existing IP address and obtain a new IP address, which solves the problem of the laptop user connecting to network resources. However, unless DNS is updated with the new IP address, the Help desk cannot connect to the laptop. IPCONFIG /RENEW will not reregister the DNS names of the laptop.

B. **Incorrect:** IPCONFIG /SETCLASSID sets the DHCP scope class for the computer, but it does not release the old IP address and obtain a new IP address. In addition, DNS names are not reregistered.

C. **Correct:** IPCONFIG /REGISTERDNS forces the laptop computer to end the lease of the IP address assigned to the laptop by DHCP, obtain a new IP address, and reregister the DNS names for the laptop. The laptop must obtain a new IP address because the laptop has moved from one network segment to another. In some instances, the users might not shut down their laptop and might move between meetings with the power on. The IP configuration is not updated if the user moves without performing some type of shutdown process. When a new IP address is obtained, the DNS servers must be updated with the new IP address. If DNS is not updated, the Help desk team cannot locate the laptop on the network.

D. **Incorrect:** IPCONFIG /RELEASE forces the laptop computer to end the lease of the IP address assigned to the laptop by DHCP. However, IPCONFIG /RELEASE does not obtain a new IP address or reregister the DNS names for the laptop.

70-218.02.03.006

▶ **Correct Answers: A**

A. **Correct:** Writing a NETSH script ensures consistency across all 50 servers because minimal user intervention is required. The NETSH script also minimizes the amount of time required for administrators to update the DHCP servers.

B. **Incorrect:** Each DHCP server database contains the specific DHCP scopes, scope options, and other DHCP database information. Backing up a DHCP database on one DHCP server and restoring the database to an existing DHCP server would destroy the DHCP scopes and scope options on the existing DHCP database.

C. **Incorrect:** Creating a superscope to accomplish the tasks requires a significant amount of user intervention. The amount of time required would be very near to, if not more than, the amount of time required by administrators to manually update each DHCP scope. In addition, because the process is manually completed, errors in the configuration might be unintentionally introduced.

D. **Incorrect:** Creating a new series of DHCP scopes requires a significant amount of user intervention. The amount of time required would be significantly more than the amount of time required by administrators to manually update each DHCP scope. In addition, because the process is manually completed, errors in the configuration might be unintentionally introduced.

70-218.02.03.007

▶ **Correct Answers: B**

A. **Incorrect:** Installing the DHCP Relay Agent on the DHCP server will cause the DHCP server to become unable to respond to DHCP requests reliably. The DHCP Server service and the DHCP Relay Agent use the same IP port to service DHCP requests. Install the DHCP Relay Agent on routers running Windows 2000 with Routing and Remote Access to provide the forwarding of DHCP traffic from clients on a network segment other than the network segment where the DHCP server is directly connected.

B. **Correct:** DHCP uses broadcast packets to exchange DHCP configuration information between DHCP clients and DHCP servers. By default, IP routers prevent broadcast packets from being forwarded across routers. Enabling DHCP/BOOTP forwarding on the routers allows the routers to forward DHCP requests from the clients on Segment A and Segment C to the DHCP server on Segment B.

C. **Incorrect:** The DHCP Relay Agent can be installed only on Windows 2000 Server or Windows 2000 Advanced Server. The client computers are already configured for automatic IP configuration. No other client configuration is required.

D. **Incorrect:** Creating a DHCP superscope does not resolve the issue. A DHCP superscope can be used to reduce administration and to support multiple subnets on the same network segment. Because only one subnet is assigned to each network segment, superscopes will not resolve the issue.

OBJECTIVE 2.4

Configure, administer, and troubleshoot DNS.

DNS is the method implemented in most operating systems for resolving user-friendly names to IP addresses (**forward lookups**) and for finding the user-friendly name associated with an IP address (**reverse lookups**). The Internet and Active Directory both use DNS to provide name resolution.

DNS is implemented in Windows 2000 as a DNS client and a DNS server. All versions of Windows 2000 include the DNS client portion of DNS. Windows 2000 Server and Windows 2000 Advanced Server include the DNS server portion of DNS.

The DNS client is responsible for receiving DNS queries from applications and services running on Windows 2000 and sending those queries to the appropriate DNS servers. The DNS client receives the reply from the DNS server and sends the response to the application or service that originally initiated the DNS query. The DNS client is an integral portion of **TCP/IP** in Windows 2000.

The DNS server, a service that runs in Windows 2000, is responsible for resolving DNS queries received from DNS clients. If the DNS server is unable to resolve the DNS query, the DNS server:

- Forwards the DNS query to another DNS server

- Reports that the DNS query was unsuccessful to the DNS client that originated the DNS query

To answer the questions in this objective, you should be able to:

- Troubleshoot TCP/IP-related issues.

- Run common TCP/IP command-line utilities (such as PING).

- Run common DNS command-line utilities (such as NSLOOKUP and DNSCMD).

- Perform common tasks in the DNS console.

- Describe how DNS performs simple and recursive forward lookups.

- Describe how DNS performs reverse lookups.

Objective 2.4 Questions

70-218.02.04.001

You are installing and configuring DNS servers in your organization. As you do so, you want to enable:

- Client computers to locate network resources by using FQDNs

- DNS resource records to be automatically updated in a secure fashion

You have installed Windows 2000 Server by using the default options. Which of the following steps must you complete to achieve these goals? (Choose all that apply.)

A. Create a primary standard forward lookup zone.

B. Create an Active Directory integrated forward lookup zone.

C. Configure the zone to support dynamic updates.

D. Configure the zone to support only secure dynamic updates.

E. Create a standard primary reverse lookup zone.

F. Create an Active Directory integrated reverse lookup zone.

70-218.02.04.002

You are troubleshooting a DNS server in your organization. The clients serviced by the DNS server are able to resolve names in zones directly managed by the DNS server, but not by names that reside in zones managed by other DNS servers. You suspect that recursive name resolution is the problem. How can you troubleshoot recursive name resolution?

A. By using the DNS console

B. By running the NETSH command

C. By running the DNSCMD command

D. By using the DSQUERY command

70-218.02.04.003

You are troubleshooting a DNS server in your organization. The DNS server is a domain controller in an Active Directory domain, and it is configured with only Active Directory integrated zones. The clients are unable to resolve FQDNs through the DNS server. From one of the client computers, you ping the DNS server successfully. You examine the DNS server and discover that the DNS Server service is not running. You attempt to start the DNS Server service, but are unable to do so. What is the most likely reason you are unable to start the DNS Server service?

A. The DNS server does not have any valid forward lookup zones.

B. The DNS server does not have any valid reverse lookup zones.

C. The DNS server is not authorized in Active Directory service.

D. The DNS server is unable to read the DNS zone stored in Active Directory.

70-218.02.04.004

The client computers configured to use the DNS server DNSServer-A for name resolution are:

- Able to resolve names managed by DNSServer-A

- Unable to resolve names managed by other DNS servers

- Unable to resolve names managed by DNS servers on the Internet

You examine the configuration of the DNS server further by examining the DNS configuration and the properties of the only network interface in the DNS server. You determine that your organization uses forwarders to recursively resolve DNS queries. The following table lists the settings of the Internet Protocol (TCP/IP) Properties for the network interfaces in Client-A, DNSServer-A, DNSServer-B, and DNSServer-C.

IP setting	Client-A	DNSServer-A	DNSServer-B	DNSServer-C
IP address	172.16.32.101	172.16.32.11	172.16.48.11	172.16.64.11
Subnet mask	255.255.252.0	255.255.252.0	255.255.252.0	255.255.252.0
Default gateway	172.16.32.1	172.16.32.1	172.16.48.1	172.16.64.1
Preferred DNS server	172.16.32.11			
Alternate DNS server	172.16.48.11			

The Root Hints and Forwarders property pages of DNSServer-A contain no entries. What is the most likely reason that the client computers are unable to resolve names managed by any DNS server other than DNSServer-A?

Examine the figure shown here.

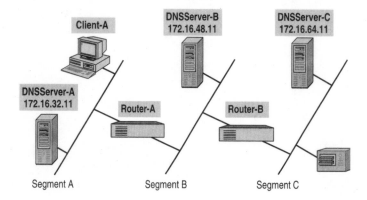

A. The preferred DNS server setting is incorrect on the DNS client.

B. The preferred DNS server setting is incorrect on DNSServer-A.

C. The configuration of DNS forwarders is incorrect on DNSServer-A.

D. The configuration of root hints is incorrect on DNSServer-A.

70-218.02.04.005

You have recently deployed new DNS servers in your organization. Now that the deployment is complete, you want to:

- Create new standard DNS zones on the new DNS servers.

- Ensure that these new DNS zones are replicated to the 140 DNS servers throughout your organization.

- Minimize any administration costs associated with the updates to DNS.

How do you update the DNS servers to achieve these objectives?

A. Write a NETSH script to create the new DNS zones on the new DNS servers and configure zone replication for the other 140 DNS servers.

B. Write a DNSCMD script to create the new DNS zones on the new DNS servers. Then write another DNSCMD script to configure zone replication for the other DNS servers.

C. Create the new zones on one of the new DNS servers. After the new zones are created and resources records are added, back up the DNS zone file database and restore the DNS zone file to the other DNS servers.

D. On each of the DNS servers in your organization, create the new DNS zones. In each of the new DNS zone, create the appropriate DNS resource records.

Objective 2.4 Answers

70-218.02.04.001

▶ **Correct Answers: B and D**

A. **Incorrect:** A primary standard forward lookup zone allows clients to locate resources by FQDNs and can be automatically updated. However, it cannot be automatically updated by using a secured method.

B. **Correct:** An Active Directory integrated forward lookup zone allows the clients to locate resources by FQDNs and can be automatically updated in a secure manner.

C. **Incorrect:** Configuring the zone to support only dynamic updates will not allow security to be enforced. You can configure standard primary zones or Active Directory integrated zones for dynamic updates.

D. **Correct:** Configuring the zone to support only secure dynamic updates ensures that only authorized users or computers can perform updates to the zone. Only Active Directory integrated zones support secure dynamic updates.

E. **Incorrect:** Reverse lookup zones allow users to query the DNS server with an IP address. The DNS server responds to the query with the FQDN of the computer that matches the IP address. The ability to perform reverse lookups was not one of the requirements.

F. **Incorrect:** Reverse lookup zones allow users to query the DNS server with an IP address. The DNS server responds to the query with the FQDN of the computer that matches the IP address. The ability to perform reverse lookups was not one of the requirements.

70-218.02.04.002

▶ **Correct Answers: A**

A. **Correct:** You can troubleshoot recursive name resolution through the DNS console. Under the Monitoring tab on the properties of the DNS server, select the test type and then click Test Now.

B. **Incorrect:** The NETSH command can be used to administer DNS, but you cannot troubleshoot recursive queries from it.

C. **Incorrect:** The DNSCMD command can be used to administer DNS, but you cannot troubleshoot recursive queries from it.

D. **Incorrect:** The DSQUERY command queries Active Directory, not DNS. You cannot query DNS with DSQUERY.

70-218.02.04.003

▶ **Correct Answers: D**

A. **Incorrect:** When DNS is initially installed, no valid forward lookup zones exist. However, DNS starts successfully without any forward lookup zones.

B. **Incorrect:** When DNS is initially installed, no valid reverse lookup zones exist. However, DNS starts successfully without any reverse lookup zones.

C. **Incorrect:** The DNS server does not need to be authorized in Active Directory service. Only DNS servers that have Active Directory integrated zones require Active Directory.

D. **Correct:** When a DNS server is configured with only Active Directory integrated zones, the DNS Server service cannot start when the DNS server is unable to read the DNS zone stored on the local Active Directory domain controller. The DNS server needs to read the zone information for all Active Directory integrated zones. In many cases, Active Directory replication might not have replicated the zone from another domain controller. You can force Active Directory replication to the nearest domain controller to ensure the local domain controller has the updated zone information. After Active Directory replication is complete, start the DNS server.

70-218.02.04.004

▶ **Correct Answers: C**

A. **Incorrect:** The preferred DNS server setting is configured to use DNSServer-A as the preferred DNS server for the DNS client. DNSServer-A is not configured properly to forward DNS queries to other DNS servers.

B. **Incorrect:** The preferred DNS server setting for DNSServer-A affects only the DNS client on DNS-Server-A, not the DNS server. The DNS client is responsible for receiving DNS queries from applications and forwarding the queries to the DNS servers configured in the IP. The DNS server is responsible for responding to queries from DNS clients, resolving the queries, and responding to the DNS clients. The DNS server on DNSServer-A is the source of the problem.

C. **Correct:** DNS forwarders are other DNS servers that can be contacted when the local DNS server cannot resolve a DNS query. The local DNS server forwards the DNS query to the servers listed on the Forwarders tab. The DNS servers on the Forwarders tab either resolve the query, forward the query to other DNS servers, or return an unsuccessful DNS query response (such as host not found). The Forwarders tab on DNSServer-A should contain DNSServer-C and DNSServer-D.

D. **Incorrect:** You can recursively resolve DNS queries by using either DNS forwarders or root hints. Typically, an organization selects only one of these methods to perform recursive DNS name resolution. The organization has standardized on using forwarding to recursively resolve DNS queries.

70-218.02.04.005

▶ **Correct Answers: B**

A. **Incorrect:** NETSH cannot be used to create scripts for managing DNS servers. You can create scripts for NETSH that can administer and manage Routing and Remote Access, DHCP, and WINS.

B. **Correct:** DNSCMD can be used to create scripts for managing DNS servers. You can create DNS zones and configure DNS replication on the DNS servers by using DNSCMD.

C. **Incorrect:** The new DNS servers are using standard DNS zones. With standard DNS zones, only one standard primary zone can exist. All other replicas of the DNS zone must be secondary zones. You cannot copy the primary zone file from one of the new DNS servers to another and create a secondary zone. The secondary zone must use DNS replication to replicate the DNS zone from the standard primary zone file. Had the organization been using Active Directory integrated zones, all DNS servers could have read/write copies of the DNS zone information.

D. **Incorrect:** Creating new DNS zones on each DNS server requires a significant amount of user intervention. In addition, each new DNS zone would have to be individually administered and would not use DNS replication to provide consistency across all the DNS servers for the zone.

O B J E C T I V E 2 . 5

Troubleshoot name resolution on client computers.

Name resolution is the process by which a user-friendly name, such as a **fully qualified domain name (FQDN)**, is resolved to an IP address. Windows 2000 supports:

- **DNS** to provide FQDN resolution for all client computers running Microsoft Windows operating systems, Macintosh operating systems, and UNIX

- **WINS** to provide NetBIOS name resolution for all client computers running Microsoft Windows operating systems and UNIX

To troubleshoot name resolution problems, you must first determine whether the name resolution problem is related to FQDN resolution or NetBIOS name resolution. FQDNs look like the names used in **Uniform Resource Locators (URLs)** on the Internet (for example, *www.contoso.com* is a FQDN). NetBIOS names are 15 characters or fewer in length and do not contain periods ".".

Unfortunately, host names and NetBIOS names can look identical (by default the host name and NetBIOS name for Windows 2000 is the same). Any application that uses the **NetBIOS over TCP/IP (NetBT)** protocol requires NetBIOS name resolution (such as file and print sharing in Windows NT 4). Any application that uses Windows Sockets (WinSock) can use either host names or NetBIOS names.

Name resolution is an integral part of TCP/IP in Windows 2000. No additional services or software is required. The FQDN and NetBIOS name resolution in Windows 2000 also caches resolved names to reduce subsequent DNS queries. For example, if a client queries DNS for an FQDN, the FQDN is cached locally on the client upon successful name resolution. On subsequent DNS queries for the same FQDN, the name is resolved from local DNS cache on the client.

To answer the questions in this objective, you should be able to:

- Troubleshoot TCP/IP-related issues.

- Run common TCP/IP command-line utilities (such as PING, IPCONFIG, and PATHPING).

- Run common name resolution command-line utilities (such as NSLOOKUP, NBSTAT, and DNSCMD).

- Perform common tasks in the DNS and WINS consoles.

- Describe how DNS performs simple and recursive forward lookups.

- Describe how DNS performs reverse lookups.

- Describe how clients perform NetBIOS name resolution with a WINS server and with broadcasts.

- Describe how the hosts and Lmhosts files are used in name resolution.

Objective 2.5 Questions

70-218.02.05.001

You are troubleshooting name resolution problems in your network. You run NSLOOKUP on Client-A and the following output is displayed:

```
C:\>nslookup fileserver-b
DNS request timed out.
    timeout was 2 seconds.
*** Can't find server name for address 172.16.32.11: Timed out
DNS request timed out.
    timeout was 2 seconds.
*** Can't find server name for address 172.16.48.11: Timed out
*** Default servers are not available
Server:  UnKnown
Address:  172.16.48.11

Name:    fileserver-b.noam.concorp.contoso.com
Address:  172.16.48.28

C:\>
```

Why does NSLOOKUP report the "Can't find server names for address" messages?

Examine the figure shown here.

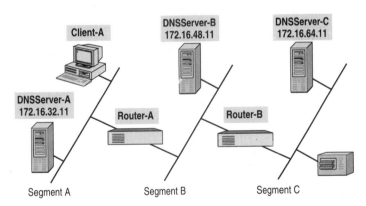

A. No resource records exist for the servers in the reverse lookup zones on the corresponding DNS server.

B. No resource records exist for the servers in the forward lookup zones on the corresponding DNS server.

C. The DNS cache on the DNS server contains outdated information.

D. The DNS cache on the client contains outdated information.

70-218.02.05.002

You are troubleshooting name resolution problems in your network. You can successfully ping other clients and servers on the network by using IP addresses. However, you are unable to ping other clients and servers on the network by using FQDNs. The following table lists the settings of the Internet Protocol (TCP/IP) Properties for the network interfaces in Client-A, DNSServer-A, DNSServer-B, and DNSServer-C.

IP setting	Client-A	DNSServer-A	DNSServer-B	DNSServer-C
IP address	172.16.32.101	172.16.32.11	172.16.48.11	172.16.64.11
Subnet mask	255.255.252.0	255.255.252.0	255.255.252.0	255.255.252.0
Default gateway	172.16.32.1	172.16.32.1	172.16.48.1	172.16.64.1
Preferred DNS server	172.16.32.12			
Alternate DNS server	172.16.48.12			

Why are you unable to ping other clients and servers on the network by using FQDNs?

Examine the figure shown here.

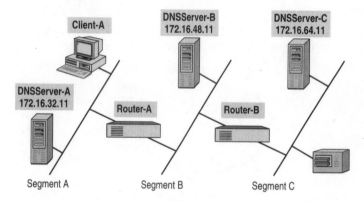

A. The default gateway setting on DNSServer-C is incorrect.

B. No resource records exist for the other clients and servers in the reverse lookup zones on DNSServer-C.

C. The primary DNS setting on Client-A is incorrect.

D. The default gateway setting on Client-A is incorrect.

70-218.02.05.003

Client-A is unable to access resources on FileServer-C. From Client-A, you can successfully ping FileServer-C by using IP addresses. However, you are unable to ping FileServer-C by using the server name. You run NBTSTAT -a on Client-A and observer the following output:

```
C:\>nbtstat -c

Local Area Connection:
Node IpAddress: [172.16.32.101] Scope Id: []

                NetBIOS Remote Cache Name Table

        Name              Type      Host Address    Life [sec]
        --------------------------------------------------------
        CLIENT-A        <20>  UNIQUE   172.16.32.101       425
        FILESERVER-C    <20>  UNIQUE   172.16.64.53        410
        WINSSERVER-B    <20>  UNIQUE   172.16.48.15        407

C:\>
```

What can you do so Client-A can access FileServer-C?

Examine the figure shown here to view the WINSServer-B WINS database entries.

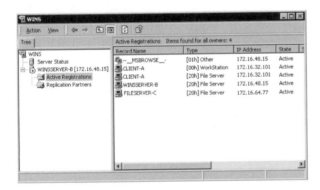

A. Delete the entry for FileServer-C in the WINS database on WINSServer-B.

B. Run the NETSH WINS SERVER CHECKNAME commands on WINSServer-B.

C. Run IPCONFIG /FLUSHDNS on Client-A.

D. Run NBTSTAT -r on Client-A.

70-218.02.05.004

Client-A is unable to access a Web site on WebServer-C by using the URL *http://www.contoso.com*. From Client-A, you can successfully ping WebServer-C by using IP addresses. However, you are unable to ping WebServer-C by using the URL. The user who reported the problem said he was able to access the Web site before. When the user was unable to access the Web site, he tried several configurations but was unsuccessful. The following is the contents of the hosts file on Client-A:

```
# Copyright (c) 1993-1999 Microsoft Corp.
#
# This is a HOSTS file used by Microsoft TCP/IP for Windows.
#
# This file contains the mappings of IP addresses to host names. Each
# entry should be kept on an individual line. The IP address should
# be placed in the first column followed by the corresponding host name.
# The IP address and the host name should be separated by at least one
# space.
#
# Additionally, comments (such as these) may be inserted on individual
# lines or following the machine name denoted by a '#' symbol.
#
# For example:
#
#      102.54.94.97      rhino.acme.com          # source server
#      38.25.63.10       x.acme.com              # x client host

127.0.0.1       localhost
172.16.64.68WebServer-C
172.16.64.11www.contoso.com
```

The following is the contents of the contoso.com.dns zone file on DNSServer-B:

```
@                         IN  SOA dnsserver-b.contoso.com.  administrator.contoso.com. (
                          5                ; serial number
                          900              ; refresh
                          600              ; retry
                          86400            ; expire
                          3600       ) ; minimum TTL
;
;   Zone NS records
;
@                         NSdnsserver-b.contoso.com.
;
;   Zone records
;
client-a                  A172.16.32.101
dnsserver-b               A172.16.48.11
webserver-c               A172.16.64.68
www                       A172.16.64.68
```

You verify that WebServer-C is running and that the Web site is available from another client computer and DNS server. What can you do so Client-A can access *www.contoso.com*?

Examine the figure shown here.

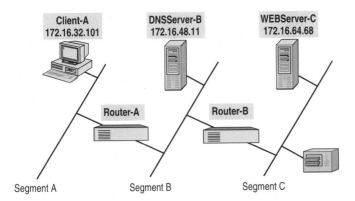

A. Delete the resource record for *www.contoso.com* in the DNS zone.

B. Delete the entry for *www.contoso.com* in the hosts file on Client-A.

C. Run IPCONFIG /FLUSHDNS on Client-A.

D. Run IPCONFIG /REGISTERDNS on Client-A.

70-218.02.05.005

A user in your organization is experiencing difficulty connecting to another user's laptop. The user who owns the laptop has shared a folder and assigned the appropriate permissions. You find that you can ping the laptop, but you are unable to locate the laptop by using the laptop's name. Upon further inquiry, you discover that the laptop was not connected to the network when the user logged on. Your organization has standardized on DNS for name resolution. What can you do to resolve the problem?

A. Run DSQUERY on the laptop.

B. Run IPCONFIG /FLUSHDNS on the laptop.

C. Run IPCONFIG /REGISTERDNS on the laptop.

D. Run NBTSTAT -RR on the laptop.

70-218.02.05.006

A coworker is trying to access shares on a file server named FileServer.noam.concorp.contoso.com. You find that you can ping the file server by IP address, but not by the file server's name. Which of the following commands gives you information that is pertinent in troubleshooting the name resolution problem? (Choose all that apply.)

A. NBTSTAT -a

B. IPCONFIG /ALL

C. NSLOOKUP FileServer.noam.concorp.contoso.com

D. ARP -a

E. NETSH WINS CHECK NAME

Objective 2.5 Answers

70-218.02.05.001

▶ **Correct Answers: A**

A. **Correct:** The NSLOOKUP command is performing recursive queries to resolve the DNS query. NSLOOKUP attempts to find the name of the DNS servers used in recursive queries by performing reverse lookups. The errors in the NSLOOKUP output are caused because NSLOOKUP cannot resolve the IP addresses of the DNS servers, used in the recursive query, to a name. Adding the appropriate resource records to the corresponding reverse lookup zone would resolve the error messages.

B. **Incorrect:** The error message is because the NSLOOKUP command is trying to perform a reverse lookup on the IP addresses of the DNS servers. Because forward lookup zones are not used in reverse lookups, the lack of resource records in the forward lookup zones is not the problem.

C. **Incorrect:** The output of the NSLOOKUP command reports the IP addresses of the DNS servers used for recursive queries. The primary DNS server for the client is unable to resolve the queries and forwards the query to other DNS servers. The DNS cache on the DNS servers caches only DNS query responses, not the names or IP addresses of other DNS servers.

D. **Incorrect:** The output of the NSLOOKUP command reports the IP addresses of the DNS servers used for recursive queries. The DNS client caches only DNS query responses, not the names of the DNS servers.

70-218.02.05.002

► **Correct Answers: C**

A. **Incorrect:** The default gateway setting on DNSServer-C is configured to use Router-A as the default gateway. Because Router-B is directly connected to the same network segment as DNSServer-C, this setting is correct.

B. **Incorrect:** Reverse lookup zones are used to resolve an IP address to an FQDN. The client computer is unable to resolve an FQDN to an IP address. Forward lookup zones are used to resolve an FQDN to an IP address.

C. **Correct:** The primary DNS setting on Client-A is configured to an IP address that does not exist in the network. The primary DNS setting of Client-A must be configured to an IP address of a DNS server on the network.

D. **Incorrect:** The default gateway setting on Client-A is configured to use Router-A as the default gateway. Because Router-A is directly connected to the same network segment as Client-A, this setting is correct.

70-218.02.05.003

► **Correct Answers: D**

A. **Incorrect:** For Client-A to access FileServer-C, Client-A must be able to resolve NetBIOS names to IP addresses. Client-A must be able to resolve the name for FileServer-C by using WINSServer-B. The WINS database on WINSServer-B lists the proper IP address for FileServer-C (172.16.64.77). The WINS database on WINSServer-B is not the problem.

B. **Incorrect:** The WINS database on WINSServer-B lists the proper IP address for FileServer-C (172.16.64.77). The WINS database on WINSServer-B is not the problem. The NETSH command will not correct the problem.

C. **Incorrect:** For Client-A to access FileServer-C, Client-A must be able to resolve NetBIOS names to IP addresses. Client-A must be able to resolve the name for FileServer-C by using WINSServer-B. NetBIOS name resolution is not affected by IPCONFIG /FLUSHDNS, only FQDN resolution.

D. **Correct:** Client-A has an outdated NetBIOS name resolution in the local NetBIOS name cache. Running NBTSTAT -r resets the cache, forcing Client-A to query WINSServer-B and retrieving the appropriate IP address for FileServer-C.

70-218.02.05.004

▶ **Correct Answers: B**

   A. **Incorrect:** The resource record in the DNS zone on DNSServer-B uses the correct IP address for WebServer-C and *www.contoso.com*. Client-A is not retrieving the information from the DNS zone because Client-A is using the hosts file on Client-A to resolve the names.

   B. **Correct:** The hosts file on Client-A lists the IP address for *www.contoso.com* as 172.16.64.11, which is incorrect. The DNS entry for *www.contoso.com* (172.16.64.68) is correct. Because Client-A checks the hosts file first, Client-A never checks the DNS entry.

   C. **Incorrect:** IPCONFIG /FLUSHDNS removes any cached DNS queries from the local DNS client. The hosts file on Client-A contains an invalid IP address for *www.contoso.com*. Removing any cached DNS queries will not correct the problem.

   D. **Incorrect:** IPCONFIG /REGISTERDNS forces the DHCP client to release the current IP configuration, renew the IP configuration, and reregister Client-A's DNS names with DNS. Reregistering Client-A's DNS names with DNS will not change how Client-A resolves *www.contoso.com*.

70-218.02.05.005

▶ **Correct Answers: C**

   A. **Incorrect:** DSQUERY performs queries against Active Directory to find Active Directory objects, such as users, groups, or computers. DSQUERY cannot be used to find the IP address of another computer. DSQUERY will not resolve the problem.

   B. **Incorrect:** IPCONFIG /FLUSHDNS removes any cached DNS queries from the laptop. The DNS cache is for queries initiated by the laptop. The problem is that other users cannot see the laptop and their DNS queries are not being resolved because the laptop did not register in DNS. Flushing the DNS cache on the laptop will not resolve the problem.

   C. **Correct:** IPCONFIG /REGISTERDNS forces the DHCP client to release the current IP configuration, renew the IP configuration, and reregister Client-A's DNS names with DNS. Reregistering Client-A's DNS names with DNS will force the laptop's DNS entries into DNS and allow the other user to see the computer name.

   D. **Incorrect:** NBTSTAT -RR clears the local NetBIOS name cache and reloads any NetBIOS name entries. Because your organization has standardized on DNS, NetBIOS names are not used. As a result, NBTSTAT -RR will not resolve the problem.

70-218.02.05.006

▶ **Correct Answers: B and C**

A. **Incorrect:** NBTSTAT -a displays the NetBIOS name cache on a computer. The file server name listed is specified as an FQDN. NetBIOS name resolution, and subsequently the NetBIOS name cache, is not used to resolve an FQDN.

B. **Correct:** IPCONFIG /ALL will display the IP configuration of the clients that cannot access the file server. You can verify the proper settings for the primary and alternate DNS server. The next step, after identifying the primary and alternate DNS servers, is to ping the primary and alternate DNS servers.

C. **Correct:** NSLOOKUP FileServer.noam.concorp.contoso.com tries to resolve the FQDN of the file server. The output from the NSLOOKUP command reports on whether the FQDN can be found in DNS. A successful response from NSLOOKUP indicates that the FQDN is found by DNS, but it might not have the right IP address. The next step, after a successful NSLOOKUP command, is to ping the FQDN.

D. **Incorrect:** ARP -a displays the contents of the ARP cache. Because the file server can be pinged, the IP connectivity is working correctly and the ARP cache is correct. The ARP command will not reveal any pertinent information.

E. **Incorrect:** NETSH WINS CHECK NAME is used to check the name records in a WINS database. The file server name listed is specified as an FQDN. NetBIOS name resolution, and subsequently WINS, is not used to resolve an FQDN.

Managing, Securing, and Troubleshooting Servers and Client Computers

Your responsibilities as an administrator most likely require you to actively manage server and client computers. One of the most basic and frequently performed tasks is installing hardware devices on server and client computers. Your users probably look to you for assistance installing the hardware devices, installing appropriate drivers, and configuring the device settings. Knowing how to effectively troubleshoot startup issues on servers and client computers caused by corrupt files or configuration errors is also an extremely important skill for administrators. You can often prevent startup issues and other server issues by monitoring a server's performance using such tools as **System Monitor**, **Event Viewer**, and **Task Manager**. Part of your management responsibilities might also include the sometimes tedious but critically important task of installing the appropriate **service packs** and **hotfixes** on computers in your network. Doing so helps ensure that the latest security fixes and performance improvements are available to your users. Understanding how to perform these tasks is key to managing server and client computers on your network.

Tested Skills and Suggested Practices

The skills that you need to master the Managing, Securing, and Troubleshooting Servers and Client Computers objective domain on the *Managing a Microsoft Windows 2000 Network Environment* exam include:

- **Installing and configuring server and client computer hardware.**

    - Practice 1: Note the hardware devices on a Windows 2000 computer such as the network adapter, sound card, compact disc read-only memory (CD-ROM) drive, and other storage devices. Verify that each device's manufacturer and model is Windows 2000–compliant on the Microsoft Hardware Compatibility List (HCL) at *http://www.microsoft.com/hcl/default.asp*.

    - Practice 2: Use Add/Remove Hardware in Control Panel to uninstall a Windows 2000–compliant Plug and Play (PnP) device from a Windows 2000 computer. Choose a device that is not critical to the operation of the computer. Use Device Manager to review all installed devices. Note that Device Manager does not list the device you uninstalled. Scan for hardware changes so Windows 2000 finds the device and reinstalls it on your computer.

    - Practice 3: Use Device Manager to view the properties for devices on your computer. Review the resource allocation for hardware devices such as a modem, network card, or Universal Serial Bus (USB) device. Choose a device that is not critical to the operation of the computer and update the device driver. Keep the currently installed driver if the Upgrade Device Driver Wizard explains that a suitable driver is already installed. Use the Driver Details button to view information about the device driver.

- **Troubleshooting starting servers and client computers.**

    - Practice 1: Start a Windows 2000 computer using an advanced boot option such as Safe Mode or Safe Mode with Networking by pressing F8 during startup. Restart the computer and use the Enable Boot Logging option from the Windows Advanced Options Menu. Restart the computer normally and examine the boot log file (NTBTLOG.TXT in the system root directory) to identify the files Windows 2000 attempts to load at startup.

    - Practice 2: Start the Recovery Console by starting the computer from the Windows 2000 Setup CD-ROM. Review the available Help commands by typing **help** at the command prompt. Do not use the commands unless you are resolving an actual startup problem, because the Recovery Console is a powerful tool that can damage the operating system if you use it improperly. Type **exit** to close the Recovery Console and restart your computer.

- **Monitoring and troubleshooting server health and performance.**

  - Practice 1: Access the Performance console from the Administrative Tools program group. Using the System Monitor snap-in, add several counters to monitor memory and cache performance. View the real-time counter values on the System Monitor graph.

  - Practice 2: Access the Performance console from the Administrative Tools program group. Use the Performance Logs and Alerts snap-in to define settings for counter logs using the same counters you used in Practice 1. Configure the logs to automatically start and stop at a time you choose. After you collect the performance logs, view the data using System Monitor.

  - Practice 3: Use Event Viewer from Administrative Tools. View information contained in the default Windows 2000 logs—application, security, and system. From the system log, select an event and view the event's properties. If you or a systems administrator has created an Audit Policy, view the associated security log.

  - Practice 4: Use Task Manager to view information about applications and processes running on a Microsoft Windows 2000 server. Use the Performance tab to monitor real-time performance data, including information about kernel usage. Use the Applications tab to select an application and then go to that application's process. Set a process's priority from the Processes tab.

- **Installing and managing Windows 2000 updates.**

  - Practice 1: Determine whether a Windows 2000 computer has the latest service pack installed by running the WINVER.EXE program from the Run dialog box. If applicable, download the latest service pack from *http://windowsupdate.microsoft.com* and run UPDATE.EXE to replace the existing files with the new files from the service pack.

  - Practice 2: Create a master source for distributing service pack files using slipstreaming. Download the service pack files to the folder containing the Windows 2000 installation files. Then apply the service pack by running UPDATE.EXE with the -s: *distribution_folder* switch (where *distribution_folder* is the name of the folder that contains the Windows 2000 installation files). This procedure replaces the existing Windows 2000 files with the appropriate files from the service pack.

Further Reading

This section lists supplemental readings by objective. We recommend that you study these sources thoroughly before taking exam 70-218.

Objective 3.1

Microsoft Corporation. *MCSA Training Kit: Managing a Microsoft Windows 2000 Network Environment*. Redmond, Washington: Microsoft Press, 2002. Review Lesson 1 in Chapter 2, "Managing Client and Server Computers."

Microsoft Corporation. *Windows 2000 Server Resource Kit*. Volume: *Microsoft Windows 2000 Server Operations Guide*. Redmond, Washington: Microsoft Press, 2000. Chapter 14, "Troubleshooting Strategies." (View the information contained in this chapter for free at *http://www.microsoft.com/windows2000/techinfo/reskit/default.asp*.)

Microsoft Corporation. *MCSE Training Kit: Microsoft Windows 2000 Professional*. Redmond, Washington: Microsoft Press, 2000. Review Lessons 4 and 5 in Chapter 4, "Using Windows Control Panel."

Microsoft Corporation. *Microsoft Windows 2000 Administrator's Pocket Consultant*. Redmond, Washington: Microsoft Press, 2000. Read Chapter 2, "Managing Microsoft Windows 2000 Workstations and Servers."

Objective 3.2

Microsoft Corporation. *MCSA Training Kit: Managing a Microsoft Windows 2000 Network Environment*. Redmond, Washington: Microsoft Press, 2002. Review Lesson 4 in Chapter 2, "Managing Client and Server Computers."

Microsoft Corporation. *Windows 2000 Server Resource Kit*. Volume: *Microsoft Windows 2000 Server Operations Guide*. Redmond, Washington: Microsoft Press, 2000. Review Chapter 13, "Repair, Recovery, and Restore," Chapter 14, "Troubleshooting Strategies," and Chapter 15, "Startup Process." (View the information contained in these chapters for free at *http://www.microsoft.com/windows2000/techinfo/reskit/default.asp*.)

Microsoft Corporation. *MCSE Training Kit: Microsoft Windows 2000 Server*. Redmond, Washington: Microsoft Press, 2000. Read Lesson 4 in Chapter 12, "Reliability and Availability."

"Windows 2000 Safe-Mode Boot and Recovery Console" describes Safe Mode and Recovery Console, and provides examples of their use. (Download this white paper for free at *http://www.microsoft.com/windows2000/techinfo/administration/management/safemode.asp*.)

Objective 3.3

Microsoft Corporation. *MCSA Training Kit: Managing a Microsoft Windows 2000 Network Environment.* Redmond, Washington: Microsoft Press, 2002. Review Lesson 1 in Chapter 6, "Monitoring Server Health and Security."

Microsoft Corporation. *Windows 2000 Server Resource Kit.* Volume: *Microsoft Windows 2000 Server Operations Guide.* Redmond, Washington: Microsoft Press, 2000. Review Chapter 5, "Overview of Performance Monitoring," and Chapter 14, "Troubleshooting Strategies." (View the information contained in these chapters for free at *http://www.microsoft.com/windows2000/techinfo/reskit/default.asp.*)

Microsoft Corporation. *MCSE Training Kit: Microsoft Windows 2000 Server.* Redmond, Washington: Microsoft Press, 2000. Review Lessons 3 and 5 in Chapter 13, "Monitoring and Optimization."

Microsoft Corporation. *Microsoft Windows 2000 Administrator's Pocket Consultant.* Redmond, Washington: Microsoft Press, 2000. Review Chapter 3, "Monitoring Processes, Services, and Events."

Objective 3.4

Microsoft Corporation. *MCSA Training Kit: Managing a Microsoft Windows 2000 Network Environment.* Redmond, Washington: Microsoft Press, 2002. Review Lesson 2 in Chapter 2, "Managing Client and Server Computers."

Microsoft Corporation. *MCSE Training Kit: Microsoft Windows 2000 Server.* Redmond, Washington: Microsoft Press, 2000. Review Appendix C, "Installing Service Packs."

"Windows 2000 Service Pack 2 Installation and Deployment Guide" is a good source of information and procedures for deploying service packs. (Download the guide for free at *http://www.microsoft.com/windows2000/techinfo/planning/incremental/sp2guide.asp.*)

OBJECTIVE 3.1

Install and configure server and client computer hardware.

As an administrator, part of your responsibilities might require you to assist users with installing and configuring hardware devices such as CD-ROM drives, printers, network adapters, display adapters, and keyboards. In many cases, installing hardware in a Windows 2000 environment is no more complex than plugging in the hardware and letting Windows 2000 automatically detect and install a **Plug and Play (PnP) device**. However, if Windows 2000 does not automatically detect the new hardware device or the device doesn't work correctly, you must know the appropriate troubleshooting and configuration steps. Many of the same steps you use for client computers are also applicable to servers in your organization.

Your understanding of configuring hardware starts with knowing how to install hardware devices using Add/Remove Hardware in Control Panel. You must then be able to load the correct driver for the device. The final installation step is to make sure the device properties and settings are properly configured. For example, you must make sure the system resources used by the device, such as **input/output (I/O)** port addresses or **interrupt request (IRQ) line numbers**, do not conflict with other devices on the computer. You should know how to use **Device Manager** to update device drivers and how to install unsigned device drivers. Device Manager is located under System Tools in the Computer Management snap-in. **Driver Signing** notifies Windows 2000 users whether the drivers they are installing are compatible with Windows 2000. You can configure Windows 2000 to warn or prevent users from installing unsigned drivers.

A frequent cause of hardware problems is using hardware that is not compatible with Windows 2000. To help prevent incompatibilities, Microsoft publishes the **Hardware Compatibility List (HCL)**, which is a compilation of system hardware Microsoft has tested with Windows 2000. One way to prevent hardware problems is to make sure you are using a device make and model listed in the HCL. Another method to ensure hardware compatibility is to use the compatibility-mode option integrated with

Windows 2000 Setup. You use this option before installing Windows 2000 to examine the computer's hardware and software for known problems Setup might encounter. The option produces a report describing any hardware files or upgrade packs the computer might need to successfully run Windows 2000.

Regular maintenance of hardware devices is also part of an administrator's responsibilities. For some computers, creating, configuring, and activating a **hardware profile** is appropriate. A hardware profile stores configuration settings for a set of devices and services. For example, you might want to optimize a laptop's hardware profile to support switching between a docking station and stand-alone use. To make sure the hardware in your organization operates correctly, you need to have a thorough understanding of how to configure these hardware options.

Objective 3.1 Questions

70-218.03.01.001

You are configuring a user's Windows 2000 computer and you need to make sure the hardware is working properly. You also want to perform the following tasks:

- Change the hardware configuration settings.

- Identify the device drivers loaded for each device and install updated drivers if necessary.

- Identify any device conflicts and change advanced settings and properties for the devices.

Which tool is appropriate for performing these tasks?

A. The System Information snap-in.

B. The Add/Remove Hardware Wizard.

C. Device Manager.

D. None of these tools allow you to perform the tasks.

70-218.03.01.002

One of your coworkers has an external USB CD-ROM configured on her Microsoft Windows 2000 Professional computer. The CD-ROM is no longer working properly, and the coworker is asking you for assistance. You suspect that the CD-ROM driver needs updating. How can you best update the driver?

A. Use Device Manager to disable the CD-ROM, and then restart the computer.

B. Use Device Manager to access the CD-ROM's Properties dialog box to update the driver.

C. Use Device Manager to scan for hardware changes.

D. Use the Add/Remove Hardware Wizard in Control Panel to remove the CD-ROM, and then restart the computer.

70-218.03.01.003

You are configuring a new laptop computer and docking station for one of your coworkers. The computer is running Windows 2000 Professional, and all hardware is PnP compliant. How do you enable the computer to recognize docked and undocked hardware profiles?

A. You must create new hardware profiles using Hardware Profiles from the Hardware tab in the System Properties dialog box.

B. You configure each individual device to be recognized by the profile using Hardware Profiles from the Hardware tab in the System Properties dialog box.

C. You customize the existing *Profile 1 (Current)* profile using Device Manager.

D. You do not need to enable the computer to recognize these profiles.

70-218.03.01.004

One of your users is attempting to add an external compact disc-rewritable (CD-RW) drive to his Windows 2000 Professional computer. Microsoft has not signed the device driver for the CD-RW, and the user has been unable to install the hardware. How can you configure the computer so the user can install the unsigned driver?

A. Set the Driver Signing option to Warn.

B. Set the Driver Signing option to Block.

C. Use Device Manager to access the device's Properties dialog box to modify the device's properties to allow an unsigned driver.

D. Use the Add/Remove Hardware Wizard in Control Panel to install the device and the driver.

70-218.03.01.005

A user in your organization has a Windows 2000 Professional laptop computer with a built-in network adapter. You want to configure the computer so the network adapter is unavailable when the user is away from the office and not connected to the organization's network. You decide to create a new hardware profile to accomplish this task, so you log on as administrator. First, you create a second hardware profile named "Undocked." You then configure Windows 2000 so the user must select an appropriate profile when the computer starts. Then you restart the laptop and select the new profile. What do you do next?

A. Use the Add/Remove Hardware Wizard to uninstall the network adapter.

B. Use the Add/Remove Hardware Wizard to disable the network adapter.

C. Use Device Manager to remove the network adapter.

D. Use Device Manager to disable the network adapter.

70-218.03.01.006

A user in your organization has asked you for assistance installing a new modem on her computer. The computer has Windows 2000 Professional installed. You are unsure whether the modem is Plug and Play (PnP) compliant. What methods are appropriate for installing the modem? (Choose all that apply.)

A. Use the Network Connection Wizard from the Network and Dial-Up Connection folder.

B. Use Device Manager.

C. Use the Add/Remove Hardware Wizard in Control Panel.

D. Use the Add/Remove Programs Wizard in Control Panel.

E. Use the Phone and Modem Options program in Control Panel.

Objective 3.1 Answers

70-218.03.01.001

▶ **Correct Answers: C**

A. **Incorrect:** Although you can use System Information to troubleshoot hardware devices by displaying system configuration information, this is not the appropriate tool for the specified tasks. System Information is a snap-in you can use to collect and view configuration information about your system. For example, you can display hardware resource settings to troubleshoot conflicts. However, you cannot use System Information to change hardware configuration settings, install device drivers, or change advanced settings as you can with Device Manager.

B. **Incorrect:** You use the Add/Remove Hardware Wizard to add, remove, and troubleshoot new hardware devices. It is most appropriate for finding and installing new Plug and Play (PnP) hardware. You cannot use the Add/Remove Hardware Wizard to identify device drivers and change advance settings for devices.

C. **Correct:** Device Manager is the appropriate tool for these tasks because it provides you with a graphical view of the hardware installed on your computer. To determine whether a hardware device is working correctly, access Device Manager under System Tools in Computer Management. Device Manager lists all devices on the computer; each device that has problems displays corresponding status information. Using Device Manager, you can change a device's configuration settings, manage and update device drivers, and change advanced settings. When you need to manually change device configurations, Device Manager allows you to identify free resources and assign a device to that resource. You can also disable devices or reallocate resources to free up additional resources for other devices. You must be logged on as a member of the Administrators group to change resource settings.

D. **Incorrect:** This is incorrect for the reasons stated in answer C.

70-218.03.01.002

▶ **Correct Answers: B**

A. **Incorrect:** Disabling the CD-ROM and restarting the computer does not update the device driver. When you disable a device, the device driver is no longer loaded when you start the computer. You must enable the device to allow the device drivers to be loaded, and in this case the system would load the original driver.

B. **Correct:** The best way to update the CD-ROM driver in this situation is to use Device Manager to access the CD-ROM's properties and install an updated device driver. First, be sure to have the manufacturer's latest driver available. To install the updated driver, click the Update Driver button on the Drivers tab of the device's Properties dialog box. You then use the Update Device Driver Wizard to update the driver.

C. **Incorrect:** Scanning for hardware changes does not update the device driver. You use the Scan for Hardware Changes option in Device Manager to scan for PnP-compliant hardware connected to the computer. This does not reinstall a PnP device if the CD-ROM is already installed, and it does not update the driver. If you scan for hardware changes in this situation, Device Manager will most likely not find any new hardware.

D. **Incorrect:** Although it is possible to use the Add/Remove Hardware Wizard to update a device driver, it is not the most efficient method and might not work. To use this method, you must first uninstall the CD-ROM and drivers, connect the CD-ROM to the computer, and possibly restart the computer to allow Windows 2000 to detect the CD-ROM. This method will possibly reinstall the existing drivers if they are found on the computer; if not, you are then prompted for the updated driver.

70-218.03.01.003

▶ **Correct Answers: D**

A. **Incorrect:** Although you create a new profile in the Hardware Profiles dialog box, it is not necessary for this configuration.

B. **Incorrect:** You cannot configure individual devices using Hardware Profiles.

C. **Incorrect:** Although you can customize the devices associated with each profile using Device Manager, this step is unnecessary.

D. **Correct:** If a portable computer and docking station are fully PnP compliant, you do not need to create new hardware profiles and you do not need to designate which profile to use when the computer starts. Windows 2000 automatically creates the docked profile and the undocked profile when it detects the hardware dock ID and serial number. Using PnP enumeration, the operating system automatically selects the correct hardware profile based on whether the laptop is docked or undocked. Portable computers that are not fully PnP compliant might require you to manually create the hardware profile.

70-218.03.01.004

▶ **Correct Answers: A**

A. **Correct:** You access the Driver Signing option from the Hardware tab in System Properties. Because Windows 2000 is preventing the user from installing an unsigned device driver, it is likely the Driver Signing option has been set to Block. To allow the unsigned driver to be installed, you must change the option to Warn or Ignore. The Warn option notifies the user if a driver has not been signed and allows the user to cancel the installation. The Ignore option allows all files to be installed, regardless of whether they have been signed.

B. **Incorrect:** Although you need to configure the Driver Signing option in this situation, setting the option to Block prevents all unsigned drivers from being installed.

C. **Incorrect:** Although you can use Device Manager to access a hardware device's properties, modifying those properties does not allow you to install an unsigned driver.

D. **Incorrect:** Using the Add/Remove Hardware Wizard allows you install hardware devices and the appropriate drivers. You cannot use the wizard to allow the installation of unsigned drivers if they are blocked.

70-218.03.01.005

▶ **Correct Answers: D**

A. **Incorrect:** You use the Add/Remove Hardware Wizard when you intend to remove the device completely from the computer. Because you cannot physically remove the built-in network adapter, Windows 2000 will likely detect the device and attempt to install it the next time you start the computer. For this scenario, you must keep the device connected to the computer.

B. **Incorrect:** Although disabling the network adapter is the correct approach, the Add/Remove Hardware Wizard does not have a feature to disable hardware devices.

C. **Incorrect:** Do not uninstall the device from the computer. Because the network adapter is built in, Windows 2000 will likely recognize it and attempt to install it when you start the computer again. Even if it were possible to physically remove the network adapter from the computer, this method is inappropriate because you would need to reinstall the device each time the user wants to connect to the network.

D. **Correct:** You use Device Manager to disable and enable devices in specific profiles. Because you are currently in the "Undocked" hardware profile, any hardware configuration changes you make are implemented in the profile. When you disable the network adapter, the device drivers for the device are not loaded when you start the computer.

70-218.03.01.006

▶ **Correct Answers: C and E**

A. **Incorrect:** The Network Connection Wizard assists you with creating new connection types, such as connections between your computer and the Internet, a network, or another computer. It can set up a dial-up connection, but it cannot help you with the initial installation of the modem.

B. **Incorrect:** You use Device Manager to check the properties of installed devices and to scan for hardware changes, but you cannot use Device Manager to initially install the modem. You might use the Scan for Hardware Changes option if the modem is not working correctly and you first uninstall it.

C. **Correct:** You can use the Add/Remove Hardware Wizard to add the modem by starting the Add a New Device option to search for new hardware. If the modem is PnP compliant, after you connect it to the computer, the Install New Modem screen appears and automatically detects the modem. If it does not automatically detect the modem, you can choose Add A New Device and then manually select the modem from a list of known devices.

D. **Incorrect:** The Add/Remove Programs Wizard installs, removes, or updates software, so it is not appropriate for installing new hardware devices such as a modem.

E. **Correct:** You can use the Phone and Modem Options program to configure dialing rules and settings for a modem. You can also add new modems by clicking Add in the Modems tab in the Phone And Modem Options dialog box. This opens the Install New Modem screen of the Add/Remove Hardware Wizard. From this screen, you add the modem in the same way as adding modems from the Add/Remove Hardware Wizard.

OBJECTIVE 3.2

Troubleshoot starting servers and client computers.

Server and client computer startup problems occur for an assortment of reasons, such as configuration errors, missing drivers, or corrupt files. Before you can begin troubleshooting these startup issues, you need to have a thorough understanding of the boot process. After you are comfortable with this process, you can then proceed to use several tools and methods to troubleshoot and optimize the computer's startup.

To troubleshoot startup, you might need to start the computer using an advanced boot option such as **Safe Mode**, which loads only default computer settings such as video and mouse drivers. Another commonly used advanced boot option is to start the computer with the **Last Known Good Configuration** option. This option provides a good way to recover from a damaged configuration because it starts Windows 2000 using the registry information Windows saved at the last shutdown.

If using advanced boot options such as Safe Mode does not correct the problem, try using the Windows 2000 **Recovery Console** to troubleshoot the computer. The Recovery Console is a powerful command-line console you can use to start, configure, and stop services. Using this tool, you can also perform other tasks such as formatting hard disk drives or copying critical files to the computer.

If Safe Mode and Recovery Console do not resolve the startup problem, consider using the **Emergency Repair Disk (ERD)** option in Backup. You prepare the ERD beforehand and use it to make basic repairs to the system files. Another troubleshooting method you can use if a computer fails to start properly is to create a **parallel installation** of Windows 2000. By installing a second copy of the operating system into a different folder or partition, you can select either installation at startup to troubleshoot the computer or recover data from the hard disk. A good disaster recovery plan includes strategies to back up and restore the operating system and system state data. Because a catastrophic computer event can occur without warning, regularly backing up systems and data is one of the most important tasks for an administrator. Windows 2000 provides the Windows 2000 Backup and Recovery Tools, which includes the Backup Wizard, a tool that allows you to easily back up and restore data. You generally restore data using the assistance of the Restore Wizard. To properly restore data, you must have the correct permissions, be able to select the appropriate backup sets, and determine any additional necessary settings.

You can also take advantage of other Windows 2000 tools for troubleshooting and configuring a computer such as the **Startup and Recovery** feature. You can find Startup and Recovery under the Advanced tab under System in Control Panel. You use this feature for computers with **dual boot** configurations to indicate which operating system it uses by default at startup. You also use the Startup and Recovery feature to determine what actions the computer performs if the system stops unexpectedly because of a severe error. For example, you can configure the system to send the contents of the system memory to a file for debugging if the system fails.

Objective 3.2 Questions

70-218.03.02.001

You want to start Windows 2000 with the registry information that was saved at the last shutdown. Which Safe Mode option do you use?

A. Enable Boot Logging

B. Debugging Mode

C. Last Known Good Configuration

D. Safe Mode with Networking

70-218.03.02.002

A Windows 2000 Professional computer is having trouble starting. You believe that a specific device driver is preventing the computer from starting properly. You want to use a tool to troubleshoot and repair the computer installation. Which methods can you use to troubleshoot the computer? (Choose all that apply.)

A. Safe Mode

B. Startup and Recovery

C. Recovery Console

D. Device Manager

E. System Monitor

70-218.03.02.003

You have recently installed Windows 2000 Professional for several users running Microsoft Windows 98. During Windows 2000 Setup, you elected to use a multiple boot configuration, leaving Windows 98 installed. Windows 2000 Professional is the default operating system, but your users currently select which operating system they want to use at startup. You now want users to begin using Windows 2000 Professional exclusively, but you do not want to uninstall Windows 98. You decide to prevent users from selecting an operating system at startup. How do you configure each computer so it accomplishes your goal?

A. Use the WINNT32.EXE command to change the Windows 2000 Professional setup to be the default operating system.

B. Configure the Startup and Recovery settings so the list of operating systems does not appear for the dual boot configuration.

C. Configure the Recovery Console settings to set the default operating system.

D. You cannot disable the startup choice. You must uninstall Windows 98.

70-218.03.02.004

You are responsible for maintaining a Windows 2000 server running some critical applications for your organization. To help you troubleshoot the server if the computer does not start correctly, you decide to install Windows 2000 Recovery Console. What steps do you take to enable Recovery Console as a startup option?

A. From Add/Remove Programs in Control Panel, use the Windows Components Wizard to add the Recovery Console service.

B. From the System program in Control Panel, click the Advanced tab and click the Startup And Recovery button. Enable the Recovery Console option in the Startup And Recovery dialog box.

C. Use the Windows 2000 Server setup files to install the Recovery Console by adding the /cmdcons parameter to the WINNT32.EXE command.

D. No action is required because Windows 2000 automatically installs Recovery Console by default.

70-218.03.02.005

A user with a Windows 2000 Professional computer asks for your help. His monitor screen is flickering and having trouble correctly displaying the desktop. Based on this description, you suspect that the driver for the monitor is corrupt. You want to accomplish the following goals:

■ To start the computer with a basic video graphics adapter (VGA) display driver rather than the currently installed driver.

■ To have access to the computer's locally attached CD-ROM drive in case you need access to the Windows 2000 installation disk.

■ To have access to a network share containing monitor drivers in case you need to install a new driver.

You decide to use an advanced boot option, and choose to restart the computer using Safe Mode. What does this solution provide?

A. This solution provides for all the goals.

B. This solution provides access only to the CD-ROM drive. It does not provide a basic VGA display driver and access to the network.

C. This solution provides a basic VGA display driver and access to the CD-ROM. It does not provide access to the network.

D. This solution provides for none of the goals.

70-218.03.02.006

You are troubleshooting a Windows 2000 server that is not starting correctly. You suspect that the registry has been corrupted, so you want to check the registry to make sure it is intact. You decide to use an emergency repair disk (ERD) you recently created. Which method can you use?

A. Use the ERD with the Manual Repair option.

B. Use the ERD with the Fast Repair option.

C. Use the ERD with the Registry Repair option.

D. You cannot use the ERD to check the registry.

70-218.03.02.007

You administer a Windows 2000 server acting as a file server for critical accounting spreadsheets. You recently backed up the C:\Documents And Settings\Username\My Documents folder, the C:\Budget folder, the D:\Receivables folder, and the D:\Payables folder. You learn that the files in the folders are now corrupt.

You have the following permissions to the folders:

- Full Control permission on C:\Documents And Settings\Username\My Documents

- Read permission on C:\Budget

- Modify permission on D:\Receivables

- Read permission on D:\Payables

Which folder or folders can you restore? (Choose all that apply.)

A. C:\Documents And Settings\Username\My Documents

B. C:\Budget

C. D:\Receivables

D. D:\Payables

E. You cannot restore any of the folders.

Objective 3.2 Answers

70-218.03.02.001

▶ **Correct Answers: C**

A. **Incorrect:** Although Enable Boot Logging is a Safe Mode option, it is used to start Windows 2000 while logging to a file all the installed drivers and services loaded by the system. All the Safe Mode options automatically log the drivers and services to a file named NTBTLOG.TXT. This option is useful for troubleshooting startup problems, but it does not start Windows 2000 with the last saved registry information.

B. **Incorrect:** Debugging Mode is not appropriate because it starts Windows 2000 in kernel debug mode for system analysis. Software developers usually use this mode to send debug information through a serial cable to another computer.

C. **Correct:** Last Known Good Configuration mode starts the computer by using the registry information that was saved at the last shutdown. You use this mode when a computer has been incorrectly configured. However, you lose any changes you made since the computer last started successfully, so use this mode with caution. Using this mode restores information in the registry key HKLM\System\CurrentControlSet only. Any changes you have made in other registry keys remain.

D. **Incorrect:** Safe Mode with Networking starts the computer with only the minimum drivers and files it needs along with network connectivity. You will not have access to printers and many other devices. It starts the computer with the most recent registry information.

70-218.03.02.002

▶ **Correct Answers: A and C**

A. **Correct:** You can use Safe Mode to bypass the driver and troubleshoot the computer. Safe Mode starts the computer with a minimal system configuration that provides basic access to the computer. When Windows 2000 starts in Safe Mode, it loads only the essential operating system files and drivers. To start in Safe Mode, press the F8 key during the operating system selection phase to display the Boot menu.

B. **Incorrect:** You cannot use the Startup and Recovery feature to troubleshoot and repair the installation. Startup and Recovery determines what actions the computer performs if the system stops unexpectedly because of a severe error. For example, you can configure the computer to send an alert to an administrator if the system suddenly stops.

C. **Correct:** The Windows 2000 Recovery Console provides access to the computer's local disk so you can run recovery and troubleshooting commands. Using the Recovery Console DISABLE command from the command-line interface, you can disable the driver and restart the computer to determine whether it is causing the problem.

D. **Incorrect:** Although you can use Device Manager to update the device driver, it is not the appropriate tool for this situation. To use Device Manager, you must first be able to successfully start the computer.

E. **Incorrect:** System Monitor is not an appropriate tool for troubleshooting device drivers. You use System Monitor to collect and view real-time data about memory, disk, processor, network, and other computer activity.

70-218.03.02.003

▶ **Correct Answers: B**

A. **Incorrect:** You most likely used this command to initially set up Windows 2000 on the users' computers. Although you can use WINNT32.EXE to install Windows 2000 to a new directory, this process continues to allow users to choose their operating system at startup. You still need to configure the computers using a method such as the Startup and Recovery settings.

B. **Correct:** Because more than one operating system is installed, the system displays a boot menu when the user first turns on the computer. By default, the system chooses one of the operating systems and displays a countdown timer. In this case, disable the countdown timer so the system automatically starts Windows 2000 Professional. To do this, open System in Control Panel. On the Advanced tab, click Startup And Recovery. Under System startup, in the Default operating system list, ensure that Windows 2000 Professional is the default system. Clear the Display List of Operating Systems check box, or set the number of seconds in the list to zero.

C. **Incorrect:** Recovery Console is a tool to gain access to a computer when it does not start correctly. There is no Recovery Console feature that allows you to set the default startup choice.

D. **Incorrect:** You can disable the operating system startup choice by modifying the Startup and Recovery options.

70-218.03.02.004

▶ **Correct Answers: C**

A. **Incorrect:** You cannot add the Recovery Console from the Windows Components Wizard. The Windows Components Wizard allows you to add, remove, and configure Windows 2000 components from the installation files. You must enable Recovery Console by running Windows 2000 Setup with the appropriate switch.

B. **Incorrect:** You use the Startup and Recovery feature to determine what actions the computer performs if the system stops unexpectedly because of a severe error, such as sending the contents of the system memory to a file for debugging. You cannot install the Recovery Console from this dialog box.

C. **Correct:** The WINNT32 /CMDCONS command starts the Setup routine and installs Recovery Console. This installs the files to the system partition into a folder named \Cmdcons. The Recovery Console allows you to gain access to the hard disk of the server without starting Windows 2000, so you can troubleshoot the computer if it does not start properly. The Recovery Console allows you to obtain limited access to NTFS, FAT16, and FAT32 volumes without starting the graphical interface.

D. **Incorrect:** Windows 2000 does not automatically install the Recovery Console by default.

70-218.03.02.005

▶ **Correct Answers: C**

A. **Incorrect:** Starting the computer in Safe Mode does not provide access to the network. To provide network access, you must start the computer in Safe Mode with Networking. This mode is similar to Safe Mode, but provides the services necessary for accessing the network.

B. **Incorrect:** Safe Mode starts the computer with default settings and minimum device drivers including a basic VGA display driver.

C. **Correct:** Safe Mode does not fulfill the goal of accessing the network. To load the services necessary for accessing the network, you must use Safe Mode with Networking. Any Safe Mode option gives you the drivers for a basic VGA display and locally attached media devices such as CD-ROM drives and hard disks.

D. **Incorrect:** The solution provides a basic VGA display driver and the drivers necessary to support the CD-ROM.

70-218.03.02.006

▶ **Correct Answers: B**

A. **Incorrect:** If you select Manual Repair, the registry files are not checked. The Manual Repair option is recommended for advanced users or administrators to repair system files, boot sector problems, and startup environment problems.

B. **Correct:** The Fast Repair option checks and repairs the registry files by loading and unloading each registry key. If the inspection of a key is not successful, it is automatically copied from the repair directory to the folder %systemroot%\System32\Config. For the Fast Repair option to correctly check the registry, the folder %systemroot%\Repair must be accessible. In addition to checking the registry, the emergency recovery process attempts to repair problems related to system files, the boot sector on the system disk, and the startup environment. The ERD must include the computer's current configuration information.

C. **Incorrect:** Registry Repair is not a valid option with the ERD.

D. **Incorrect:** You can use an ERD to help repair Windows 2000 system files as long as the disk includes the computer's current configuration information.

70-218.03.02.007

▶ **Correct Answers: A and C**

A. **Correct:** You can use Windows Backup to restore any files and folders for which you have been granted the Full Control permission. In addition, you can restore any files and folders that you created, or for which you have been granted the Modify permission. You can also restore data if you are a member of the Administrators group or the Backup Operators group.

B. **Incorrect:** You cannot restore files or folders for which you have been granted the Read permission.

C. **Correct:** You can restore any files and folders for which you have been granted the Modify permission.

D. **Incorrect:** You cannot restore files or folders for which you have been granted the Read permission.

E. **Incorrect:** You can restore any files and folders for which you have been granted the Modify permission or the Full Control permission, but you cannot restore them if you have been granted the Read permission.

OBJECTIVE 3.3

Monitor and troubleshoot server health and performance.

Administrators perform several tasks to keep a network running efficiently. A particularly important task is monitoring a server's performance by observing trends and troubleshooting problems as they arise. For this objective, you should be familiar with the tools at your disposal to monitor and troubleshoot a server's performance.

You use the **Performance tool** to get comprehensive performance information about the server or other computers on your network. Specifically, the **System Monitor** component of the Performance tool allows you to collect performance data about the server and compare it with other computers on your network. You can view the data generated currently, or previously from a log file. Using this data, you can analyze system resource usage to plan for system upgrades or evaluate recent changes. More importantly, you use the tool to diagnose problems. The **Performance Logs and Alerts** utility is another component of the Performance tool that you can use to monitor data about hardware resources or system services. You can also configure Performance Logs and Alerts to record performance data in logs and set system alerts to notify you when a specified data value exceeds defined thresholds.

Event Viewer gathers information about events that occur with a server's hardware, software, system, and security settings. Because Windows 2000 records events in a log, you can use the event logs in Event Viewer to monitor the status of the system. You should be familiar with reading the three default event logs. This is especially true for the important security logs that record auditing events such as invalid logon attempts. The application log contains events logged by applications, and the system log contains events logged by system components. You should also understand the four types of events Event Viewer displays depending on the log: Error, Warning, Information, and Auditing.

Even though Windows **Task Manager** is a simple tool compared to the robust System Monitor, it provides an easy way to monitor the real-time performance of a server. In particular, processor activity is one of the more important issues you should monitor. You should understand how to use Task Manager's tabs to start and end applications, start and end processes, and view a computer's performance including CPU and memory usage. Using the Services administrative tool, you can start, stop, pause, or resume services on remote and local computers. You can also identify and disable unnecessary operating system services. Every service in Windows 2000 can be set to one of three states: disabled, manual, or automatic.

Objective 3.3 Questions

70-218.03.03.001

Your Windows 2000 server is running several applications. You want to understand how individual processes on the server affect system resources including CPU usage and memory usage. How can you use Task Manager to view this information?

A. Use the Applications tab.

B. Use the Performance tab.

C. Use the Processes tab.

D. You cannot use Task Manager to view specific processes.

70-218.03.03.002

You are monitoring the current performance of your Windows 2000 server. You must monitor the following:

- The amount of physical memory available to all processes

- The size of virtual memory used by all processes

- CPU usage

- CPU resources used by applications using operating system services

You decide to use the Performance tab in Task Manager. From the View menu you select Show Kernel Times. What does your solution achieve?

A. All of the required results.

B. All of the required results except the CPU resources used by applications using operating system services.

C. Only the physical memory and virtual memory performance results.

D. None of the required results.

70-218.03.03.003

You are an administrator responsible for monitoring the performance of several Windows 2000 servers. Recently, you have noticed that one server's performance is sluggish. To help determine where the bottleneck is occurring, you want to monitor the data for the computer. You want to achieve the following goals:

- You must be able to view the performance data in real time.

- You must be able to see the percentage of time the processor is busy.

- You must be able to see how much physical memory is available.

- You must be able to see how much virtual memory is available.

- You must receive administrative alerts if specified processor or memory thresholds are exceeded.

You decide to configure the System Monitor snap-in on the Performance console. You add the Processor\ % Processor Time counter and the Memory\ Available Bytes counter. Which results does your solution achieve? (Choose all that apply.)

A. The performance data is real time.

B. You can view the percentage of time the processor is busy.

C. You can view how much physical memory is available.

D. You can view how much virtual memory is available.

E. You receive administrative alerts if thresholds are exceeded.

F. You achieve none of the required results.

70-218.03.03.004

You are monitoring a Windows 2000 server. With your administrator privileges you have enabled security logging on the computer. You want to review the event logs for suspected security breaches from users randomly guessing the password. What is the appropriate action?

A. Expand the Event Viewer (Local) folder, and then click Security Log. In the details pane, look for error audits for passwords.

B. Expand the Event Viewer (Local) folder, and then click System Log. In the details pane, look for error audits for passwords.

C. Expand the Event Viewer (Local) folder, and then click Security Log. In the details pane, look for success audits for logon/logoff.

D. Expand the Event Viewer (Local) folder, and then click Security Log. In the details pane, look for failure audits for logon/logoff.

70-218.03.03.005

Your supervisor has asked you to monitor a Windows 2000 server for potential security breaches. You want to be able to view the following information for each security event:

- The action that occurred

- The success or failure of the event

- When the event occurred

- The method of access

- The method of encryption used (if any)

- The user who performed the action

You turn on security logging. The next day you start Event Viewer, open the security log, and begin reviewing individual audit entries.

Which results does your solution achieve? (Choose all that apply.)

A. You can view the action that occurred.

B. You can view the success or failure of the event.

C. You can view when the event occurred.

D. You can view the method of access.

E. You can view the user who performed the action.

F. You can view the method of encryption used for the event.

G. You achieve none of the required results.

70-218.03.03.006

Your supervisor has given you the responsibility for monitoring a Windows 2000 server. The administrator before you was monitoring the computer to determine whether processor bottlenecks are occurring on the computer.

You want to make sure the counters will tell you the following:

- The rate of processor activity

- The length of the processor queue

Using System Monitor, you review the counters added by the previous administrator.

Examine the counters in the following figure.

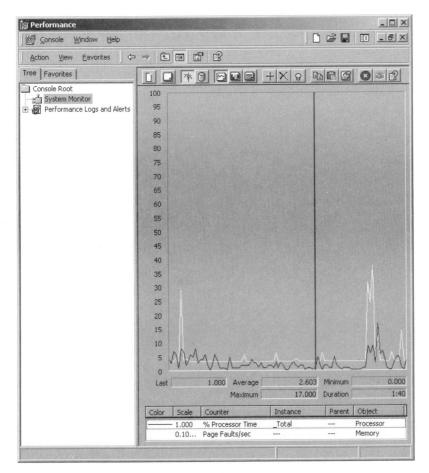

Which result do these counters achieve?

A. The counters tell you the information you want.

B. The counters tell you the rate of processor activity, but not the length of the processor queue.

C. The counters tell you the length of the processor queue, but they do not tell you the rate of the processor activity.

D. The counters do not tell you any of the information you want.

70-218.03.03.007

You administer a Windows 2000 computer acting as a DNS server. To provide maximum security, you want to disable unnecessary services running on the computer. Which method is appropriate for disabling services to prevent them from automatically starting?

A. Open Task Manager, click the Processes tab, click each process that you want to disable, and click End Process.

B. Open Task Manager, click the Processes tab, right-click each process that you want to disable, point to Set Priority, and select Disabled.

C. Open Services, right-click each service you want to disable, click Properties, and select Disabled under Startup type.

D. Open Services, right-click each service you want to disable, and then click Stop.

Objective 3.3 Answers

70-218.03.03.001

▶ **Correct Answers: C**

A. **Incorrect:** The Applications tab shows the status of applications running on the computer. You can use this tab to start programs, end programs, or switch to other programs. Although you can use the information on this tab to identify the process associated with an application, it does not display the process information you need.

B. **Incorrect:** The Performance tab displays an overview of your computer's current performance such as processor and memory usage. However, the performance measurements are for the cumulative processes rather than individual processes.

C. **Correct:** The Processes tab displays a list of running processes and measurements of their performance, such as the total processor (CPU) time or the amount of memory in use. You can view the current percentage of the CPU time used by the process, as well as the total processor time used by the process since it was started. The tab shows the amount of main memory, in kilobytes, used by each process. If the computer is not running a specific process, it runs System Idle Process, which is a percentage of time the computer is not processing other tasks.

D. **Incorrect:** Task Manager is the appropriate tool because it provides information about programs and processes running on your computer. The Processes tab of Task Manager allows you to view performance measurements for each process running on the computer.

70-218.03.03.002

▶ **Correct Answers: A**

A. **Correct:** The Performance tab in Task Manager monitors all the information you require. The Physical Memory process measure displays the amount of physical memory available to processes. The Commit Charge measure displays the size of virtual memory in use by all processes. The CPU Usage measure displays the percentage of time the processor is running a thread other than the Idle thread. By default, Task Manager does not monitor kernel mode usage, but by selecting Show Kernel Times from the View menu you can monitor CPU resources used by kernel operations. The kernel is the core of the operating system that manages items such as memory, files, and peripheral devices. The Performance tab graphs display the kernel mode processor time in red to measure CPU resources that applications use for operating system services.

B. **Incorrect:** This is incorrect for the reasons stated in answer A.

C. **Incorrect:** This is incorrect for the reasons stated in answer A.

D. **Incorrect:** This is incorrect for the reasons stated in answer A.

70-218.03.03.003

▶ **Correct Answers: A, B, and C**

A. **Correct:** System Monitor is the right tool for collecting and viewing real-time performance information on the server such as memory, disk, processor, network, and other data.

B. **Correct:** To display performance data in System Monitor, you must add counters to the graph area. You add the Processor\ % Processor Time counter to gauge the activity of the processor by showing the percentage of elapsed time a processor is busy executing a nonidle thread.

C. **Correct:** To display performance data in System Monitor, you must add counters to the graph area. The Available Bytes counter shows the amount of physical memory, in bytes, available to processes running on the computer.

D. **Incorrect:** The two performance counters you added do not show available virtual memory. To show available virtual memory, use a counter such as Memory\ Commit Limit, which shows the amount of virtual memory, in bytes, that can be committed without having to extend the paging file.

E. **Incorrect:** You cannot use System Monitor to receive administrative alerts. The Performance Logs and Alerts snap-in in the Performance console is the appropriate tool for configuring alerts. Performance Logs and Alerts has a feature that detects when a predefined counter value rises above or falls below the configured threshold and notifies you using the Messenger service.

F. **Incorrect:** This is incorrect for the reasons stated in answers A, B, and C.

70-218.03.03.004

▶ **Correct Answers: D**

A. **Incorrect:** Although the security log is the appropriate log for researching security breaches, error audits for passwords are not valid audits.

B. **Incorrect:** The system log contains events logged by the Windows 2000 system components, so this log is not appropriate for researching this type of security breach. You might use the system log to review the failure of a driver or other system component.

C. **Incorrect:** Reviewing logon/logoff events in the security log is appropriate for determining potential security breaches. However, reviewing success audits for logon/logoff finds issues in which correct logon information was used, such as when a password was stolen.

D. **Correct:** Reviewing the security log for a failure audit for logon/logoff is a method for monitoring random password hacking. Each time an attempt is made to log on to a domain account using an incorrect or invalid user ID/password combination, an event is recorded in the security log. The security log also records other security events such as creating, opening, or deleting files or other objects.

70-218.03.03.005

▶ **Correct Answers: A, B, C, and E**

A. **Correct:** Event Viewer shows what occurred by displaying a description of the event. For example, if a user (or intruder) attempts to log on using an incorrect password, a Logon Failure event is recorded. In addition, the header of the audit entry shows the type of event, such as Error, Warning, Information, Success Audit, or Failure Audit. The header also shows an event number that can help you track the event in the system.

B. **Correct:** The security log shows whether the event was successful or unsuccessful in the header information. A Success Audit displays when an audited security event is completed successfully, such as when a user logs on to a computer. A Failure Audit is recorded when an audited security event did not successfully complete, such as when a user provides an incorrect password or attempts to use an expired user account.

C. **Correct:** An event log shows the date and time an event was generated. This information appears in the header of the event entry.

D. **Incorrect:** Audit entries in the security log provide various details about the event, such as the computer name related to the event. However, the event log does not provide specific information about the method of access, such as whether the user was a remote user.

E. **Correct:** The event header displays the user name if an event is attributed to a specific user. It also displays the exact name of the computer where the logged event occurred, so you can track the source of the event.

F. **Incorrect:** The security log does not indicate whether encryption was used or the method of encryption. To log encryption programs, you might configure the application log to record this information.

G. **Incorrect:** This is incorrect for the reasons stated in answers A, B, C, and E.

70-218.03.03.006

▶ **Correct Answers: B**

A. **Incorrect:** Although the Processor\ % Processor Time counter tells you the rate of processor activity, the Memory\ Page Faults/sec counter does not tell you the length of the processor queue. Use the System\ Processor Queue Length counter to determine the processor queue length.

B. **Correct:** Processor bottlenecks occur when the processor is so busy it cannot respond to requests. You can judge whether a processor bottleneck is occurring by looking at the rate of processor activity. For example, if Processor\ % Processor Time often exceeds 80 percent, a bottleneck is occurring. Also use a counter such as System\ Processor Queue Length to determine whether a long processor queue is occurring. In this situation, the Memory\ Page Faults/sec counter is not appropriate for measuring the processor queue.

C. **Incorrect:** The counters tell you the processor activity through the Processor\ % Processor Time counter, but they do not tell you the length of the processor queue. To measure the processor queue, use a counter such as System\ Processor Queue Length.

D. **Incorrect:** The selected counters tell you some of the information you want. With the Processor\ % Processor Time counter you can understand the rate of processor activity. However, the Memory\ Page Faults/sec counter does not tell you the length of the processor queue. You must use a counter such as System\ Processor Queue Length to determine the processor queue length.

70-218.03.03.007

▶ **Correct Answers: C**

A. **Incorrect:** You cannot use Task Manager to disable services. You use Task Manager to see the status of programs that are running and to end programs that have stopped responding.

B. **Incorrect:** You cannot use Task Manager to disable services. You use Task Manager to see the status of programs that are running and to end programs that have stopped responding. In addition, Disabled is not a possible priority in Task Manager.

C. **Correct:** You configure the startup type in Services to disable services from automatically starting. Using this method, the startup type remains in effect even after you restart the computer.

D. **Incorrect:** Although it is appropriate to use Services, using this method might not keep the service stopped. The service might automatically start again when you restart the computer.

O B J E C T I V E   3 . 4

Install and manage Windows 2000 updates.

A typical task for systems administrators is keeping Windows 2000 up to date. Although it might seem tedious to install updates to Windows 2000, this is your first line of defense against the latest security threats. Security threats such as hacker attacks are becoming more complex, and networks connected to the Internet are particularly vulnerable. In addition to mitigating security threats, updating Windows 2000 ensures that you have the latest software enhancements so your systems run at peak performance.

Hotfixes address a specific issue such as a newly discovered security threat or performance issue. Because Microsoft releases hotfixes to address a single urgent issue, they do not go through the same rigorous testing as other software. As a system administrator, you must determine whether the hotfix is appropriate for your network environment, and install only those that are applicable. Because hotfixes have not been fully tested, applying a hotfix always carries the chance of causing unexpected issues. Hotfixes are also known as patches and can be downloaded from various sites including *www.microsoft.com.*

Periodically, Microsoft consolidates all its hotfixes and other enhancements into a **service pack**. Service packs are tested more thoroughly than hotfixes and are therefore distributed less frequently. For example, Microsoft Windows 2000 Service Pack 2 (SP2) is a collection of fixes that address system reliability and security issues. You apply a service pack using the UPDATE.EXE program and appropriate command-line switches. By using this program, you do not need to reapply the service pack after every system state change. However, after applying a service pack, you must continue to install necessary subsequent hotfixes as Microsoft releases them. Although service packs are cumulative, on occasion you might want to remove a service pack from a computer. You can uninstall a service pack by using Add or Remove Programs in Control Panel or by running the Uninstall program from the command prompt. You can also use Add or Remove Programs in Control Panel to uninstall a hotfix.

One way for you or users in general to install service packs and hotfixes on individual computers is through the **Windows Update** feature. Users activate Windows Update from the Start menu. The program opens Internet Explorer and takes the user to the

Windows Update Web site. The site allows users to easily install updates such as service packs and updated device drivers. As an administrator, you might want to disable this feature on your users' computers by configuring the Windows 2000 group policy setting called Disable And Remove Links To Windows Update.

If you administer clients currently running Windows 2000 Professional, it is often more appropriate to deploy service packs and hotfixes to them with several methods such as using a network distribution share, **Microsoft Systems Management Server (SMS)**, or the **Microsoft Windows Installer Service**. The Windows Installer Service is appropriate for automatically installing the software to the user's computer without the user taking any action.

If you are installing Windows 2000 to clients for the first time, it's possible to incorporate the latest service pack files during the installation using a process known as **slipstreaming**. Slipstreaming replaces the original installation files on a distribution share with newer files provided with the service pack. Performing an installation this way eliminates the need to install service packs separately. The first step to slipstream a service pack into a distribution share is to extract the service pack files by running the W2KSP2.EXE -x command. You then run the UPDATE.EXE application with the -s: *distribution_folder* parameter, where *distribution_folder* is the name of the folder where the Windows 2000 distribution share is located. You can also slipstream appropriate hotfix files into the distribution share.

Objective 3.4 Questions

70-218.03.04.001

You are troubleshooting a user's computer running Windows 2000 Professional. How do you verify that the computer has the latest service pack?

A. Run the UPDATE command. You receive notification if the latest service pack has been installed.

B. Run the WINVER command to determine the version of Windows and any service packs.

C. Use Add/Remove Windows Components to determine whether the service pack file has been installed.

D. None of these options verify that the computer has the latest service pack.

70-218.03.04.002

You have just installed Windows 2000 Server on a computer, and you want to make sure the computer has the latest service pack. Upon visiting the Microsoft Web site, you discover that there are two service packs: Service Pack 1 and Service Pack 2. After reading the documentation for both service packs, you decide you want the updates contained in Service Pack 2. Which statement is true?

A. You must install Service Pack 1 and then install Service Pack 2.

B. You must first install and then uninstall Service Pack 1 before installing Service Pack 2.

C. You should install Service Pack 2 only.

D. You should install Service Pack 2 and then install Service Pack 1.

70-218.03.04.003

You install Windows 2000 Professional on a user's new laptop. Two days later, you want to apply the latest service pack, Windows 2000 Service Pack 2. Because the laptop is not connected to the network, you bring the service pack on a CD-ROM. How do you apply the service pack?

A. By using the UPDATE command with no parameters or switches

B. By using the UPDATE command with the -s: *distribution_folder* switch

C. By using the W2KSP2 command

D. By using the W2KSP2 command with the -x switch

70-218.03.04.004

You are responsible for ensuring the Windows 2000 Professional installation and service pack files on your organization's distribution share are current. You want to integrate the service pack files with the Windows 2000 installation files so you do not have to later perform the service pack installation separately. How do you apply the service pack?

A. Apply the service pack files to the distribution share by overwriting the outdated Windows 2000 files using Windows Explorer.

B. Apply the service pack by using the UPDATE command with no parameters or switches.

C. Apply the service pack by using the UPDATE command along with the -s: *distribution_folder* switch.

D. Apply the service pack by using the UPDATE command along with the /slipstream switch.

70-218.03.04.005

Your supervisor has asked you to research ways to deploy the latest service pack to 100 users in your organization currently running Windows 2000 Professional. You know that performing a manual installation on each computer will be time consuming. Which of the following methods are appropriate for automating service pack deployment to large groups? (Choose all that apply.)

A. Windows Installer Service

B. Slipstreaming

C. Sysprep utility

D. Microsoft Systems Management Server (SMS)

E. None of these methods

70-218.03.04.006

You are an administrator responsible for maintaining several Windows 2000 Professional computers. You have just become aware of an important security hotfix you should apply to the computers. You want to accomplish the following goals:

- You want to make the hotfix available for users from a distribution share.

- You want the hotfix program to notify users if they are running a service pack version that is newer than the hotfix.

- You want the hotfix program to automatically install during all future Windows 2000 installations.

You perform the following steps:

1. On the Windows 2000 network distribution share, you create a distribution folder for the hotfix file.

2. You copy the Windows 2000 hotfix executable file to the distribution folder you just created.

3. You send e-mail to each of your users asking them to connect to the distribution share and double-click the hotfix executable file.

Which results does your solution achieve? (Choose all that apply.)

A. The hotfix is available for users from a distribution share.

B. The hotfix program notifies users if they are running a service pack version that is newer than the hotfix.

C. The hotfix program is available to automatically install during all future Windows 2000 installations.

D. The solution does not provide any of the desired results.

Objective 3.4 Answers

70-218.03.04.001

▶ **Correct Answers: B**

A. **Incorrect:** You use the UPDATE.EXE program to install the service pack after you have service pack files available for installing. This program does not tell you the information you need.

B. **Correct:** To verify that the computer has the latest service pack installed, click Start, click Run, type **winver,** and then press ENTER. The About Windows 2000 dialog box displays the Windows version number and the service pack version number if one has been installed.

C. **Incorrect:** The Add/Remove Windows Components Wizard does not tell you whether a service pack is installed. You typically use Add/Remove Windows Components to add Windows 2000 components you chose not to include in the original installation, such as networking options.

D. **Incorrect:** You can determine whether the computer has the latest service pack installed by running the WINVER command.

70-218.03.04.002

▶ **Correct Answers: C**

A. **Incorrect:** Because service packs are cumulative, it is unnecessary to install earlier service packs on a new Windows 2000 installation. Service Pack 2 contains all of the updates found in Service Pack 1.

B. **Incorrect:** For your new installation, it is appropriate to install only Service Pack 2 because it contains all the updates found in Service Pack 1. If you have already installed Service Pack 1 on an existing installation, Microsoft recommends that you install Service Pack 2 without uninstalling Service Pack 1.

C. **Correct:** This answer is correct for the reasons stated in answer A.

D. **Incorrect:** This answer is incorrect for the reasons stated in answer A.

70-218.03.04.003

▶ **Correct Answers: A**

A. **Correct:** To apply a service pack to an existing installation of Windows 2000, run the UPDATE.EXE utility from the CD-ROM by typing **update**. This replaces the existing Windows 2000 files with the appropriate new files from the service pack.

B. **Incorrect:** The UPDATE command with the -s: *distribution_folder* switch is intended for updating a central distribution point of Windows 2000 source files with the service pack files. In this case, because you are updating an existing Windows 2000 installation with the service pack from the CD-ROM, this command is not appropriate.

C. **Incorrect:** This command does not apply the service pack. The W2KSP2.EXE program extracts the individual service pack files from the archive and prompts you to choose a directory to place the extracted files and subfolders.

D. **Incorrect:** This command does not apply the service pack. You use the W2KSP2 command with the -x switch to extract the files from the archive in preparation for later slipstreaming the service pack into a Windows 2000 distribution share.

70-218.03.04.004

▶ **Correct Answers: C**

A. **Incorrect:** This method does not ensure that the service pack files are incorporated correctly into future Windows 2000 installations.

B. **Incorrect:** Although you should use the UPDATE command, you must also use the -s: *distribution_folder* switch. This installs the updated service pack files over the existing Windows 2000 files.

C. **Correct:** To apply a service pack to the Windows 2000 distribution share, you use a process known as slipstreaming. You accomplish slipstreaming using the UPDATE command with the -s: *distribution_folder* switch (where *distribution_folder* is the name of the folder where the Windows 2000 distribution share is located). This command and switch installs the updated service pack files over the existing Windows 2000 files. By using this process, you no longer need to reinstall Windows components after applying a service pack.

D. **Incorrect:** Although using the UPDATE command is appropriate, the command does not include a /slipstream switch.

70-218.03.04.005

▶ **Correct Answers: A and D**

A. **Correct:** Windows Installer Service is a Windows 2000 component that standardizes software program installations on multiple computers. You can use it to install service packs using the UPDATE.MSI package file included with Windows 2000 service pack releases. After you create the software installation package, the group policy object installs the software as the client computer starts.

B. **Incorrect:** You cannot use slipstreaming to deploy service packs to existing Windows 2000 computers. With slipstreaming, you eliminate the need for separately installing service packs on new Windows 2000 installations.

C. **Incorrect:** The SYSPREP.EXE utility is not appropriate for deploying service packs for computers with Windows 2000 already installed. You use Sysprep to install a system with Windows 2000 applications and then duplicate it to other systems in your organization.

D. **Correct:** SMS is a network management tool that provides software distribution and installation. You can use SMS to distribute service packs to client computers in a variety of ways. For example, you can simultaneously upgrade all the SMS client computers in your organization with the new service pack, or allow users to upgrade at a time they choose.

E. **Incorrect:** This is incorrect for the reasons stated in answers A and D.

70-218.03.04.006

▶ **Correct Answers: A and B**

   A. **Correct:** This procedure is the correct way to make the hotfix available to users from a distribution share. Each hotfix is an executable file that contains an integrated installation program. The hotfix executable file extracts the hotfix files and runs the HOTFIX.EXE installer. To install the hotfix from the distribution share, double-click the executable file, use the Run dialog box, or use a command prompt.

   B. **Correct:** The hotfix installation program checks the service pack version you are currently using. If the service pack version is newer than the hotfix, the installation stops and an error dialog box displays stating that the version is incorrect. If the service pack version is older than the hotfix program, the hotfix installs automatically.

   C. **Incorrect:** Although you can also slipstream hotfix releases into a Windows 2000 distribution share, there are additional steps you need to perform to make the installation work properly. For example, you must change the hotfix file names because Windows 2000 Setup requires the 8.3 naming convention for all files and folders in the distribution folder. In addition, you must create the appropriate subfolders on the distribution share and copy the appropriate hotfix binaries into the folders.

   D. **Incorrect:** Using this procedure, you can make the hotfix file available to users from a distribution share. When users run the hotfix executable file, the hotfix installation program checks the service pack version and gives the user an error if the service pack version is newer than the hotfix.

Configuring, Managing, Securing, and Troubleshooting Active Directory Organizational Units and Group Policy

The Active Directory service configuration that you use is largely based on the security and Group Policy application requirements for your organization. This chapter deals with creating user and group objects within Active Directory, securing the objects, and addressing replication problems between domain controllers. The chapter also covers issues with Group Policy application including deploying software with Group Policy, troubleshooting Group Policy application problems, and securing computers using security templates and Group Policy.

By creating user, group, and computer objects in Active Directory and using the Delegation of Authority Wizard, you can test **organizational unit (OU)** designs to ensure that you assign only the necessary permissions to OU administrators. In addition, working with multiple domain controllers can ensure that you understand replication issues that arise in Active Directory's multiple master replication model.

Finally, by defining Group Policy Objects (GPOs) in sites, domains, and OUs, you learn how to troubleshoot Group Policy application problems and determine the optimal locations to apply GPOs based on your security and application deployment needs.

Tested Skills and Suggested Practices

The skills that you need to master the Configuring, Managing, Securing, and Trouble-shooting Active Directory Organizational Units and Group Policy objective domain on the *Managing a Microsoft Windows 2000 Network Environment* exam include:

- **Creating, managing, and troubleshooting user and group objects in Active Directory.**

  - Practice 1: Practice creating user, computer, and group objects by using the Active Directory Users and Computers console.

  - Practice 2: Use Microsoft Notepad or another text editor to create an LDAP Data Interchange Format (LDIF) import file and use LDIFDE.EXE to import the users and groups into Active Directory.

  - Practice 3: Validate group memberships for global groups, domain local groups, and universal groups in both mixed mode and native mode.

  - Practice 4: Search for objects in Active Directory by using the Find command in the Active Directory Users and Computers console. Review both the Basic and Advanced Find functions.

- **Managing object and container permissions.**

  - Practice 1: Create an OU and then create some example user accounts within the OU. Use the Delegation of Administration Wizard to delegate permissions to a specific domain local group.

  - Practice 2: After the delegation is complete, review the actual permissions delegated by viewing the Advanced Properties of the OU's Security tab. Attempt to delegate permissions to specific attributes of the user object.

  - Practice 3: Load the Windows 2000 Support Tools from the Microsoft Windows 2000 Server CD-ROM. In a Microsoft Management Console (MMC) console, load the ADSIEDIT console. In the ADSIEDIT console, connect to the Configuration naming context and review the permissions that can be assigned to containers in the Configuration naming context.

- **Diagnosing Active Directory replication problems.**

  - Practice 1: Install two domain controllers in an Active Directory domain. Review the connection objects created for replication in the Active Directory Sites and Services console.

  - Practice 2: In the Active Directory Sites and Services console, define a subnet object for the Internet Protocol (IP) subnet you use for your practice network.

Create a new site object and associate the IP subnet with the site. Move the existing domain controllers to the new site from the Default_First_Site site. If available, install a new domain controller and observe which site the domain controller is placed in.

- Practice 3: Use the replication tools included in the Windows 2000 Support Tools. Use Replication Monitor to generate the replication topology and review the individual replication updates between the two domain controllers in a domain. Review the command-line switches for the REPADMIN.EXE text-based replication tool.

- Practice 4: Place the domain controllers that exist in your forest in separate sites. Configure site link and site link bridge objects to allow replication between the domain controllers.

- **Deploying software by using Group Policy.**

  - Practice 1: Deploy a software application by assigning the application in Active Directory. Then, determine whether the application is available for use or must be installed from the Add/Remove Programs icon in Control Panel. Also determine whether the application can be loaded by running a data file with an extension recognized by the application.

  - Practice 2: Deploy a software application by publishing the application in Active Directory. Then, determine whether the application is available for use or must be installed from the Add/Remove Programs icon in Control Panel. Also determine whether the application can be loaded by running a data file with an extension recognized by the application.

  - Practice 3: Perform an upgrade to an existing software package, reviewing the process required to indicate that the new package is an update for an existing package.

- **Troubleshooting end-user Group Policy.**

  - Practice 1: Create an OU structure, three layers deep, for the application of Group Policy. At each level, define GPOs that have conflicting settings and observe the default inheritance model for Group Policy settings. Use the No Override and Block Inheritance settings and observe the difference in Group Policy application.

  - Practice 2: Use GPRESULT.EXE from the Microsoft Windows 2000 Resource Kit to determine which GPOs are applied to users when they log on.

  - Practice 3: Download the FAZAM 2000, Reduced-Functionality tool available at *http://www.microsoft.com/WINDOWS2000/techinfo/reskit/tools/existing/ fazam2000-o.asp*, and investigate the effect of moving objects between OUs on Group Policy application.

- **Implementing and managing security policies by using Group Policy.**

  - Practice 1: Create a custom security template using the Security Templates MMC console.

  - Practice 2: Import the security template into the Default Domain Policy and observe how the settings affect all computers in the domain.

  - Practice 3: Create a second security template that differs in settings (other than Account Policy settings), and import the security template into an OU that contains computers accounts. Verify that the Group Policy settings applied at the OU take precedence over those settings applied at the domain.

Further Reading

This section lists supplemental readings by objective. We recommend that you study these sources thoroughly before taking exam 70-218.

Objective 4.1

Microsoft Corporation. *MCSA Training Kit: Managing a Microsoft Windows 2000 Network Environment.* Redmond, Washington: Microsoft Press, 2002. Review Lessons 1, 2, and 3 in Chapter 7, "Managing Active Directory User and Computer Objects."

Microsoft Corporation. *MCSA Training Kit: Managing a Microsoft Windows 2000 Network Environment.* Redmond, Washington: Microsoft Press, 2002. Review Lessons 1, 2, and 3 in Chapter 8, "Managing Active Directory Group Objects."

"Step-by-Step Guide to Managing Active Directory." (This white paper can be downloaded for free at *http://www.microsoft.com/windows2000/techinfo/planning/activedirectory/manadsteps.asp.*)

"Q237677: Using LDIFDE to Import/Export Directory Objects to the Active Directory." (This Knowledge Base article can be downloaded for free at *http://support.microsoft.com/support/kb/articles/q237/6/77.asp.*)

"Importing and Exporting Directory Information." (This online Help documentation can be read at *http://www.microsoft.com/WINDOWS2000/en/server/help/sag_ad_ldif_csv.htm.*)

Objective 4.2

Microsoft Corporation. *MCSA Training Kit: Managing a Microsoft Windows 2000 Network Environment.* Redmond, Washington: Microsoft Press, 2002. Review Lessons 1, 2, and 4 in Chapter 12, "Active Directory Service Administration."

Microsoft Corporation. *MCSA Training Kit: Managing a Microsoft Windows 2000 Network Environment*. Redmond, Washington: Microsoft Press, 2002. Review Lesson 4 in Chapter 8, "Managing Active Directory Group Objects."

"Step-by-Step Guide to Using the Delegation of Control Wizard." (This white paper can be downloaded for free at *http://www.microsoft.com/windows2000/techinfo/ planning/activedirectory/delegsteps.asp.*)

Objective 4.3

Microsoft Corporation. *MCSA Training Kit: Managing a Microsoft Windows 2000 Network Environment*. Redmond, Washington: Microsoft Press, 2002. Review Lessons 1, 2, and 3 in Chapter 11, "Replicating Active Directory."

"Step-by-Step Guide to Active Directory Sites and Services." (This white paper can be downloaded for free at *http://www.microsoft.com/windows2000/techinfo/planning/ activedirectory/adsites.asp.*)

Microsoft Corporation. *Windows 2000 Server Resource Kit*. Volume: *Distributed Systems Guide*. Redmond, Washington: Microsoft Press, 2000. (This book can be downloaded for free at *http://www.microsoft.com/windows2000/techinfo/reskit/en-us/ default.asp.*) Review Chapter 6, "Active Directory Replication."

Objective 4.4

Microsoft Corporation. *MCSA Training Kit: Managing a Microsoft Windows 2000 Network Environment*. Redmond, Washington: Microsoft Press, 2002. Review Lesson 3 in Chapter 10, "Managing Resources with Active Directory Service."

"Software Installation and Maintenance." (This white paper can be downloaded for free at *http://www.microsoft.com/windows2000/techinfo/administration/management/ siamwp.asp.*)

"Step-by-Step Guide to Software Installation and Maintenance." (This white paper can be downloaded for free at *http://www.microsoft.com/windows2000/techinfo/planning/ management/swinstall.asp.*)

Objective 4.5

Microsoft Corporation. *MCSA Training Kit: Managing a Microsoft Windows 2000 Network Environment*. Redmond, Washington: Microsoft Press, 2002. Review Lessons 1, 2, and 4 in Chapter 9, "Using Group Policies."

"Troubleshooting Group Policy in Windows 2000." (This white paper can be downloaded for free at *http://www.microsoft.com/windows2000/techinfo/howitworks/ management/gptshoot.asp.*)

Microsoft Corporation. *Windows 2000 Server Resource Kit*. Volume: *Distributed Systems Guide*. Redmond, Washington: Microsoft Press, 2000. (This book can be downloaded for free at *http://www.microsoft.com/windows2000/techinfo/reskit/en-us/ default.asp*.) Review Chapter 25, "Troubleshooting Change and Configuration Management."

Objective 4.6

Microsoft Corporation. *MCSA Training Kit: Managing a Microsoft Windows 2000 Network Environment*. Redmond, Washington: Microsoft Press, 2002. Review Lesson 3 in Chapter 9, "Using Group Policies."

"Security Configuration Tool Set." (This white paper can be downloaded for free at *http://www.microsoft.com/windows2000/techinfo/howitworks/security/sctoolset.asp*.)

"Step-by-Step Guide to Using the Security Configuration Tool Set." (This white paper can be downloaded for free at *http://www.microsoft.com/windows2000/techinfo/ planning/security/secconfsteps.asp*.)

OBJECTIVE 4.1

Create, manage, and troubleshoot user and group objects in Active Directory.

All security in a Windows 2000 network derives from **user**, **computer**, and **group objects**. When you create user, computer, and group objects, the major decisions you must make include where the objects are created in the Active Directory structure and how to secure the Active Directory structure so only the required people can modify existing objects.

Computer accounts might occasionally need to be reset in the Active Directory Users and Computers console. The resetting of the computer account is only required if the computer becomes separated from the domain and must be rejoined.

The primary tool you use for user and group object management is the Active Directory Users and Computers Microsoft Management Console (MMC) snap-in. Become familiar with the console and the creation process for both user and group objects. Also ensure that you know how to find objects within Active Directory by using the Find function within the snap-in.

When designing security for file and printer access, remember the two common methods for security assignments:

- A-G-DL-P. In this model, user accounts are gathered into global groups. The global groups are included in the membership of domain local groups, and the domain local groups are assigned permissions to the resource.

- A-G-U-DL-P. In this model, user accounts are still gathered into global groups. In the event multiple domains exist in the forest, the global groups from separate domains are then gathered into a single universal group. This universal group is included in the membership of a domain local group in the domain where the file or print resource exists, and the domain local group is assigned permissions to the resource.

To answer the questions in this objective, you should be familiar with the various methods available to create user and group objects in Active Directory. Be sure to spend time creating the objects in the Active Directory Users and Computers MMC snap-in. Consider creating **template accounts** that contain the default settings you require, and copying these accounts when you create new accounts. Finally, attempt to create accounts in a batch method using the LDIFDE.EXE and CSVDE.EXE utilities.

Objective 4.1 Questions

70-218.04.01.001

Your company has entered into negotiations to acquire a competing company. The competing company has an Active Directory that contains 500 users, and you are assigned the task of planning the merger of the user account information into your Active Directory.

The IT manager has decided not to migrate existing group and security identifier (SID) information from the competing company's Active Directory. What tools can you use to generate the 500 user accounts in a batch format? (Choose all that apply.)

A. Active Directory Migration Tool (ADMT)

B. Active Directory Domains and Trusts

C. Active Directory Users and Computers

D. CSVDE.EXE

E. Local Users and Groups

F. LDIFDE.EXE

70-218.04.01.002

The marketing department's network administrator has just announced she is leaving the company to accept a position with a competing company. You immediately pull out your checklist of goals for when a network administrator leaves the company. The goals include:

- Ensuring that the new network administrator maintains the same level of access as the previous administrator

- Minimizing the configuration changes required

- Blocking the current marketing department's network administrator from further network access

- Auditing all access by the marketing department's network administrator account

To meet these goals, you delete the marketing department's network administrator's user account immediately and create a new account when you hire the replacement network administrator. To audit use by the network administrator, you enable auditing in a GPO linked to the OU where the user account of the marketing department's network administrator is located.

Which goals are met by the preceding actions?

A. The network administrator maintains the same level of access as the previous administrator.

B. You minimize the configuration changes required.

C. You block the current network administrator from further network access.

D. You audit all access by the marketing department's network administrator.

E. The installation does not allow any of the desired functionality.

70-218.04.01.003

You are the network administrator and have just deployed a file server named FSERVER in the east.nwtraders.com domain as shown in the following figure. The file share you are creating, BRIEFS, must be secured so only members of the legal department can access it. The following groups exist in Active Directory and the local SAM database of the FSERVER computer.

Examine the figure shown here.

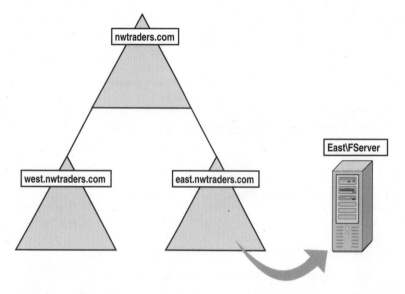

- Each domain contains a global group named LegalDept that contains all members of the legal department in the domain.

- Each domain contains a domain local group named LegalPerms that is assigned permissions to resources in that domain.

- The user accounts for the legal department are all stored in an OU named Legal in each of the three domains.

- The local SAM database of the FSERVER computer contains a local group named LegalAccess.

If all three domains in the nwtraders.com forest are in mixed mode, what is the recommended strategy for assigning permissions to the BRIEFS file share?

A. In each domain, make users in that domain's Legal OU members of the LegalPerms domain local group in that domain. In the East domain, add the three LegalPerms domain local groups to the membership of the East\LegalDept global group. Finally, assign the East\LegalDept group permissions to the BRIEFS file share at the FSERVER computer.

B. In each domain, make users in that domain's Legal OU members of the LegalDept global group. In the East domain, add the three LegalDept global groups to the membership of the East\LegalPerm domain local group. Finally, assign the East\LegalPerm domain local group permissions to the BRIEFS file share at the FSERVER computer.

C. In each domain, make users in that domain's Legal OU members of the LegalDept global group. At the FSERVER computer, add the three LegalDept global groups to the membership of the FSERVER\LegalAccess local group. Finally, assign the FSERVER\LegalAccess local group permissions to the BRIEFS file share at the FSERVER computer.

D. In each domain, make users in that domain's Legal OU members of the LegalPerms domain local group. At the FSERVER computer, add the three LegalPerms domain local groups to the membership of the FSERVER\LegalAccess local group. Finally, assign the FSERVER\LegalAccess local group permissions to the BRIEFS file share at the FSERVER computer.

70-218.04.01.004

You are the network administrator and have just deployed a file server named FSERVER in the east.nwtraders.com domain as shown in the following figure. The file share you are creating, BRIEFS, must be secured so only members of the legal department can access the file share. The following groups exist in Active Directory and the local SAM database of the FSERVER computer.

Examine the figure shown here.

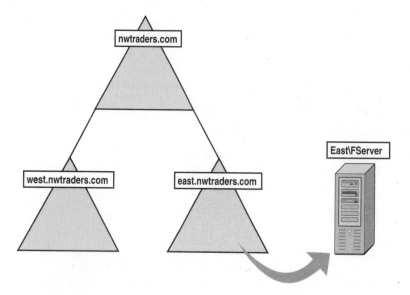

- Each domain contains a global group named LegalDept that contains all members of the legal department in the domain.

- Each domain contains a domain local group named LegalPerms that is assigned permissions to resources in that domain.

- The user accounts for the legal department are all stored in an OU named Legal in each of the three domains.

- The local SAM database of the FSERVER computer contains a local group named LegalAccess.

If all three domains in the nwtraders.com forest are in native mode, what is the recommended strategy for assigning permissions to the BRIEFS file share?

A. In each domain, make users in that domain's Legal OU members of the LegalPerms domain local group in that domain. In the East domain, add the three LegalPerms domain local groups to the membership of the East\LegalDept global group. Finally, assign the East\LegalDept group permissions to the BRIEFS file share at the FSERVER computer.

B. In each domain, make users in that domain's Legal OU members of the LegalDept global group. In the East domain, add the three LegalDept global groups to the membership of the East\LegalPerm domain local group. Finally, assign the East\LegalPerm domain local group permissions to the BRIEFS file share at the FSERVER computer.

C. In each domain, make users in that domain's Legal OU members of the LegalDept global group. At the FSERVER computer, add the three LegalDept global groups to the membership of the FSERVER\LegalAccess local group. Finally, assign the FSERVER\LegalAccess local group permissions to the BRIEFS file share at the FSERVER computer.

D. In each domain, make users in that domain's Legal OU members of the LegalPerms domain local group. At the FSERVER computer, add the three LegalPerms domain local groups to the membership of the FSERVER\LegalAccess local group. Finally, assign the FSERVER\LegalAccess local group permissions to the BRIEFS file share at the FSERVER computer.

70-218.04.01.005

The membership in the Auditors universal group is modified because a new auditor was hired. Before the modification is performed, the IT manager asks how the modification of the universal group membership will affect replication. What statement describes the replication that is caused by adding the user account to the universal group?

A. The change in the universal group membership is replicated to all domain controllers in the domain where the universal group is defined and to all global catalog servers in the forest.

B. The change in the universal group membership is replicated only to the global catalog servers in the forest.

C. The change in the universal group membership is replicated to all domain controllers in the forest.

D. The change in the universal group membership is replicated only to domain controllers in the domain where the universal group is defined.

Objective 4.1 Answers

70-218.04.01.001

▶ **Correct Answers: A, D, and F**

A. **Correct:** The ADMT can be used to create user accounts from one Active Directory forest without migrating SID information.

B. **Incorrect:** Active Directory Domains and Trusts is used to establish and manage trust relationships between domains; it provides no functionality for performing batch processing of user accounts.

C. **Incorrect:** The Active Directory Users and Computers console does not perform batch processing. Each of the 500 accounts would have to be manually created.

D. **Correct:** If the user information is imported into a comma separated value format file, the CSVDE.EXE utility can be used to import the information into Active Directory.

E. **Incorrect:** The Local Users and Groups console is used to define users and groups in the local Security Accounts Manager (SAM) database of member servers and stand-alone computers. In addition, the Local Users and Groups console does not allow batch creation of accounts.

F. **Correct:** If the user information is imported into an LDIF file format, the LDIFDE.EXE utility can be used to import the information into Active Directory.

70-218.04.01.002

▶ **Correct Answers: C**

A. **Incorrect:** The only way to guarantee that the network administrator has the same level of access as the previous administrator is to rename the existing administrator account.

B. **Incorrect:** The creation of a new user account adds additional work because permissions must be reassigned, group memberships defined, and delegation of administration performed for the new user account.

C. **Correct:** The deletion of the current network administrator's user account immediately blocks that user from accessing the network.

D. **Incorrect:** The auditing GPO must be defined at the OU where the computer is used and managed by the marketing department network administrator. Enabling auditing for the OU where the user account exists does not accomplish the goal.

E. **Incorrect:** The goal to block the current network administrator from further network access is met when the current account is deleted from Active Directory.

70-218.04.01.003

▶ **Correct Answers: C**

  A. **Incorrect:** Domain local groups cannot be members of global groups. In addition, a domain local group cannot cross domain boundaries. Domain local groups can be used only in the domain where the domain local group exists.

  B. **Incorrect:** Domain local groups cannot be used as member servers in a mixed mode domain. Domain local groups are recognized by member servers only in native mode domains.

  C. **Correct:** In a mixed mode domain, the recommended strategy is to gather all user accounts into global groups in their domain. The global groups are then made members of a local group in the local SAM database of the member server. Finally, the local group is assigned permissions to the resource.

  D. **Incorrect:** Domain local groups cannot be added to the membership of local groups in a member server's SAM database.

70-218.04.01.004

▶ **Correct Answers: B**

  A. **Incorrect:** Domain local groups cannot be members of global groups. In addition, a domain local group cannot cross domain boundaries. Domain local groups can be used only in the domain where the domain local group exists.

  B. **Correct:** Permissions can be assigned to domain local groups in a native mode domain. When you collect the user accounts into global groups in each domain and then make the three global groups members of the East\LegalPerm group, group membership best practices are followed.

  C. **Incorrect:** In native mode domains, it is recommended that you assign permissions to domain local groups created in Active Directory rather than creating separate local groups in each file server's SAM database.

  D. **Incorrect:** Domain local groups cannot be added to the membership of local groups in a member server's SAM database.

70-218.04.01.005

▶ **Correct Answers: A**

A. **Correct:** When a universal group's membership is modified, the change is replicated to both the domain controllers in the domain where the universal group exists and to all global catalog servers in the forest.

B. **Incorrect:** In addition to replicating a universal group's membership to all global catalog servers, the membership change is also replicated to the domain controllers in the domain where the universal group exists.

C. **Incorrect:** Changes in universal group membership are replicated to all global catalog servers in the forest, not to all domain controllers in the forest. The change is also replicated to all domain controllers in the domain where the universal group is defined.

D. **Incorrect:** In addition to being replicated to all domain controllers in the domain where the universal group is defined, the membership change is also replicated to all global catalog servers in the forest.

O B J E C T I V E   4 . 2

Manage object and container permissions.

Active Directory allows **delegation of administration** to specific OUs and hierarchies of OUs in your organization. When implementing your OU structure, you must ensure that the OU structure meets your administration goals, and allows administration of specific department's or regions's OUs to be delegated to users or groups in the organization.

The most common method of performing the delegation is by using the Delegation of Administration Wizard in the Active Directory Users and Computers MMC snap-in. When running the wizard, you must choose which **security principals** (users, computers, or security groups) you are delegating permissions to and then decide which permissions to assign. Remember that you can choose to delegate permissions to the entire container, specific **object classes**, or even specific attributes of a class when using the wizard.

When delegating the permissions, remember the best practices for permissions:

- For containers in the domain-naming context, delegate permissions to domain local groups in the domain.

- For attributes that are published to the global catalog, ensure that Read permissions are assigned to global groups or universal groups to ensure that users in other domains can read the information in the global catalog.

- For containers in the Configuration or Schema naming contexts, assign permissions to global groups or universal groups. Domain local groups work in these naming contexts only when a single domain exists in the forest. Remember that domain local groups can be used only in the same domain where the domain local group is defined.

To answer the questions in this objective, become familiar with the Delegation of Authority Wizard and assigning advanced permissions to an OU or to the domain in the Active Directory Users and Computers console. When working in the console, notice the way the OU design affects the Delegation of Authority Wizard. The delegation of administration requirements might also result in changes to the OU design.

Objective 4.2 Questions

70-218.04.02.001

You are implementing your organization's security plan and must use the Delegation of Administration Wizard to delegate administrative permissions to departmental administration groups. The following goals must be met using the Delegation of Administration Wizard.

- The engineering department administrators must be able to manage user, computer, and group objects for their department.

- The IT department administrators must be able to manage user, computer, and group objects for the entire organization.

- The human resources department must be able to manage only address and staffing attributes for all user accounts in the organization.

- The accounting department administrators must be able to manage all user accounts in the accounting department.

- The desktop administrators must be able to manage all workstations in the domain.

To meet the objectives, you perform the following tasks:

- You create all user, computer, and group objects for the human resources and IT departments in the Workstations, Groups, and Staff OUs.

- You create the user, computer, and group objects for the accounting and engineering departments in the Accounting and Engineering OUs located within the Workstations, Groups, and Staff OUs.

- At the domain, you delegate the ability to manage user, group, and computer objects to the Eng Admins domain local group.

- At the Domain Controllers OU, you delegate the ITAdmins domain local group the ability to manage user, group, and computer objects.

- At the OU=Accounting, OU=Staff OU, you delegate the AccountAdmins domain local group the ability to manage user accounts.

- At the domain, you delegate the HumResources domain local group the ability to manage staffing attributes.

- At the domain, you delegate the ability to manage computer accounts to the DesktopAdmins domain local group.

The following OU structure is used in your organization's domain.

Examine the figure shown here.

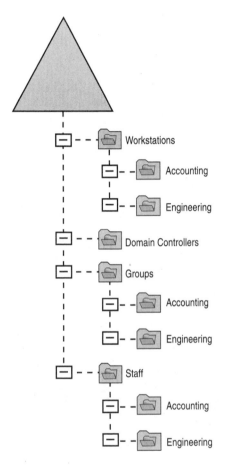

What objectives are met by your actions? (Choose all that apply.)

A. The engineering department administrators can manage only user, computer, and group objects for their department.

B. The IT department administrators can manage users, computers, and group objects for the entire organization.

C. The human resources department can manage only address and staffing attributes for all user accounts in the organization.

D. The accounting department administrators can manage only all user accounts in the accounting department.

E. The desktop administrators can manage only workstation accounts in the domain.

70-218.04.02.002

Northwind Traders has two domains in the forest, which are named corporate.nwtraders.com and production.nwtraders.com. The OUs defined in the two domains are shown in the following figure.

Examine the figure shown here.

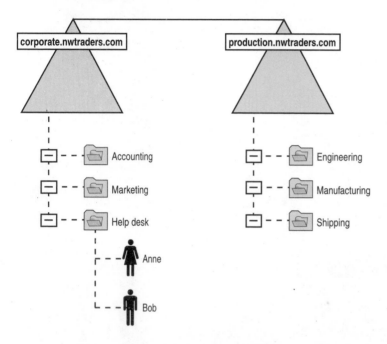

Anne and Bob work on the Help desk of Northwind Traders and must be able to reset passwords for all user accounts in the organization. Where must you assign the Reset Password permission for the Help desk personnel? (Choose all that apply.)

A. The Help desk OU

B. The production.nwtraders.com domain

C. The corporate.nwtraders.com domain

D. The Domain Controllers OU in both domains

E. The Configuration naming context

70-218.04.02.003

Your organization has decided to delegate the ability to create and link GPOs to all department administrators. The department administrators should be able to create GPOs only in the GPOCentral OU and link GPOs to OUs they manage. What must you do to provide this ability to the department administrator for the marketing department?

A. Make the DeptAdmins global group a member of the Group Policy Creator Owners global group. At the GPOCentral OU, delegate the DeptAdmins global group the ability to Manage Group Policy links and delegate Full Control permissions for the Marketing OU to the MarketingAdmins domain local group.

B. At the GPOCentral OU, delegate the DeptAdmins global group the ability to Manage Group Policy links and delegate Full Control permissions for the Marketing OU to the MarketingAdmins domain local group.

C. Make the DeptAdmins global group a member of the Group Policy Creator Owners global group. At the domain, delegate the DeptAdmins global group the ability to Manage Group Policy links and delegate Full Control permissions for the Marketing OU to the MarketingAdmins domain local group.

D. Make the DeptAdmins global group a member of the Domain Admins global group. At the GPO Central OU, delegate the DeptAdmins global group the ability to Manage Group Policy links and delegate full control permissions for the Marketing OU to the MarketingAdmins domain local group.

70-218.04.02.004

You want to delegate the ability to publish updated certificate revocation lists (CRLs) to the CN=CDP, CN=Public Key Services, CN=Services, CN=Configuration, DC=nwtraders, DC=com container to the CRLPublishers group in the sub.nwtraders.com domain. What group scope can you use for the group when assigning permissions to this container? (Choose all that apply.)

A. A domain local group in the nwtraders.com domain

B. A domain local group in the sub.nwtraders.com domain

C. A global group in the nwtraders.com domain

D. A global group in the sub.nwtraders.com domain

E. A universal group in either the nwtraders.com or sub.nwtraders.com domain

Objective 4.2 Answers

70-218.04.02.001

▶ **Correct Answers: C and D**

A. **Incorrect:** The EngAdmins domain local group is assigned too many rights. The EngAdmins domain local group can manage user, computer, and group objects for the entire domain, not just for the engineering department.

B. **Incorrect:** The ITAdmins domain local group is not assigned permissions at the correct location. To manage user, computer, and group objects, the delegation should be performed at the domain, not at the Domain Controllers OU.

C. **Correct:** By delegating the ability to manage staffing attributes at the domain to the HumResources domain local group, this objective is met.

D. **Correct:** By delegating permissions to manage user accounts at the OU=Accounting, OU=Staff OU, the AccountAdmins domain local group can manage the accounting department's user accounts.

E. **Incorrect:** The desktop administrators can manage all computer accounts, including domain controller accounts if they are delegated the ability to manage computer accounts at the domain. The delegation should be performed at the Workstations OU, not at the domain.

70-218.04.02.002

▶ **Correct Answers: B and C**

A. **Incorrect:** The Reset Password permission must be defined at both the production.nwtraders.com and corporate.nwtraders.com domains, not at the OU where the Help desk personnel accounts exist.

B. **Correct:** The Reset Password permission needs to be set in the production.nwtraders.com domain to allow passwords to be reset for user accounts in the production.nwtraders.com domain.

C. **Correct:** The Reset Password permission needs to be set in the corporate.nwtraders.com domain to allow passwords to be reset for user accounts in the corporate.nwtraders.com domain.

D. **Incorrect:** The Reset Password permission must be defined at both the production.nwtraders.com and corporate.nwtraders.com domains, not at the OU where the domain controller accounts exist.

E. **Incorrect:** The Reset Password permission must be defined at both the production.nwtraders.com and corporate.nwtraders.com domains, not at the Configuration naming context. Permissions assigned to the Configuration naming context do not affect user objects.

70-218.04.02.003

▶ **Correct Answers: A**

A. **Correct:** Membership in the Group Policy Creator Owners group allows the DeptAdmins to create GPOs. The other delegations limit creation of GPOs in the GPOCentral and management of objects in the Marketing OU to the MarketingAdmins group.

B. **Incorrect:** To create new GPOs in the GPOCentral OU, the DeptAdmins global group must be a member of the Group Policy Creator Owners group.

C. **Incorrect:** This solution results in an excess of permissions. By delegating the ability to Manage Group Policy links at the domain, the department administrators are able to manage Group Policy links in all OUs, not just the OU representing their department.

D. **Incorrect:** This solution results in an excess of permissions. By making the DeptAdmins global group a member of the Domain Admins global group, the department administrators are now administrators of the domain and can manage any objects in the domain, not just in the OU created for their department.

70-218.04.02.004

▶ **Correct Answers: D and E**

A. **Incorrect:** You should never assign permissions to the Configuration naming context to domain local groups when multiple domains exist in the forest, because the domain local group would be recognized only by the domain in which the domain local group exists.

B. **Incorrect:** This answer is incorrect for the reasons stated in answer A.

C. **Incorrect:** The CRLPublishers group is in the sub.nwtraders.com domain. You can add security principals only from the same domain to global groups. Because the CRLPublishers group exists in the sub.nwtraders.com domain, you cannot make the CRLPublishers members of the group if it is in the nwtraders.com domain.

D. **Correct:** Permissions that are assigned to global groups can be resolved by any domain in the forest. Assigning permissions to global groups is the preferred method to assign permissions to the Configuration naming context.

E. **Correct:** Universal groups are recognized by any domain because the membership is stored in the global catalog, and they can be used to assign permissions to the Configuration naming context.

O B J E C T I V E   4 . 3

Diagnose Active Directory replication problems.

Active Directory uses **multimaster replication**. This means no single copy of the Active Directory database in a domain takes precedence over the other copies. A change made at one domain controller is replicated to the other domain controllers in the domain, and changes can be performed at any domain controller in the domain. This can result in replication latency issues. For example, an account that is created at one domain controller will not be available for authentication at other domain controllers until the account and its attributes are replicated to the other domain controllers.

The use of a multimaster domain can result in problems if the **replication topology** breaks down. To troubleshoot Active Directory replication problems, you must understand the basics of Active Directory replication. Review how the Knowledge Consistency Checker, the Inter-Site Topology Generator, and bridgehead servers are used to generate a replication topology between the domain controllers in your forest.

Active Directory replication is optimized through the definition of sites. When replication is performed between sites, the actual size of the replicated data decreases to 15 percent of the original data size. When you define sites, you must also define subnets that are associated with each site, site links that define the connections, and protocols used to replicate between the sites.

In some cases, site link bridges must be defined to connect site links. This is required only in cases in which the network is not fully routed and when the definition of a site link bridge allows connectivity between remote sites.

To answer the questions in this objective, become familiar with the tools that allow management of replication in the forest. These include Active Directory Sites and Services, Replmon from the Windows 2000 Support Tools, and Repadmin from the Windows 2000 Support Tools. Become familiar with the options available in each tool and what actions can be performed with each tool. Also be sure to review what restrictions exist for the available replication protocols. Remember that Simple Mail Transfer Protocol (SMTP) replication can be used only between sites when different domains exist at the two sites.

Objective 4.3 Questions

70-218.04.03.001

Your organization uses two domains, DomainA and DomainB, and exists at two separate sites. An SMTP site link is defined between the two sites, and the domain controllers are placed as shown in the following figure.

Examine the figure shown here.

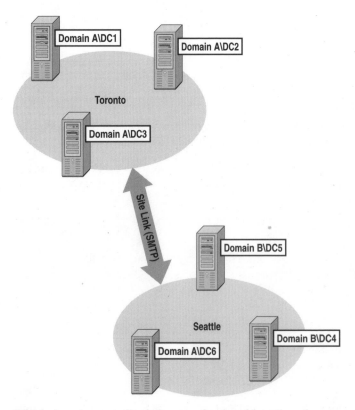

Which domain controller is incorrectly placed based on the current site topology implemented for the organization?

A. DomainA\DC1

B. DomainA\DC2

C. DomainA\DC3

D. DomainB\DC4

E. DomainB\DC5

F. DomainA\DC6

70-218.04.03.002

You are responsible for troubleshooting replication problems between DC1, a domain controller at your Washington site, and DC2, a domain controller at your Malaysia site. A direct wide area network (WAN) connection exists between the two sites, but the amount of traffic using the site link appears to be lower than expected.

Assuming that the site link costs between sites are configured as shown in the following figure, what paths are used for replication between the Washington and Malaysia sites? (Choose all that apply.)

Examine the figure shown here.

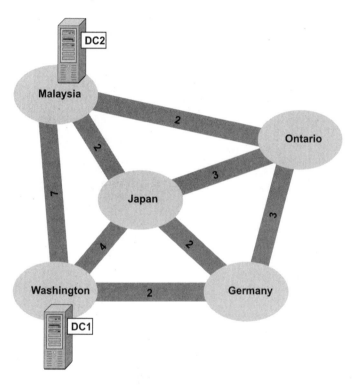

A. Washington to Malaysia

B. Washington to Japan to Malaysia

C. Washington to Germany to Japan to Malaysia

D. Washington to Germany to Ontario to Malaysia

E. Washington to Germany to Ontario to Japan to Malaysia

70-218.04.03.003

You are responsible for configuring the replication topology for Active Directory replication. You must configure site links, connection objects, and bridgehead servers to ensure that replication does not fail between sites. These are your goals:

- You must provide multiple paths of replication between sites to ensure that failure of a single WAN link does not result in replication failure.

- All replication to and from the hub site of Virginia must take place through a new domain controller named Zeus.

- If the Zeus server is unavailable, all replication to the Virginia site must fail over to the Athena server.

- The replication solution must allow for the fact that the link between Virginia and Bermuda might not always be available.

To meet these goals, you perform the following tasks:

- At each remote site, you manually configure a single domain controller as the preferred bridgehead server for replication.

- At each remote site, you manually configure a connection object for the Zeus server.

- At the Virginia site, you configure the Zeus server as the preferred bridgehead server for both RPC and SMTP replication.

- At the Virginia site, you manually configure connection objects to the bridgehead servers at each remote site.

- You configure an SMTP site link between the Bermuda and Virginia sites. The Bermuda site uses a separate domain.

Which goals are met by the preceding actions? (Choose all that apply.)

A. Provide multiple paths of replication between sites to ensure that failure of a single WAN link does not result in replication failure.

B. All replication to and from the Virginia site must take place through a new domain controller named Zeus.

C. If the Zeus server is unavailable, all replication to the Virginia site must fail over to the Athena server.

D. The replication solution must allow replication to work between the Bermuda and Virginia sites if the link is temporarily unavailable.

E. All goals are met by the preceding actions.

70-218.04.03.004

You are investigating a remote user logon problem and believe that the trouble might be caused by replication problems with the remote domain controller. What tools can you use to troubleshoot the replication problem? (Choose all that apply.)

A. Active Directory Users and Computers

B. Active Directory Sites and Services

C. Active Directory Domains and Trusts

D. Replication Monitor

E. REMOTE.EXE

70-218.04.03.005

When are you required to define a site link bridge to ensure that replication takes place between sites in your forest?

A. Site link bridges are used when two or more site links exist. The site links must be connected using site link bridges.

B. A site link bridge translates replication traffic between SMTP site links and RPC site links.

C. Site link bridges must be defined in networks that are not fully routed.

D. Site link bridges are required to define the shortest route between remote sites connected by two or more site links.

70-218.04.03.006

There are three domain contollers named DC1, DC2, and DC3 that exist in your Active Directory domain. A member of the Administrators domain local group is creating a new user account named ANNE1 in the Temporary OU while connected to DC1. At the same time, another Administrator deletes the Temporary OU and all objects in the OU while connected to DC3. Where will the ANNE1 user account exist after all replication takes place between DC1, DC2, and DC3?

A. The LostAndFound container

B. The Temporary OU

C. The Users container

D. The object is deleted because of the deletion of the Temporary OU at DC3.

Objective 4.3 Answers

70-218.04.03.001

▶ **Correct Answers: F**

A. **Incorrect:** This domain controller is placed with two other domain controllers for DomainA at the Toronto site. It will be unable to replicate with DC6 at the Seattle site, because intersite replication between domain controllers in the same domain must use remote procedure calls (RPCs), not SMTP.

B. **Incorrect:** This answer is incorrect for the reasons stated in answer A.

C. **Incorrect:** This answer is incorrect for the reasons stated in answer A.

D. **Incorrect:** This domain controller is placed with two other domain controllers for DomainB at the Seattle site. It can replicate with all domain controllers in the forest because only domain controllers for DomainA exist at the Toronto site, allowing for SMTP replication to work.

E. **Incorrect:** This answer is incorrect for the reasons stated in answer D.

F. **Correct:** DC6 will be unable to replicate changes to the other domain controllers in the DomainA domain because intersite replication between domain controllers in the same domain must use RPCs, not SMTP replication.

70-218.04.03.002

▶ **Correct Answers: B and C**

A. **Incorrect:** The transitive cost of this site link is 7, which is a higher site link cost than two other replication paths. This explains why less traffic than expected is being transmitted over the dedicated WAN link between the Washington and Malaysia sites.

B. **Correct:** The transitive cost of this site link is 6, which is the lowest cost site link between the Washington and Malaysia sites. The site link between Washington to Germany to Japan to Malaysia is also 6, so the replication would be evenly divided between the two paths.

C. **Correct:** This answer is correct for the reasons stated in answer B.

D. **Incorrect:** The transitive cost of this site link is 7, which is a higher site link cost than two other replication paths.

E. **Incorrect:** The transitive cost of this site link is 10, which is a higher site link cost than other replication paths.

70-218.04.03.003

► **Correct Answers: B and D**

A. **Incorrect:** The replication model you deployed is a spoke and hub operation where all replication to a remote site is from the Virginia hub site.

B. **Correct:** You accomplished this by manually configuring bridgehead servers at the remote sites, designating Zeus as the bridgehead server for the Virginia site, and manually configuring connection objects at each bridgehead server to predefine replication traffic.

C. **Incorrect:** The Athena server is not designated as a preferred bridgehead server. If the Zeus server fails, all replication to the Virginia site will fail until either Zeus is restarted or Athena is designated as a preferred bridgehead server.

D. **Correct:** The use of SMTP replication between the Virginia and Bermuda sites allows for replication over an unreliable link. SMTP replication can be used because a separate domain is implemented at the Bermuda site.

E. **Incorrect:** The proposed actions allow only two objectives to be met.

70-218.04.03.004

► **Correct Answers: B and D**

A. **Incorrect:** Active Directory Users and Computers is used to manage many aspects of Active Directory, but not Active Directory replication.

B. **Correct:** You can view connection objects for each domain controller in the forest using Active Directory Sites and Services by viewing the connection objects in each server's NTDS Settings container.

C. **Incorrect:** Active Directory Domains and Trusts is used to manage trust relationships between domains, not to troubleshoot replication problems.

D. **Correct:** This graphical tool is provided in the Windows 2000 Support Tools and allows you to troubleshoot replication problems between domain controllers. Replication Monitor includes a graphical view of your replication topology and the ability to view individual replication updates.

E. **Incorrect:** REMOTE.EXE allows remote command-line execution, and does not provide any troubleshooting capabilities for replication problems. REMOTE.EXE is typically used for remote blue screen debugging procedures.

70-218.04.03.005

▶ **Correct Answers: C**

A. **Incorrect:** By default, site links are transitive and there is no need to define site link bridges to connect site links. The only time you need to define a site link bridge is when you operate in a network that is not fully routed.

B. **Incorrect:** A site link bridge does not act as a gateway translating replication traffic between SMTP and RPC links. SMTP replication is sent as SMTP from start to end, and it is not translated midstream. The same is true for RPC replication.

C. **Correct:** Site link bridges define replication paths between sites in a network that is not fully routed. This scenario exists when a network segment is not reachable using the network routing table and must be defined by bridging individual site links.

D. **Incorrect:** Site link bridges do not optimize replication, but instead define replication paths between two sites in networks that are not fully routed.

70-218.04.03.006

▶ **Correct Answers: A**

A. **Correct:** The user object was created in the Temporary OU, but the OU was deleted at a different DC. When the deletion of the OU and the creation of the user object is replicated, the replication results in the user account being placed in the LostAndFound container.

B. **Incorrect:** The deletion of the Temporary OU at DC3 will be replicated to both DC1 and DC2. The user account will be placed in the LostAndFound container because the actual OU where the object was created no longer exists.

C. **Incorrect:** The object must be created in the Users container for the object to exist in the Users container. Because the Temporary OU was deleted, the user object will exist in the LostAndFound container after replication takes place.

D. **Incorrect:** The deletion of the Temporary OU took place at a different OU. The ANNE1 user object is valid, but it cannot exist in the created naming context because of the deletion of the OU. This does not result in the deletion of the user object but, instead, places the user object in the LostAndFound container.

O B J E C T I V E   4 . 4

Deploy software by using Group Policy.

Group Policy allows you to distribute software to both computers and users without having to assign additional permissions to the users and computers. Software deployment is part of the change and configuration management features in Windows 2000.

Group Policy allows you to deploy applications to users and computers. When you are deploying applications, the first decision is whether to publish or assign applications. The differences between published and assigned applications are as follows:

- A **published application** is made available to a user or computer in the Add/Remove Programs icon in Control Panel. A published application is typically used for common applications that are not required by all users within an organization or department. The application can be installed only through invocation by opening a document with an extension associated with the application, or by choosing to install the application from Add/Remove Programs.

- An **assigned application** appears in the Start menu of a user or computer object in the Group Policy container where the application is assigned. If assigned to a user, the application installs when the user clicks the application in the Start menu, or when a user opens a document with an extension associated with the application. If assigned to a computer, the application installs when the computer starts.

In addition to knowing how applications can be deployed using Group Policy, be sure you know how application settings can be modified using transform files, how .zap files allow applications without Windows Installer packages to be deployed, and how Windows Installer packages allow deployed applications to be upgraded and automatically repaired.

To answer the questions in this objective, practice deploying applications using Group Policy. Be sure to both assign applications and publish applications so you can compare the differences between the two deployment methods and deploy the applications to both computers and users. When deploying the applications, be sure to review all options available for software deployment.

Objective 4.4 Questions

70-218.04.04.001

Your organization's Active Directory uses a single domain and the OU structure shown in the following figure.

Examine the figure shown here.

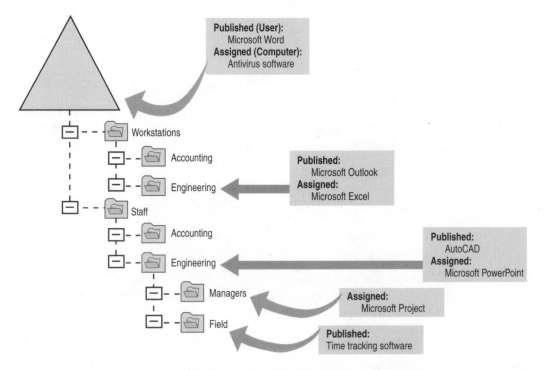

Assuming that your laptop computer is located in the OU=Engineering, OU=Workstations OU and that your user account exists in the OU=Field, OU=Engineering, OU=Staff OU, what programs are available in your Start menu when you log on to the network, based on the software deployment configuration shown in the figure? (Choose all that apply.)

A. Word

B. Antivirus software

C. Outlook

D. Excel

E. AutoCAD

F. PowerPoint

70-218.04.04.002

Your organization's Active Directory uses a single domain and the OU structure shown in the following figure. Examine the figure shown here.

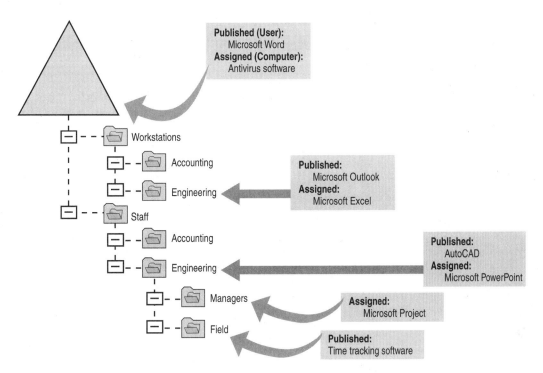

Assuming that your laptop computer is located in the OU=Engineering, OU=Workstations OU and that your user account exists in the OU=Field, OU=Engineering, OU=Staff OU, what programs are available in Add/Remove Programs in Control Panel, based on the software deployment configuration shown in the figure? (Choose all that apply.)

A. Word

B. Antivirus software

C. Outlook

D. Excel

E. AutoCAD

F. PowerPoint

G. Time tracking software

70-218.04.04.003

You want to use Group Policy to install the antivirus software used by your organization. If you want to ensure that the antivirus software is installed without user intervention on all Windows 2000–based computers, what method do you use?

A. Assign the antivirus software at the domain to all users.

B. Publish the antivirus software at the domain to all users.

C. Assign the antivirus software at the domain to all computers.

D. Publish the antivirus software at the domain to all computers.

70-218.04.04.004

Each department in your organization uses Word but implements different templates and default settings. Assuming that Group Policy is used to deploy Word, how do you deploy Word to ensure that the different default settings are implemented for each department?

A. Create separate Windows Installer packages for each department that define the default settings required for that department. Configure separate GPOs for each department that define which Windows Installer package is applied for that department.

B. Create a transform file (.mst) that defines the default settings for each department. Place the transform files in a separate network share, and reference the transform share and the Windows Installer package share in each GPO that assigns Word.

C. Create a transform file (.mst) that defines the default settings for each department. Create a separate Windows Installer package for each transform file. After Word is deployed to all users in the organization, deploy the transform file packages to apply the default settings for each department.

D. Create a transform file (.mst) that defines the default settings for each department. Place the transform files in the network share that contains the Windows Installer package, and configure in each GPO that assigns Word the specific transform file to use for the deployment.

70-218.04.04.005

Your company wants to deploy Microsoft Office 97 using published applications in Group Policy. One of the network administrators wants to configure Office 97 to automatically repair itself if important files are accidentally deleted from the application. How do you do this?

A. Create a Windows Installer package that defines what files can be repaired automatically. Deploy this custom .msi file using Group Policy.

B. Create a transform file (.mst) that defines what files can be repaired automatically by Group Policy.

C. Create a .zap file that defines what files can be repaired automatically by Group Policy.

D. None of the above.

Objective 4.4 Answers

70-218.04.04.001

▶ **Correct Answers: B, D, and F**

A. **Incorrect:** Word is published to users at the domain. Published applications appear in Add/Remove Programs and are not available from the Start menu until after they are installed.

B. **Correct:** The antivirus software is assigned to all computers in the domain and is installed after the computer restarts.

C. **Incorrect:** Outlook is published to computers at the OU=Engineering, OU=Workstations OU. Published applications appear in Add/Remove Programs and are not available from the Start menu until after they are installed.

D. **Correct:** Excel is assigned to all computers in the OU=Engineering, OU=Workstations OU and is installed after the computer restarts.

E. **Incorrect:** AutoCAD is published to users in the OU=Engineering, OU=Staff OU. Published applications appear in Add/Remove Programs and are not available from the Start menu until after they are installed.

F. **Correct:** PowerPoint is assigned to all users in the OU=Engineering, OU=Staff OU and is available on the Start menu when the user logs on to the network.

70-218.04.04.002

► **Correct Answers: A, C, E, and G**

A. **Correct:** Word is published to users at the domain. Published applications appear in Add/Remove Programs.

B. **Incorrect:** The antivirus software is assigned to all computers in the domain and is installed after the computer restarts. Assigned applications do not appear in Add/Remove Programs in Control Panel.

C. **Correct:** Outlook is published to computers at the OU=Engineering, OU=Workstations OU and appears in Add/Remove Programs in Control Panel.

D. **Incorrect:** Excel is assigned to all computers in the OU=Engineering, OU=Workstations OU and does not appear in Add/Remove Programs in Control Panel.

E. **Correct:** AutoCAD is published to users in the OU=Engineering, OU=Staff OU. Published applications appear in Add/Remove Programs in Control Panel.

F. **Incorrect:** PowerPoint is assigned to all users in the OU=Engineering, OU=Staff OU and does not appear in Add/Remove Programs in the Control Panel.

G. **Correct:** The time tracking software is published to users in the OU=Field, OU=Engineering, OU=Staff OU. Published applications appear in Add/Remove Programs in Control Panel.

70-218.04.04.003

► **Correct Answers: C**

A. **Incorrect:** Assigning the application at the domain to all users results in the antivirus software being installed only when the user invokes the application, which can delay the deployment of the software.

B. **Incorrect:** Publishing the antivirus software results in the software being available in Add/Remove Programs in Control Panel. Publishing does not automatically install the application.

C. **Correct:** When you assign the antivirus software to computers at the domain, the software is installed when the computer restarts.

D. **Incorrect:** This answer is incorrect for the reasons stated in answer B.

70-218.04.04.004

▶ **Correct Answers: D**

A. **Incorrect:** Assigning the application at the domain to all users results in the antivirus software being installed only when the user invokes the application, which can delay the deployment of the software.

B. **Incorrect:** Publishing the antivirus software results in the software being available in Add/Remove Programs in Control Panel. Publishing does not automatically install the application.

C. **Incorrect:** Transform files are applied only at the installation of the software. The deployment of the transform files as described would not result in the default settings for Word being applied.

D. **Correct:** Separate transform files can be created for each customized installation of the application. The transform files must be installed in the same distribution folder as the Windows Installer package and are applied at installation.

70-218.04.04.005

▶ **Correct Answers: D**

A. **Incorrect:** Custom Windows Installer packages can be created by only using third-party software such as Veritas WinINSTALL. Office 97 does not ship with a Windows Installer package.

B. **Incorrect:** Transform files define the default settings for a Windows Installer package and are applied at installation time, not after the application is installed.

C. **Incorrect:** These files allow non–Windows 2000 certified applications to be published in Group Policy. The .zap file describes what command line to use to install the application and what file extensions are used by the application; it does not provide repair features.

D. **Correct:** Office 97 can be deployed only using a .zap file with the default tools, and .zap files do not support the auto-repair feature available in Windows Installer packages.

Troubleshoot end-user Group Policy.

Group Policy application troubleshooting is rooted in understanding that Group Policies are applied in a default manner. The order is as follows:

1. Any local policy settings defined at the Windows 2000 computer are applied.

2. If they exist, GPOs defined at the site are applied.

3. If they exist, GPOs defined at the domain are applied.

4. If they exist, GPOs defined at the OU level are applied. The OU Group Policies are applied from the furthest OU to the OU where the object exists.

Be aware that troubleshooting Group Policy becomes more complex when the **No Override** and **Block Inheritance** flags are set for GPOs. Remember that when the two flags are in conflict, the No Override flag always takes precedence.

In addition to knowing how inheritance affects Group Policy application, also study which permissions are required for the Group Policy to successfully apply. Unless a user or computer is assigned both the Read and Apply Group Policy permissions for a GPO, the Group Policy settings will not be successfully applied.

To answer the questions in this objective, review the order in which Group Policies are applied. Be sure to investigate how Group Policy application is affected when No Override and Block Inheritance is added to the mix. Review the tools provided in the Windows 2000 Resource Kit Supplement One to troubleshoot Group Policy application. The tools you should review include GPRESULT.EXE, GPOTOOL.EXE, and FAZAM Lite. Know the features of each tool, and under what circumstances you use each tool in troubleshooting Group Policy application issues.

Objective 4.5 Questions

70-218.04.05.001

You are troubleshooting a Group Policy application problem and are trying to determine why Group Policy settings are not applied as expected. Your domain has deployed the Group Policies shown in the following figure.

Examine the figure shown here.

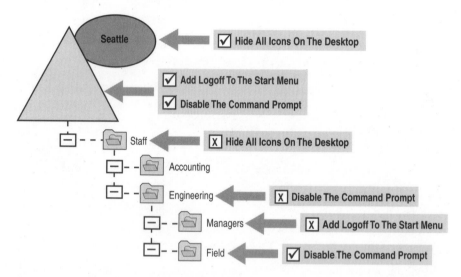

The following Group Policy settings are defined:

- At the Seattle site, a user Group Policy is configured that enables the Hide All Icons On The Desktop policy.

- At the domain, a user Group Policy is configured that enables the Add Logoff To The Start Menu policy and the Disable The Command Prompt policy.

- At the Staff OU, a user Group Policy is configured that disables the Hide All Icons On The Desktop policy.

- At the Engineering OU, a user Group Policy is configured that disables the Disable The Command Prompt policy.

- At the Managers OU, a user Group Policy is configured that disables the Add Logoff To The Start Menu policy.

- At the Field OU, a user Group Policy is configured that enables the Disable The Command Prompt policy.

Assuming that the user account you are troubleshooting is located in the Managers OU and the default Group Policy application model is used, what are the expected effective policy settings? (Choose all that apply.)

A. Icons are not visible on the desktop.

B. Icons are visible on the desktop.

C. Logoff is not available on the Start menu.

D. Logoff is available on the Start menu.

E. The command prompt is disabled.

F. The command prompt is enabled.

70-218.04.05.002

You are trying to determine whether GPOs are successfully replicated to all domain controllers in your domain. What tool from the resource kit can assist you in comparing the GPOs at all domain controllers?

A. GPRESULT.EXE

B. GPOTOOL.EXE

C. Group Policy MMC

D. FAZAM Lite

70-218.04.05.003

You are unsure where a Group Policy setting that is affecting your user environment is set. What tool can you use to determine what GPOs are applied to the user and computer account? (Choose all that apply.)

A. GPRESULT.EXE

B. GPOTOOL.EXE

C. Group Policy MMC

D. FAZAM Lite

E. Active Directory Users and Computers

70-218.04.05.004

What permissions must be assigned to a security principal for a GPO for the policies defined in the GPO to be applied to the security principal? (Choose all that apply.)

A. Full Control

B. Read

C. Write

D. Create All Child Objects

E. Apply Group Policy

Objective 4.5 Answers

70-218.04.05.001

► **Correct Answers: B, C, and F**

    A. **Incorrect:** The Hide All Icons On The Desktop policy was set to a disabled state at the Staff OU and was not defined in any OUs closer to the Managers OU; therefore, the effective state of this policy would be disabled.

    B. **Correct:** The Hide All Icons On The Desktop policy was set to a disabled state at the Staff OU and was not defined in any OUs closer to the Managers OU, resulting in the desktop icons being visible.

    C. **Correct:** At the Managers OU, the Add Logoff To The Start Menu policy is disabled, resulting in the Logoff option not being available on the Start menu.

    D. **Incorrect:** The Add Logoff To The Start Menu policy is disabled at the Managers OU, resulting in this policy being the effective policy. The Logoff option is not available on the Start menu.

    E. **Incorrect:** The Disable The Command Prompt policy is disabled at the Engineering OU, resulting in the command prompt being available to a user account in the Managers OU.

    F. **Correct:** The Disable The Command Prompt policy is disabled at the Engineering OU. Although the policy is enabled at the Field OU, it does not affect a user account created in the Managers OU.

70-218.04.05.002

▶ **Correct Answers: B**

A. **Incorrect:** GPRESULT.EXE indicates which GPOs are applied to a user or computer.

B. **Correct:** The GPOTOOL.EXE utility allows you to check GPO consistency and replication from a command line and is included in the Windows 2000 Server Resource Kit.

C. **Incorrect:** The Group Policy MMC console allows you to define and review GPOs, but it does not allow you to analyze where individual Group Policy settings are defined.

D. **Incorrect:** FAZAM Lite, available in the Windows 2000 Resource Kit Supplement One, is a resultant set of policy tool that shows what GPOs were applied and what the effective policy is for a user or computer.

70-218.04.05.003

▶ **Correct Answers: A and D**

A. **Correct:** GPRESULT.EXE indicates which GPOs are applied to a user or computer. To determine user Group Policy settings, type **gpresult /u *username***.

B. **Incorrect:** The GPOTOOL.EXE utility allows you to check GPO consistency and replication from a command line. It does not indicate which GPOs are applied to a specific user or computer.

C. **Incorrect:** The Group Policy MMC console allows you to define and review GPOs. It does not allow you to determine which GPOs are applied to a specific user or computer based on their location in Active Directory.

D. **Correct:** FAZAM Lite, available in the Windows 2000 Resource Kit Supplement One, is a resultant set of policy tool that shows what GPOs were applied and what the effective policy is for a user or computer.

E. **Incorrect:** Active Directory Users and Computers can be used to create and edit GPOs that are linked to domains and OUs, but it cannot be used to determine where Group Policy settings are applied to a specific user account.

70-218.04.05.004

▶ **Correct Answers: B and E**

   A. **Incorrect:** Although the Full Control permission would provide you with the necessary Read and Apply Group Policy permissions, this would be an excess permission assignment.

   B. **Correct:** A security principal must be assigned the Read permission to read the contents and settings defined in a GPO. The permission can be assigned directly to the security principal or to a group object in which the security principal has membership.

   C. **Incorrect:** The Write permission allows a security principal to modify any linked GPOs for the Group Policy container.

   D. **Incorrect:** The Create All Child Objects permission allows a security principal to define new Group Policy Links for a Group Policy container.

   E. **Correct:** A security principal must be assigned the Apply Group Policy permission to have the contents and settings defined in a GPO applied. The permission can be assigned directly to the security principal or to a group object in which the security principal has membership.

OBJECTIVE 4.6

Implement and manage security policies by using Group Policy.

The first fact to realize about security policies is that they are applied to **computer accounts**, even though several of the settings directly affect users, such as password settings.

The second fact you must understand about security policies is where to apply them in the Active Directory structure. Typically, security policies are applied at the OU where the user or computer account exists. The only exception to this rule is with the application of account policies. Account policies are applied at the domain, not at the OU where the user or computer accounts exist. In other words, if you require different account policies in your organization, you must implement separate domains. Specifically, the following settings make up the account policy settings:

- Password policy settings define minimum and maximum password lengths, how frequently you have to change passwords, and whether passwords must be complex.

- Account lockout policy defines under what circumstances an account will be locked out because of password failures and when the account will be reset.

- Kerberos policy defines lifetimes for Kerberos ticket-granting tickets and service tickets, clock variance tolerance, and whether logon restrictions are enforced at all times.

Although you can apply password and account lockout policies at an OU, these settings affect only the local **Security Accounts Manager (SAM)** database of the computer accounts within the OU, not the user accounts that exist in the OU.

To answer the questions in this objective, review the various security policies that are applied using Group Policy. Review the default security templates that are included with Windows 2000 and in what circumstances they should be applied. Also review the use of the SECEDIT command to force the application of user and computer policy to occur quicker than the defaults of 5 minutes for domain controllers and 90 minutes for Microsoft Windows 2000 Professional computers and Windows 2000 member servers.

Objective 4.6 Questions

70-218.04.06.001

You are responsible for defining the account policies for the organization. Your company wants to implement the following account policies:

- Passwords must be at least nine characters long.

- Passwords must be a combination of three of the following four forms: uppercase letters, lowercase letters, numbers, and symbols.

- Six unique passwords must be used before a previous password can be reused.

- An account must be locked out until an administrator unlocks the account.

What action must you take to implement these account policies using Group Policy?

A. Define the account policies at the domain under computer configuration.

B. Define the account policies at the domain under user configuration.

C. Define the account policies at the Domain Controllers OU under computer configuration.

D. Define the account policies at the Domain Controllers OU under user configuration.

70-218.04.06.002

You recently implemented changes in Group Policy settings for computer configurations applied at the Engineering OU. You want to test the new settings at a computer located in the Engineering OU to verify that they are defined correctly. What process can be performed to speed up the application of the new Group Policy settings?

A. At the command prompt, type **repadmin /applypolicy machine_policy**.

B. From Administrative Tools, open the Local Computer Policy console. In the console, right-click Security Settings and then click Refresh.

C. At the command prompt, type **secedit /refreshpolicy machine_policy**.

D. You cannot speed up Group Policy application. Wait 90 minutes for the next application interval.

70-218.04.06.003

The corporate security team has defined default security configuration for the typical roles played by computers on the network. Configurations have been defined for desktops, laptops, file servers, domain controllers, and application servers. You have defined the following security templates:

- DESKTOPS.INF, which contains security settings for desktop computers

- LAPTOPS.INF, which contains security settings for laptop computers

- FILESERV.INF, which contains security settings for file servers

- DOMCONTROL.INF, which contains security settings for domain controllers

- APPSERV.INF, which contains security settings for application servers

Assuming that the following figure represents the OUs used by your organization, what must you do to apply the security templates consistently to all computers in each security role?

Examine the figure shown here.

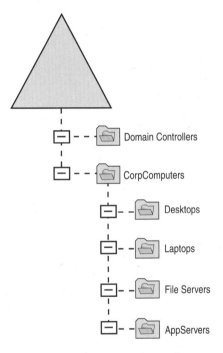

A. Place the computers for each category into the matching OU. At each computer, apply the security template using the Security Configuration and Analysis console.

B. Place the computers for each category into the matching OU. Create a GPO in each OU that runs a Computer Startup script that applies the matching security template.

C. Place the computers for each category into the matching OU. Create a GPO in each OU, and import the security template for that OU into the user configuration of the GPO.

D. Place the computers for each category into the matching OU. Create a GPO in each OU, and import the security template for that OU into the computer configuration of the GPO.

70-218.04.06.004

After a recent attack on your network, the general manager has requested that audit logs be maintained to track all access to network resources. Specifically, the following goals must be met by the auditing:

- All logon attempts to the domain must be audited.

- All logon attempts to the local SAM database of the Web server must be audited.

- All access to the files stored on the Corporate Web site must be audited. (During the attack, the Corporate Web site was altered by the attacker.)

- All account modification attempts in Active Directory must be audited. (During the attack, an existing user account was modified to make the user account a member of the Administrators group.)

- All modifications to audit settings must be logged at all computers in the domain. (The attacker attempted to prevent analysis of its attack by modifying audit settings.)

The OU structure used by your organization is shown in the following figure.

Examine the figure shown here.

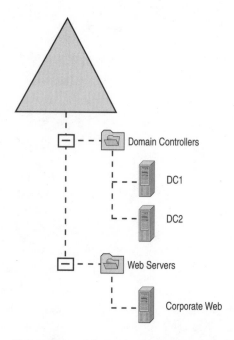

To meet the objectives, you complete the following tasks:

- At the Domain Controllers OU, you enable success and failure auditing for account logon events.

- At the Web Servers OU, you enable success and failure auditing for logon events.

- At the Web Servers OU, you enable success and failure auditing for object access.

- At the Domain Controllers OU, you enable success and failure auditing for directory service access.

- At the Domain Controllers OU and at the Web Servers OU, you enable success and failure auditing for policy change.

What goals are *not* met by your actions? (Choose all that apply.)

A. All logon attempts to the domain must be audited.

B. All logon attempts to the local SAM database of the Web server must be audited.

C. All access to the files stored on the Corporate Web site must be audited.

D. All account modification attempts in Active Directory must be audited.

E. All modifications to audit settings must be logged at all computers in the domain.

70-218.04.06.005

Your organization wants to increase the security settings for its domain controllers. Your organization uses a mix of Windows 98, Windows NT 4 Workstation, and Windows 2000 Professional client computers, and will continue to do so for the upcoming year.

You want to use Group Policy to ensure that the security template you use will be continually applied to the Windows 2000 domain controllers. What security template must you import into Group Policy to increase the base security settings and still allow communication with the Windows 98 and Windows NT 4 clients?

A. BASICDC.INF

B. COMPATWS.INF

C. SECUREDC.INF

D. HISECDC.INF

Objective 4.6 Answers

70-218.04.06.001

▶ **Correct Answers: A**

A. **Correct:** Account policies are defined at the domain for computers and are applied to all user accounts in the domain.

B. **Incorrect:** Account policies are defined under computer configuration, not user configuration, at the domain.

C. **Incorrect:** Account policies are defined at the domain, not at the Domain Controllers OU, in a Windows 2000 domain. Account policies are domain-wide settings that cannot be changed at a specific OU.

D. **Incorrect:** Account policies are defined at the domain, not at the Domain Controllers OU, in a Windows 2000 domain. In addition, account policies are a computer configuration setting, not a user configuration setting.

70-218.04.06.002

▶ **Correct Answers: C**

A. **Incorrect:** REPADMIN.EXE is used to force replication between domain controllers, and to check replication status. It cannot be used to trigger Group Policy application.

B. **Incorrect:** The Local Computer Policy console allows you to define local policy settings. You cannot trigger Group Policy application from this console.

C. **Correct:** The SECEDIT command allows you to trigger Group Policy application for both computer and user settings using the /refreshpolicy parameter.

D. **Incorrect:** The SECEDIT command allows you to refresh Group Policy settings. Alternatively, you can also restart the computer. At restart, the computer Group Policy settings are reapplied.

70-218.04.06.003

▶ **Correct Answers: D**

A. **Incorrect:** The Security Configuration and Analysis console does allow the application of a security template but does not ensure continued application of the security template. The security template must be imported into Group Policy.

B. **Incorrect:** You do not use Computer Startup scripts to apply predefined security templates. Instead, import the security template settings into the computer configuration component of the GPO.

C. **Incorrect:** Security templates contain computer configuration information, not user configuration information. The security templates must be imported into the computer configuration section of the GPO.

D. **Correct:** Security templates can be imported into the computer configuration section of a GPO to ensure consistent application of the security template settings.

70-218.04.06.004

▶ **Correct Answers: C and D**

A. **Incorrect:** The auditing of account logon events at the domain controllers OU ensures that all interactive and network logon events are audited. This meets the objective.

B. **Incorrect:** The auditing of logon events at the Web Servers OU ensures that all local logon events are audited for the Corporate Web server. This meets the objective.

C. **Correct:** Not all steps are completed by your actions. In addition to enabling success and failure auditing for object access, you must also enable auditing in the NT file system (NTFS) properties of the Web server's content folder. Auditing must be enabled for the Everyone group for all actions to meet the objectives. The current actions do not meet this objective.

D. **Correct:** Directory service access does not audit the account modification events—it audits all connection attempts to Active Directory. To meet the objective, success and failure auditing for account management must be enabled. The current actions do not meet the objective.

E. **Incorrect:** Enabling success and failure auditing of policy change at both the Domain Controllers OU and at the Web Servers OU meets the objective.

70-218.04.06.005

▶ **Correct Answers: A**

A. **Correct:** The BASICDC.INF security template ensures that default Windows 2000 security is applied to the domain controllers, but it does not implement security technologies that are not compatible with Windows 98 and Windows NT 4 Professional clients.

B. **Incorrect:** The COMPATWS.INF security template reduces security on a Windows 2000–based computer to allow non–Windows 2000 compliant software to run, and it results in reduced security for the Windows 2000 domain controllers.

C. **Incorrect:** The SECUREDC.INF security template is an incremental security template that implements security technologies that are not compatible with Windows 98 and Windows NT 4 computers, and it should not be deployed until these computers are upgraded to Windows 2000 Professional or replaced with Windows 2000 Professional computers.

D. **Incorrect:** The HISECDC.INF security template is an incremental security template that enforces security technologies that are not compatible with Windows 98 and Windows NT 4 computers and should not be deployed until these computers are upgraded to Windows 2000 Professional or replaced with Windows 2000 Professional computers.

Configuring, Securing, and Troubleshooting Remote Access

The Microsoft Windows 2000 platform greatly extended Routing and Remote Access from earlier Microsoft platforms. Most companies will benefit from having IT personnel who are capable of configuring and troubleshooting remote access and **virtual private network (VPN)** connections. Because the Routing and Remote Access service is disabled by default, you need to enable it in the Routing and Remote Access management console by right-clicking your server in the console tree and then clicking Configure And Enable Routing And Remote Access. This invokes the Routing and Remote Access Server Setup Wizard and presents you with these preconfigured server options, each of which requires specific hardware configurations to support the type of server being configured:

- An Internet Connection Server enables clients on the internal network to access the Internet without exposing internal Internet Protocol (IP) addresses using either **Internet Connection Sharing (ICS)** or a Windows 2000 network router with the **Network Address Translation (NAT)** routing protocol.

- A **Remote Access Service (RAS)** server provides direct dial-in access to the internal network for external clients.

- A VPN server provides indirect access to the internal network for external clients through the Internet.

- A network router enables clients on the internal network to access external networks, passing IP packets unaltered from clients on the internal network to external networks, including the Internet.

Providing users with access to the Internet has become more important than ever. Microsoft Windows 2000 Server provides several options for this purpose. It is important to understand the concepts behind these technologies in order to configure and troubleshoot both the servers and clients.

You can enable remote administration of any Windows 2000 Server by installing **Terminal Services** in remote administration mode. This provides a desktop environment for the administration of the Windows 2000 Server from a remote client computer.

Tested Skills and Suggested Practices

The skills that you need to master the Configuring, Securing, and Troubleshooting Remote Access objective domain on the *Managing a Microsoft Windows 2000 Network Environment* exam include:

- **Configuring and troubleshooting remote access and virtual private network (VPN) connections.**

  - Practice 1: Install an advanced Remote Access server using the Routing and Remote Access Server Setup Wizard. Specify a range of IP addresses to be used by the RAS server to assign to clients. Configure the server to allow inbound connections and configure VPN ports.

  - Practice 2: Configure outbound VPN connections by using the Network Connection Wizard.

  - Practice 3: Configure demand-dial and persistent VPN connections for branch offices in the Routing and Remote Access console.

- **Troubleshooting a remote access policy.**

  - Practice 1: Install Internet Authentication Service (IAS) and create a remote access policy using IAS administration. Register IAS in the Active Directory service, and specify all RAS servers as Remote Authentication Dial-in Internet User Service (RADIUS) clients.

  - Practice 2: Edit the default remote access policy to allow all clients access to the RAS server by changing the Deny Remote Access setting to Grant Remote Access.

  - Practice 3: Create a remote access policy using the Routing and Remote Access management console. Configure a Remote Access Profile for the remote access policy and apply a policy filter so RAS dial-in clients are disconnected after a period of idle time, and RAS clients are allowed to use only VPN connections.

- Practice 4: Configure the Windows-Groups attribute for the conditions of a RAS policy so the policy affects only members of a certain group. Change the order in which policies are processed.

- **Implementing and troubleshooting Terminal Services for remote access.**

  - Practice 1: Install Terminal Services in remote administration mode. Install the Terminal Services Client on a separate computer, and create a Terminal Services session.

  - Practice 2: Use Terminal Services Configuration to create and configure a connection. Use Terminal Services Manager to take remote control of a client session using the connection.

  - Practice 3: Make changes to a domain controller's BOOT.INI file so you are able to remotely start a domain controller running Terminal Services (in remote administration mode) in directory services repair mode.

  - Practice 4: Explore the default client settings for a terminal server connection. Change the default so settings are determined by the user account, not the connection client settings.

- **Configuring and troubleshooting Network Address Translation (NAT) and Internet Connection Sharing (ICS).**

  - Practice 1: Configure NAT on a server using the Routing and Remote Access Server Setup Wizard. Within the Routing and Remote Access management console, edit the NAT properties and configure the Address Assignment and Name Resolution tabs.

  - Practice 2: Enable ICS by using the Sharing tab in the Properties dialog box of a dial-up, VPN, or incoming connection in My Network Places.

  - Practice 3: View the Properties dialog box of a network interface with ICS enabled. Configure ICS to allow external users from the Internet to connect to an internal Web server and allow external users to connect to a server on the intranet.

Further Reading

This section lists supplemental readings by objective. We recommend that you study these sources thoroughly before taking exam 70-218.

Objective 5.1

Microsoft Corporation. *MCSA Training Kit: Managing a Microsoft Windows 2000 Network Environment*. Redmond, Washington: Microsoft Press, 2002. Review Lessons 1, 2, and 5 in Chapter 18, "Remote Client Access."

Microsoft Corporation. *Windows 2000 Server Resource Kit*. Volume: *Internetworking Guide*. Redmond, Washington: Microsoft Press, 2000. Review Chapter 7, "Remote Access," and Chapter 9, "Virtual Private Networking."

Microsoft Corporation. "Windows 2000 Virtual Private Networking Scenario." (This white paper can be downloaded for free at *http://www.microsoft.com/WINDOWS2000/ techinfo/howitworks/communications/remoteaccess/w2kvpnscenario.asp*.)

Objective 5.2

Microsoft Corporation. *MCSA Training Kit: Managing a Microsoft Windows 2000 Network Environment*. Redmond, Washington: Microsoft Press, 2002. Review Lesson 3 in Chapter 18, "Remote Client Access."

Microsoft Corporation. *Windows 2000 Server Resource Kit*. Volume: *Internetworking Guide*. Redmond, Washington: Microsoft Press, 2000. Review Chapter 8, "Internet Authentication Services."

Microsoft Windows 2000 Server Online Help. This resource provides a rich array of information for configuring as well as troubleshooting remote access policies. Search help for "Remote Access Policies."

Objective 5.3

Microsoft Corporation. *MCSA Training Kit: Managing a Microsoft Windows 2000 Network Environment*. Redmond, Washington: Microsoft Press, 2002. Review Lesson 4 in Chapter 6, "Monitoring Server Health and Security."

Microsoft Corporation. *Windows 2000 Server Resource Kit*. Volume: *Deployment Planning Guide*. Redmond, Washington: Microsoft Press, 2000. Review Chapter 16, "Deploying Terminal Services."

Microsoft Windows 2000 Server Online Help. This resource provides a rich array of information for configuring, deploying, and troubleshooting Terminal Services. Search help for "Terminal Services."

Objective 5.4

Microsoft Corporation. *MCSA Training Kit: Managing a Microsoft Windows 2000 Network Environment*. Redmond, Washington: Microsoft Press, 2002. Review Lesson 4 in Chapter 18, "Remote Client Access."

Microsoft Corporation. *MCSE Training Kit: Microsoft Windows 2000 Network Infrastructure Administration*. Redmond, Washington: Microsoft Press, 2000. Review Chapter 12, "Supporting Network Address Translation (NAT)."

Microsoft Corporation. *Windows 2000 Server Resource Kit*. Volume: *Internetworking Guide*. Redmond, Washington: Microsoft Press, 2000. Review Chapter 3, "Unicast IP Routing."

Microsoft Corporation. *Windows 2000 Professional Resource Kit*. Redmond, Washington: Microsoft Press, 2000. Review Chapter 21, "Local and Remote Network Connections."

Microsoft Windows 2000 Server Online Help. This is a good resource for information about deployment, configuration, and troubleshooting of NAT. Search help for "Network Address Translation."

OBJECTIVE 5.1

Configure and troubleshoot remote access and virtual private network (VPN) connections.

This objective deals with the concepts, configuration, and troubleshooting tools available for remote access and **virtual private networks (VPNs)**. The configuration of remote access and VPNs should be planned before implementation. Determine your communications and security requirements, and map these to Windows 2000 Routing and Remote Access features. Identify whether you will allow clients to dial in directly to RAS servers, or if you will require them to use the Internet to connect to VPN servers.

A **Remote Access Service (RAS)** server is configured to support clients that are dialing in directly to that server. The RAS server must be equipped with a modem or other device that supports dial-in connections. The configuration on the RAS server determines whether the dialed-in clients will have access to the entire network, thereby acting as a gateway, or whether the client will have access to only the RAS server itself. You configure how each dialed-in client is assigned an IP address during the setup of the RAS server. There are two ways in which a client can receive an IP address—either using **Dynamic Host Configuration Protocol (DHCP)** services configured on the RAS server, or by defining a range of IP addresses that the RAS server assigns to dial-in clients. You grant users permission to dial in on the Dial-In tab of their user account.

A VPN server also provides users with external access to a private network. The VPN server, unlike the RAS server, requires a connection to the Internet. Using tunneling protocols, such as **Layer 2 Tunneling Protocol (L2TP)** and **Point-to-Point Tunneling Protocol (PPTP)**, the client and server communicate over the Internet using encryption technologies that provide privacy for transmissions.

There are many areas in the configuration of the RAS server and the VPN server in which problems might arise. In addition, there can be client connection issues. An understanding of the mechanisms involved and how they relate and interoperate is essential when troubleshooting RAS and VPN. Also, you need to be familiar with the tools that are available for troubleshooting and how to use them. Windows 2000 Online Help is an excellent resource for troubleshooting RAS and VPN.

Objective 5.1 Questions

70-218.05.01.001

You are setting up a VPN server for your company to allow users to connect to the local area network (LAN) from the Internet. You run the Routing and Remote Access Server Setup Wizard on a multihomed Windows 2000 Server with an external (Internet) network interface card (NIC) and an internal (intranet) NIC. You select the Virtual Private Network Server option from the Common Configurations page and accept the default settings. Now, you can no longer ping the IP address of the external NIC from the internal network. All other Internet communications are working properly. Which of the following solutions resolves this?

A. In the Routing and Remote Access management console, expand IP Routing and then expand General, right-click your external interface, select Properties, and use the Input and Output buttons to configure Internet Control Message Protocol (ICMP) filters.

B. Configure the default gateway on the client from which you are pinging with the internal IP address of the VPN server.

C. In the Routing and Remote Access management console, expand IP Routing and then expand General, right-click your internal interface, select Properties, and use the Input and Output buttons to configure ICMP filters.

D. Configure the default gateway on the router between the client and the VPN server with the internal IP address of the VPN server.

70-218.05.01.002

Your company operates a manufacturing business with a main corporate campus in Miami and branch offices and distribution partners throughout the United States. You are setting up the VPN server for the Miami campus.

You want to accomplish the following goals:

- Avoid forwarding potentially unwanted Internet traffic to the intranet.

- Use a tunneling protocol that supports only mutual computer authentication.

- Provide simultaneous VPN remote access for 200 employees.

- Use a static address pool from which to assign IP addresses to clients.

You use the Routing and Remote Access Server Setup Wizard to configure settings for your VPN server. You choose to manually configure your server. In the Routing and Remote Access management console, you right-click Ports and select Properties. You set the maximum WAN Miniport (L2TP) ports to 200 and the maximum WAN Miniport (PPTP) to 1. To disable the one PPTP port, you clear the two check boxes on the Configure Device – WAN Miniport (PPTP) configuration page.

Which results does your installation achieve? (Choose all that apply.)

A. You avoided forwarding potentially unwanted Internet traffic from the Internet to the intranet.

B. You used a tunneling protocol that supports only mutual computer authentication.

C. You provided simultaneous VPN remote access for 200 employees.

D. You used a static address pool from which to assign IP addresses to clients.

E. The installation does not meet any of the required results.

70-218.05.01.003

Your Microsoft Windows 2000 Professional clients connecting to the internal network using VPN connections complain they are unable to reach network locations beyond the VPN server after they log on. How should you troubleshoot this issue? (Choose all that apply.)

A. Verify that the VPN server is enabled for remote access.

B. Using the PING command, verify that the host name or IP address of the VPN server is reachable.

C. Verify that the LAN protocols used by remote access VPN clients are enabled to allow access to the network to which the VPN server is attached.

D. Verify the IP address pools of the VPN server.

E. Verify that packet filtering on a router interface between the VPN client and the VPN server is not preventing the forwarding of tunneling protocol traffic.

70-218.05.01.004

How does a RAS server obtain and assign IP addresses when it has been configured to use DHCP to obtain client addresses? (Choose all that apply.)

A. The DHCP client component on the RAS server obtains 10 IP addresses from its configured DHCP server.

B. The RAS server uses the last IP address obtained for the RAS interface.

C. The DHCP server component on the RAS server obtains 30 IP addresses from its configured DHCP server.

D. The RAS server uses the first IP address obtained for the RAS interface.

E. A RAS server can be configured only with a static IP address and a static address pool.

70-218.05.01.005

Your company operates a manufacturing business with a main corporate campus in Miami and branch offices and distribution partners throughout the United States. You want to connect the Atlanta and Chicago branch offices to the corporate office by using on-demand router-to-router VPN connections. Both offices have a small number of employees who need only occasional connectivity with the corporate office. You are setting up the RAS server in the Chicago branch office.

Examine the figure shown here.

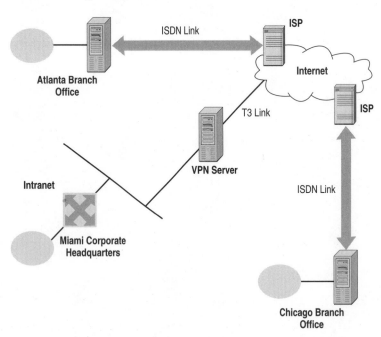

You want to accomplish the following goals:

- Set up a one-way initiated connection that is always initiated by the branch office router to the Internet and to the corporate VPN server.

- Configure the VPN server at the corporate office to drop the connection if it is not used for 10 minutes.

- Ensure that only PPTP-based traffic is allowed on the connection to the Internet.

- Configure the RAS server so only the MS-CHAP v2 authentication protocol is used.

On the Chicago server, you use the Routing and Remote Access Server Setup Wizard to configure your RAS server manually. After the wizard finishes and the Routing and Remote Access service is started, you use the Demand-Dial Interface Wizard to create and configure a demand-dial interface for the connection to the Internet service provider (ISP) using the Connect Using a Modem, ISDN Adapter, Or Other

Physical Device connection type. You do not check the Add User Account So A Remote Router Can Dial In box on the Protocols And Security page. You configure the appropriate credentials for authenticating to the ISP. On the Networking tab on the Properties dialog box of the ISP demand-dial interface, you configure the Type Of VPN Server I Am Calling as PPTP. You use the Demand-Dial Interface Wizard to create and configure a demand-dial interface for the Router-to-Router VPN connection using the Connect Using Virtual Private Networking connection type. You do not check the Add User Account So A Remote Router Can Dial In box on the Protocols And Security page. You configure the appropriate credentials for authenticating to the corporate VPN server.

Which results does your solution achieve? (Choose all that apply.)

A. You set up a one-way initiated connection that is always initiated by the branch office router to the Internet and to the corporate VPN server.

B. You configured the demand-dial interfaces to drop the connection if it is not used for 10 minutes.

C. You ensured that only PPTP-based traffic is allowed on the connection to the Internet.

D. You configured the RAS server so only the MS-CHAP v2 authentication protocol is used.

E. Your solution does not achieve any of the required results.

70-218.05.01.006

By default, Windows 2000 remote access VPN clients have the Automatic Server Type option selected. In which order do they try to establish a VPN connection?

A. First a PPTP-based VPN connection, and then an L2TP over IPSec connection

B. First a Point-to-Point Protocol (PPP)–based VPN connection, and then a PPTP-based connection

C. First a Microsoft Challenge Handshake Authentication Protocol (MS-CHAP) connection, and then a Password Authentication Protocol (PAP) connection

D. First an L2TP over IPSec–based VPN connection, and then a PPTP-based VPN connection

70-218.05.01.007

All your remote access clients are Windows 2000 Professional computers. You suspect there might be a breach of security, and someone is capturing authentication credentials on the wire. Which authentication protocol should you ensure is disabled on your RAS server to make it more secure?

A. MS-CHAP

B. SPAP

C. CHAP

D. PAP

Objective 5.1 Answers

70-218.05.01.001

▶ **Correct Answers: A**

A. **Correct:** Because of the default PPTP and L2TP over Internet Protocol Security (IPSec) packet filtering that is configured on the Internet interface of the answering router (the external interface), ICMP packets used by the PING command are filtered out. To enable ping capability on the answering router, you need to add an input filter and an output filter that allow traffic for IP protocol 1 (ICMP traffic).

B. **Incorrect:** Because all other Internet communication is working, it is not a default gateway issue.

C. **Incorrect:** The ICMP filters on a VPN server configured with the default settings are applied to the external interface only, so there is no need to configure filters on the internal interface.

D. **Incorrect:** Because all other Internet communication is working, it is not a default gateway issue.

70-218.05.01.002

▶ **Correct Answers: B and C**

A. **Incorrect:** You need to configure PPTP and L2TP over IPSec packet filters on the Internet interface of the VPN server to prevent potentially unwanted Internet traffic to the intranet.

B. **Correct:** By implementing L2TP, you accomplished this goal. PPTP does not support mutual computer authentication. Only L2TP supports this feature. By setting the Maximum PPTP ports to one (zero is not allowed) and clearing the check boxes to allow Remote Access connections and Demand-Dial Routing connections, you virtually disable PPTP.

C. **Correct:** When you are manually configuring the Routing and Remote Access server, the default number of L2TP ports is 5. By setting the maximum to 200, you provided simultaneous access for 200 employees.

D. **Incorrect:** The default setting for IP address assignment is to use DHCP. This can be configured inside the Routing and Remote Access management console by right-clicking the computer icon in the console tree pane and selecting Properties. In the Properties dialog box, select the IP tab. If you want to configure a static pool of IP addresses, you select the static address pool and configure the range of IP addresses you want to use for your connections.

E. **Incorrect:** With this installation, you used a tunneling protocol that supports only mutual computer authentication and provided simultaneous VPN remote access for 200 employees.

70-218.05.01.003

▶ **Correct Answers: C and D**

A. **Incorrect:** Because the clients are able to connect to the VPN server, the server is already enabled for remote access, so this is not a practical verification.

B. **Incorrect:** Because the clients are able to connect to the VPN server, this is not a useful verification because the PING command verifies connectivity only. This might work if the symptom is that a connection attempt is rejected when it should be accepted.

C. **Correct:** For remote access VPNs, verify that either IP is enabled for routing, or the Entire Network option is selected for other LAN protocols (NWLink and NetBEUI) in the Routing and Remote Access server Properties for the LAN protocols being used by the VPN clients.

D. **Correct:** If the VPN server is configured to use a static IP address pool, verify that the routes to the range of addresses defined by the static IP address pools are reachable by the hosts and routers of the intranet. If not, an IP route consisting of the VPN server static IP address pools, as defined by the IP address and mask of the range, must be added to the routers of the intranet or you must enable the routing protocol of your routed infrastructure on the VPN server. If the routes to the remote access VPN client subnets are not present, remote access VPN clients cannot receive traffic from locations on the intranet. Routes for the subnets are implemented either through static routing entries or through a routing protocol, such as Open Shortest Path First (OSPF) or Routing Information Protocol (RIP).

If the VPN server is configured to use DHCP for IP address allocation and no DHCP server is available, the VPN server assigns addresses from the Automatic Private IP Addressing (APIPA) address range from 169.254.0.1 through 169.254.255.254. Allocating APIPA addresses for remote access clients works only if the network to which the VPN server is attached is also using APIPA addresses.

E. **Incorrect:** Because clients are connecting to the VPN server, they are able to establish a tunnel so this is not the case. This is a practical test only if the client is unable to establish a tunnel with the VPN server. IP packet filtering can be configured from the Advanced TCP/IP Settings and from the Routing and Remote Access snap-in. Check both places for filters that might be excluding VPN connection traffic.

70-218.05.01.004

▶ **Correct Answers: A and D**

   A. **Correct:** When the RAS server is configured to use DHCP to obtain IP addresses, the Routing and Remote Access service instructs the DHCP client component to obtain 10 IP addresses from a DHCP server.

   B. **Incorrect:** This answer is incorrect for the reasons stated in answer D.

   C. **Incorrect:** This answer is incorrect for the reasons stated in answer A.

   D. **Correct:** The RAS server uses the first IP address obtained from DHCP for the RAS interface and uses the subsequent addresses to assign to TCP/IP-based remote access clients.

   E. **Incorrect:** A RAS server can be configured to use either DHCP or a static IP address pool to obtain IP addresses.

70-218.05.01.005

▶ **Correct Answers: A and C**

   A. **Correct:** By using the Demand-Dial Interface Wizard to create both a connection to the ISP and to the corporate VPN server using the appropriate credentials, and not configuring dial-in properties, you accomplished the first goal.

   B. **Incorrect:** Because you did not change the default, the demand-dial interface drops the connection if it is not used for five minutes. This is configured on the Options tab of the created demand-dial interface.

   C. **Correct:** By setting the type of VPN server to PPTP on the Networking tab on the ISP demand-dial interface Properties dialog box, you accomplished this goal.

   D. **Incorrect:** By default, the authentication methods allowed are MS-CHAP and MS-CHAPv2. This is configured from the Routing and Remote Access management console by clicking Authentication Methods on the Security tab of the RAS server Properties dialog box.

   E. **Incorrect:** This answer is incorrect for the reasons stated in answers A and C.

70-218.05.01.006

▶ **Correct Answers: D**

A. **Incorrect:** This answer is incorrect for the reasons stated in answer D.

B. **Incorrect:** PPP is the Internet standard for transmission of IP packets over serial lines, not a tunneling protocol used by VPNs.

C. **Incorrect:** MS-CHAP and PAP are authentication protocols, not tunneling protocols used by VPNs.

D. **Correct:** By default, Windows 2000 remote access VPN clients have the Automatic Server Type option selected, which means they try to establish an L2TP over IPSec–based VPN connection first, and then a PPTP-based VPN connection. If either the PPTP or L2TP Server Type option is selected, verify that the selected tunneling protocol is supported by the VPN server as well.

70-218.05.01.007

▶ **Correct Answers: D**

A. **Incorrect:** With MS-CHAP, the RAS server requires only the MD4 hash of the password to validate the challenge response. The actual password is neither stored on the RAS server nor sent across the wire in plain text to the RAS server.

B. **Incorrect:** The Shiva Password Authentication Protocol (SPAP) is a reversible encryption mechanism employed by Shiva remote access servers. Only the encrypted password is sent across the wire to the RAS server.

C. **Incorrect:** With Challenge Handshake Authentication Protocol (CHAP), the encrypted password is sent across the wire to the RAS server using a one-way encryption scheme to hash the response to a challenge issued by the RAS server.

D. **Correct:** PAP is a simple, plain text authentication scheme. The user name and password are requested by the RAS server and returned by the remote access client in plain text. A person capturing the PAP packets between the RAS server and remote access client can easily determine the remote access client's password.

O B J E C T I V E 5 . 2

Troubleshoot a remote access policy.

Through **remote access policies**, it is possible to achieve a very granular level of control over who can access, how they can access, and when they can access a RAS or VPN server. Understanding how policies are applied will allow you to provide customized access to the various users and groups in your organization.

To apply and use remote access policies effectively and efficiently, you must have a clear understanding of how they operate. First, remote access policies are not stored in Active Directory but only on the RAS server to which the policy will apply. This is so policies can vary according to RAS server capabilities. A remote access policy consists of three components that work with Active Directory to provide secure access to RAS servers. These components are:

- Conditions—A list of parameters that are matched to the parameters of the client connecting to the server.

- Permissions—The three dial-in permissions are Deny Access, Allow Access, and Control Access Through Remote Access Policy (which is available only in native mode operation).

- Profiles—Authentication and encryption protocol settings that are applied to the connection.

These three components together determine whether a RAS server accepts or rejects a connection attempt.

To answer the questions in this objective, you should understand the policy evaluation logic and the order in which policies (if there are multiple policies) apply. You should also understand the default remote access policy, which denies access to all users, and you should understand the behavior of policies in **mixed mode** and **native mode**. In mixed mode, the Control Access Through Remote Access Policy permission does not exist. It is available only on servers operating in native mode. In mixed mode, a user who has a dial-in permission set to Allow Access still needs to meet the conditions of the remote access policy on the RAS server. When you are converting from mixed to native mode, the permissions for all users with a dial-in setting of Deny Access are changed to Control Access Through Remote Access Policy. Permissions for all users with a dial-in setting of Allow Access remain set to Allow Access. If the default remote access policy remains unaltered and no other policies exist, the conversion to native mode has no effect on users' remote access permissions.

If there are multiple policies, the first policy to meet the conditions of a connection attempt is processed and no further policies are evaluated. Also, it is important to understand the effect policy order has on the connection attempt. For example, if a user has membership in two groups, and one group has been denied access while the other is granted access, the connection is accepted or rejected depending on the order of the policies. If the policy that accepts access is before the policy that denies access, the connection attempt is accepted.

Objective 5.2 Questions

70-218.05.02.001

You have one Windows 2000 RAS server on your network. You have three user groups—GroupA, GroupB, and GroupC. You create three policies—PolA, PolB, and PolC—and have them apply to a user based on group membership using the Routing and Remote Access console. You ensure the default remote access policy is the last policy to be evaluated.

You want to accomplish the following goals:

- Group A, using PolA, must dial in to a specific phone number.

- Group B, using PolB, must use only Integrated Services Digital Network (ISDN) connections to dial in.

- Group C, Using PolC, must authenticate using a smart card.

- A fourth policy must run last, denying access to any user who has not met conditions of any of the three policies.

You take the following steps:

1. In the Routing and Remote Access console, you open the Properties dialog box of remote access policy PolA. On the Settings tab, you click Edit Profile. In the Dial-In Constraints, select the Restrict Dial-In To This Number Only check box, and type a phone number.

2. In the Routing and Remote Access console, you open the Properties dialog box of remote access policy PolB. You add the Framed-Protocol attribute and select PPP as a condition.

Which result or results does your solution achieve? (Choose all that apply.)

A. Group A, using PolA, is restricted to dial in to a specific phone number.

B. Group B, using PolB, is allowed to connect using only an ISDN connection.

C. Group C, using PolC, is configured only to allow users to authenticate using a smart card.

D. You use a fourth policy denying access to any user who has not met conditions of any of the three policies.

E. Your solution does not achieve any of the required results.

70-218.05.02.002

You have set up a Windows 2000 RAS member server in a Windows 2000 native mode domain, and you have decided on the administration by policy in a Windows 2000 native mode domain model—all users have their dial-in permissions set to Control Access Through Remote Access Policy. You have enabled and configured Routing and Remote Access, but no clients are able to connect. What is a possible step you can take to allow all clients to connect?

A. Assign the group Everyone the Allow permission to the RAS connection.

B. Change the default RAS policy to Grant Remote Access Permission.

C. Remove the group Everyone from the access control list (ACL) of the connection.

D. Leave the default policy as is and below the default policy create a new remote access policy immediately that grants dial-in permission.

70-218.05.02.003

You have five RAS servers on your network. You want to create policies once and have them apply to all five servers. How can you accomplish this?

A. Create a remote access policy on one server, and then use the file replication service to copy it to the remaining servers.

B. Create an organizational unit (OU) in Active Directory, and place all five RAS servers in the new OU. Configure and apply a group policy on the OU containing the RAS servers.

C. Install and configure IAS on a server that will be used to create and centralize policies for the RAS servers. Configure each RAS server as a RADIUS client of the IAS server.

D. Install and configure Internet Information Services (IIS) on a server that will be used to create and centralize policies for the RAS servers. Configure each RAS server to receive remote access policy from the configured server in the Routing and Remote Access console.

70-218.05.02.004

Which default location stores authentication requests, including access-accept and access-reject events, received by the Routing and Remote Access server?

A. %SYSTEMROOT%\LOGFILES

B. %SYSTEMROOT%\SYSTEM32\LOGFILES

C. %SYSTEMROOT%\LASLOG

D. %SYSTEMROOT%\SYSTEM32\LASLOG

70-218.05.02.005

You want to use the administration by policy in your Windows 2000 mixed mode single domain. You enable Routing and Remote Access and use the wizard to configure a RAS server with all the defaults. You want to prevent dial-in access for all vendors and allow all regular employees of your company no restrictions on dialing in. You create a Windows 2000 group named Vendors and make all vendor user accounts members of this group. You use the built-in Windows group Domain Users for all employees. You create two policies as follows and you make no further changes:

Policy 1

- Policy Name: Reject Vendor Connections

- Windows Groups: Vendors

- Permissions: Deny Remote Access

- Order: First policy to be evaluated

Policy 2

- Policy Name: Allow Access If Dial-In Permission Is Enabled

- Windows Groups: Domain Users

- Permissions: Allow remote access

- Order: Second policy to be evaluated

The default policy is left in third place. All employees are complaining they cannot dial in. What is the cause of this?

A. The profile settings of Policy 2 are preventing users from dialing in.

B. The default dial-in permissions on user accounts are preventing users from dialing in.

C. The default remote access policy called Allow Access If Dial-In Is Enabled is preventing users from dialing in.

D. The conditions of Policy 1 are preventing domain users from dialing in.

70-218.05.02.006

You are the administrator of a Windows 2000 network and need to configure a Routing and Remote Access server and remote access policies.

You have three groups of users with the following requirements:

- Any user who is a member of both GroupB and GroupC should be allowed to connect between 8 A.M. and 8 P.M. Monday through Friday.

- Any user who is a member of both GroupA and GroupB should connect using only a VPN connection.

- GroupA should be restricted to dialing in using only VPN connections.

- GroupB should be allowed to connect between 8 A.M. and 8 P.M. Monday through Friday.

- GroupC should not be allowed access at any time.

You create PolicyA with a condition set to VPN connections for the NAS-Port-Type attribute. You add GroupA to the Windows-Groups attribute as a condition, and select the Grant Remote Access Permission. You create PolicyB and configure a condition set to 8 A.M. to 8 P.M. Monday through Friday. For the Day-and-Time-Restrictions attribute, you add GroupB to the Windows-Groups attribute as a condition and select the Grant Remote Access Permission. You create PolicyC with default settings, add GroupC to the Windows-Groups attribute as a condition, and select the Deny Remote Access Permission. You place the policies so PolicyC is evaluated first, PolicyB second, and PolicyA third.

Which result or results does your solution achieve? (Choose all that apply.)

A. Any user who is a member of both GroupB and GroupC is allowed access from 8 A.M. to 8 P.M. Monday through Friday.

B. Any user who is a member of both GroupA and GroupB must use a VPN connection.

C. GroupA is restricted to dialing in using only VPN connections.

D. GroupB is not allowed to connect between 8 A.M. and 8 P.M. Monday through Friday.

E. GroupC is not allowed access at any time.

70-218.05.02.007

You installed a Windows 2000 member server into a native mode domain. You configure this server as a RAS server. Dial-in permissions for all user accounts are set to Control Access Through Remote Access Policy. You want to allow all users non-restricted dial-in access to the RAS server, any time on any day, in the most administratively efficient manner. How can you achieve this goal?

A. Create a remote access policy and configure it to Grant Remote Access Permission if the conditions are met.

B. Create a group and add all users to the group. Create a remote access policy that is configured with the condition attribute Windows-Groups and add the group created. Select the Grant Remote Access Permission for the policy.

C. Apply a Group policy to the container in which the Domain Users group resides.

D. Change the Deny Remote Access Permission in the default remote access policy to Grant Remote Access Permission.

Objective 5.2 Answers

70-218.05.02.001

▶ **Correct Answers: A and D**

A. **Correct:** Configuring a specific number is part of the connection profile, and the steps are correct.

B. **Incorrect:** Adding the Framed-Protocol and selecting PPP as a condition was not the goal for PolB. To meet the goal for PolB, the profile of the connection must be configured to accept ISDN connections only.

C. **Incorrect:** The default setting for the Extensible Authentication Protocol (EAP) is Smart Card or Certificate. You must also edit the profile using the Authentication tab to select EAP.

D. **Correct:** Because the default remote access policy denies access to all users and you have ensured that it is in the last position, this goal was met.

E. **Incorrect:** The solution satisfies two of the four goals.

70-218.05.02.002

▶ **Correct Answers: B**

A. **Incorrect:** Permissions cannot be assigned to a RAS connection.

B. **Correct:** If you use the native mode administration model and do not add any remote access policies and do not change the default remote access policy (named Allow Access If Dial-In Permission Is Enabled), no users are allowed remote access. By default, the remote access permission on the default remote access policy is set to Deny Remote Access Permission. If you change the setting to Grant Remote Access Permission, all users are allowed remote access.

C. **Incorrect:** Groups cannot be added to a specific connection.

D. **Incorrect:** The default policy is set to deny access to a user if the user meets the policy conditions. Because the default policy is first to be processed and all users meet the conditions of the default policy, the connection is rejected and no other policy is checked. If a user does not meet the conditions of a policy, the next policy is checked in order (from top to bottom).

70-218.05.02.003

▶ **Correct Answers: C**

A. **Incorrect:** This cannot be done.

B. **Incorrect:** Group Policy in Active Directory cannot be used to apply remote access policies.

C. **Correct:** IAS can be used to create and implement policies on all RAS servers that are configured as RADIUS clients to the IAS server.

D. **Incorrect:** IIS cannot be used for this purpose.

70-218.05.02.004

▶ **Correct Answers: B**

A. **Incorrect:** This answer is incorrect for the reasons stated in answer B.

B. **Correct:** This is the default location for storing authentication requests, including access-accept and access-reject events, received by the Routing and Remote Access server.

C. **Incorrect:** This answer is incorrect for the reasons stated in answer B.

D. **Incorrect:** This answer is incorrect for the reasons stated in answer B.

70-218.05.02.005

▶ **Correct Answers: B**

A. **Incorrect:** There have been no changes to the profile of Policy 2. Because, by default, there are no restrictions set in the profile of a policy, this is not preventing the users from dialing in.

B. **Correct:** The default dial-in permission setting for all user accounts in a mixed mode domain is set to Deny Access. To use the administration by policy in a Windows 2000 mixed mode domain, you must change the default dial-in permission on accounts to Allow Access. In this case, users cannot gain access because the default has not been changed to Allow Access.

C. **Incorrect:** The conditions of a policy are the first component evaluated when a client dials in. In this case, conditions of Policy 1 are checked first. Because no conditions match, the conditions of Policy 2 are evaluated next. The Domain Users group has been granted access, and no further policies are checked. The next component evaluated is the user account dial-in permissions. If the dial-in permission is set to Deny Access, the connection attempt is rejected. Because the default dial-in permission for each user account was not changed to Allow Access, the connection attempt is rejected.

D. **Incorrect:** The conditions of Policy 1 are not applied to the Domain Users group—only to the Vendors group.

70-218.05.02.006

▶ **Correct Answers: C and E**

A. **Incorrect:** Because PolicyC is evaluated first and the Windows-Groups condition is met, no further policies are evaluated and the user (belonging to GroupC) connection is rejected.

B. **Incorrect:** Because PolicyB is evaluated before PolicyA, the Windows-Groups condition is met with PolicyB and no further policies are evaluated. PolicyB allows any kind of connection between 8 A.M. and 8 P.M. Monday through Friday.

C. **Correct:** Because the NAS-Port-Type attribute was defined as VPN for the condition in PolicyA and GroupA was added to the Windows-Groups attribute as a condition, GroupA is able to connect using only VPN connections.

D. **Incorrect:** Because the Day-and-Time-Restrictions type attribute has been defined as a condition in PolicyB and GroupB was added to the Windows-Groups attribute as a condition, GroupB is able to connect between 8 A.M. and 8 P.M. Monday through Friday.

E. **Correct:** Because you added GroupC to the Windows-Groups attribute as a condition for PolicyC and selected Deny Access, none of the members of GroupC are able to connect.

70-218.05.02.007

▶ **Correct Answers: D**

A. **Incorrect:** Creating a Remote Access policy and then configuring it with the Grant Remote Access Permission does not meet the goal because it involves significant administrative overhead.

B. **Incorrect:** Creating a group and a Remote Access policy and then configuring it with the Grant Remote Access Permission does not meet the goal because it involves significant administrative overhead.

C. **Incorrect:** Group policy cannot be used to control remote access in this fashion.

D. **Correct:** This is the fastest and therefore the most administratively efficient way to provide remote access for all users.

OBJECTIVE 5.3

Implement and troubleshoot Terminal Services for remote access.

There are clearly many advantages to having remote administration capability for Windows 2000 servers. **Terminal Services**, when installed in remote administration mode, is designed to have very low consumption of resources. This very small performance impact and low bandwidth usage provides an ideal platform for conducting remote server administration. This administration can be done from any system on which a Terminal Services client was installed. Because of the low bandwidth consumption, remote administration can be done using a modem and a dial-up connection.

To answer the questions in this objective, you should understand the difference between installing Terminal Services in **remote administration mode** and **application mode**. In application mode, there are significantly more server resources consumed because the server is running applications in a multi-user environment. Each user that runs an application on the server is allocated a specific amount of memory and CPU resources to support the user session.

You also need to understand when and how to use the Terminal Services management tools: Terminal Services Manager and Terminal Services Configuration. An understanding of the Terminal Services Client and how a connection is established is required, as well as how to control applied client connection settings. There are two methods of controlling client settings—in the user's Active Directory user account on the Sessions and Environment tabs, and through the connection properties within the Terminal Services Configuration console. If you choose to control configuration through Terminal Services Configuration, the user's Account settings are ignored. The default is to use the user's account settings, in which case the connection settings are ignored.

Objective 5.3 Questions

70-218.05.03.001

You are the administrator of a Windows 2000 network and need to configure Terminal Services using a dial-up connection to accomplish the following goals:

- You want to perform remote administration on member server ABC on your corporate network from home.

- You want to perform remote administration on member server ABC on your corporate network from several other clients within your corporate network.

- You want Terminal Services to end your session when you connect from home if the session is idle for more than five minutes.

- You want Terminal Services to end your session when you connect from within your corporate network if the session is idle for more than one hour.

You set up Terminal Services in remote administration mode on member server ABC on your corporate Windows 2000 domain network. You set up a dial-in connection to your corporate Routing and Remote Access router from which you can access the entire network. You install the terminal service client for both your computer at home and the designated clients on your corporate network and use the Terminal Services Client Connection Manager to create a connection with the IP address of the ABC server.

Which result or results does your configuration achieve? (Choose all that apply.)

A. You can perform remote administration on member server ABC on your corporate network from home.

B. You can perform remote administration on member server ABC on your corporate network from several other clients within your corporate network.

C. Terminal Services will end your session when you connect from home if a session is idle for more than five minutes.

D. Terminal Services will end your session when you connect from within your corporate network if it is idle for one hour.

70-218.05.03.002

You have several users in a remote office who need to access and run the AccountingApp application on the terminal server at the corporate office. They will use a modem to dial up a Routing and Remote Access server located at the corporate office to connect to the corporate network. All computers, clients as well as the server, are members of the same domain.

You need to accomplish the following goals:

- The Accounting group should be able to run the AccountingApp application remotely using its Terminal Services client.

- You want to end a disconnected session after 15 minutes of idle time.

- You do not want to allow more than five users to connect to the terminal server at a time.

- You want to configure the same user account to automatically log users on to the terminal server.

- You want to specify the AccountingApp program to start after the automatic logon event.

You ensure that all user accounts that are members of the Accounting group have the Allow Logon To Terminal Server check box selected on the Terminal Services Profile tab of their individual user accounts. You use Terminal Services Configuration to edit the properties of the default RDP-TCP connection. You choose Properties from the shortcut menu. On the Permissions tab, you add the Accounting group and assign the Guest Access permission. On the Network Adapter tab, you click OK to accept the default for maximum connections. On the Sessions tab, you select the Override User Settings check box and leave the defaults in place.

Which result or results does your configuration achieve? (Choose all that apply.)

A. The Accounting group is able to run the AccoutingApp remotely.

B. A disconnected session will be ended after 15 minutes of idle time.

C. No more than five users can connect to the terminal server at a time.

D. The same account is configured for all users to automatically log on to the terminal server.

E. The AccountingApp Program starts after the automatic logon event.

70-218.05.03.003

You improve the performance of a terminal server by taking which of the following steps?

A. Enabling Active Desktop in the Server Settings

B. Changing Terminal Services to application mode

C. Clearing the Disable Wallpaper check box on the Environment tab of the connection's Properties dialog box

D. On the Network Adapter tab of the connection's Properties dialog box, selecting and configuring Maximum Connections

70-218.05.03.004

You have a firewall between your remote access Terminal Services clients and your terminal server. Which TCP port do you need to open on the firewall to allow client access to the terminal server?

A. 8080

B. 3000

C. 3333

D. 3389

70-218.05.03.005

You installed the Terminal Services Client on your computer at home. You are using a 56K modem to dial in to your network's Routing and Remote Access server that has been configured to allow you access to the entire network. You use Terminal Services Client Connection Manager to create a connection to the terminal server named RemoteAdmin. After you connect to the RAS server, you use the RemoteAdmin connection to connect to an administrative server on which you installed Terminal Services and the Windows 2000 Administration tools. When you connect, the response time is very slow and tasks are taking too long to complete. How can you configure the RemoteAdmin connection to improve performance? (Choose all that apply.)

A. In the Terminal Services Client Connection Manager, select the connection properties for the RemoteAdmin connection. On the Connection Options tab, select Enable Data Compression.

B. In the Terminal Services Client Connection Manager, select the connection properties for the RemoteAdmin connection. On the Connection Options tab, select Full Screen.

C. In the Terminal Services Client program, select the RemoteAdmin connection and select Enable Data Compression.

D. In the Terminal Services Client Connection Manager, verify the connection properties for the connection used. On the Connections Options tab, the default setting, which is Cache Bitmaps To Disk, should be selected.

E. In the Terminal Server administration tool, configure the client connection to compress data and cache bitmaps.

70-218.05.03.006

You have a Microsoft Exchange server on your network with Terminal Services installed in administration mode with all the default settings. A first-tier Exchange administrator needs help with a procedure that needs to be executed on the Exchange server. She is accessing the Exchange server console through a Terminal Services session. You have also logged on using a Terminal Services session. When you try to gain remote control of the Exchange administrator's session, you receive a Terminal Services error message. Which steps can you take to resolve this? (Choose all that apply.)

A. On the Client Settings tab of the connection properties in Terminal Services Configuration, clear the Use Connection Settings From User Settings check box.

B. On the Remote Control tab of the connection properties in Terminal Services Configuration, select the Use Remote Control With The Following Settings option and then select the Interact With The Session option.

C. On the Exchange administrator's user account properties, select the Enable Remote Control check box on the Remote Control tab.

D. In Terminal Services Manager, right-click the Exchange administrator's session and select Properties. On the Permissions tab, grant your user account the Remote Control permission.

E. On the Exchange administrator's user account Properties dialog box, select the Disable Remote Control check box on the Remote Control tab.

70-218.05.03.007

You are the administrator of a Windows 2000 network with two domains and several domain controllers. You have installed Terminal Services in remote administration mode on all domain controllers. You need to be able to perform directory service repair functions on the domain controllers by using the directory service restore mode remotely. How can you accomplish this?

A. Create a new entry in the BOOT.INI file on each Windows 2000 domain controller to permit Windows 2000 to be started in offline repair mode.

B. Install Terminal Services in remote administration mode and select Domain Controller as the type of server on which administration will be performed.

C. Change the registry value Dsrepair under the TermServices key to a 1.

D. In Terminal Services Configuration under Server Settings, right-click Terminal Server Mode and change to Domain Controller Administration.

70-218.05.03.008

A Terminal Services client user is complaining that she is not able to print to her locally attached printer when running a Terminal Services application session. When not connected to a terminal server, she is able to print. How can you troubleshoot this? (Choose all that apply.)

A. Verify that the correct printer driver is installed on the client computer and that the Sharing tab is configured for sharing.

B. Verify that on the Environment tab of the user's account Properties page the appropriate boxes are selected under Client Devices.

C. Verify that the appropriate print permissions were assigned either directly to the user account, or to a group of which the user is a member.

D. Verify that on the Client Settings tab of the connection properties in Terminal Services Configuration the Use Connection Settings From User Settings check box is selected.

E. Verify that the Not Shared option on the Sharing tab of the Properties dialog box of the client printer is selected.

Objective 5.3 Answers

70-218.05.03.001

► **Correct Answers: A and B**

A. **Correct:** By configuring a dial-in connection to the Routing and Remote Access server, which connects you to the entire corporate network, and creating a connection configured with the IP address of the member server ABC, you accomplished this goal.

B. **Correct:** You installed the Terminal Services Client on the client computers within the network from which you need to perform remote administration; therefore, this goal was accomplished.

C. **Incorrect:** You need to configure the Sessions tab of the Properties dialog box of your user account with Idle Session Limit to 5 Minutes and When A Session Limit Is Reached Or Connection Is Broken to End Session to accomplish this goal.

D. **Incorrect:** You need to configure the Sessions tab of the Properties dialog box of your user account with Idle Session Limit to 1 Hour and When A Session Limit Is Reached Or Connection Is Broken to End Session to accomplish this goal.

70-218.05.03.002

▶ **Correct Answers: D and E**

A. **Incorrect:** To meet this requirement, you click Always Use The Following Logon Information on the Logon Settings tab and type the credentials to be used by all members of the Accounting group and clear the Always Prompt For Password check box. On the Environment tab, you select the Override Settings From User Profile And Client Connection Manager Wizard check box, and you fill in the Program Path And File Name field for the AccountingApp. Because you used the Permissions tab of the connection properties to add the Accounting group, they will be able to connect to the terminal server and run the AccountingApp. Guest Access is the minimum permission required to run an application on the terminal server.

B. **Incorrect:** If you select the Override User Settings check box and leave the defaults in place on the Sessions tab, the Idle Session Limit will be set to Never.

C. **Incorrect:** The default setting on the Network Adapter tab is set to Unlimited Connections.

D. **Correct:** By configuring the Logon Settings tab to Always Use the Following Logon Information and typing the credentials to be used by all members of the Accounting group and clearing the Always Prompt For Password check box, you accomplished this requirement.

E. **Correct:** By selecting the Override Settings From User Profile And Client Connection Manager Wizard and typing the Program Path And File Name for the AccountingApp, you accomplished this requirement.

70-218.05.03.003

▶ **Correct Answers: D**

A. **Incorrect:** Enabling Active Desktop consumes more server resources.

B. **Incorrect:** Application mode is more resource intensive than remote administration mode.

C. **Incorrect:** By default, the Disable Wallpaper check box is selected to conserve resources. Clearing this box would consume more server resources.

D. **Correct:** Restricting the number of sessions improves performance because fewer sessions are demanding system resources.

70-218.05.03.004

▶ **Correct Answers: D**

A. **Incorrect:** This answer is incorrect for the reason stated in answer D.

B. **Incorrect:** This answer is incorrect for the reason stated in answer D.

C. **Incorrect:** This answer is incorrect for the reason stated in answer D.

D. **Correct:** The correct port used by clients to connect to a Terminal Services server is 3389.

70-218.05.03.005

▶ **Correct Answers: A and D**

A. **Correct:** Using the Terminal Services Client Connection Manager, you can configure connections with different options. Because this connection is over a slow modem link, it should be configured to compress data.

B. **Incorrect:** This option will not affect performance.

C. **Incorrect:** You cannot select a created and configured connection from Terminal Services Client. The Terminal Services Client is used to connect to a terminal server by name or by browsing.

D. **Correct:** Using the Client Connection Manager, you can configure connections with different options. Because this connection is over a slow modem link, it should be configured to cache frequently used bitmaps to disk, which is the default setting.

E. **Incorrect:** Data compression and cache bitmaps can be configured using only Client Connection Manager.

70-218.05.03.006

▶ **Correct Answers: B and C**

A. **Incorrect:** This setting does not have any effect on remote control. This action will override the user account client settings.

B. **Correct:** This setting overrides any setting on the user account Remote Control tab. Because the Use Remote Control With The Following Settings and the Interact With The Session options were chosen, this allows you to take control over every user session, regardless of the settings in their user accounts.

C. **Correct:** The default setting for the connection on the Remote Control tab is Use Remote Control With User Default User Settings. This means the settings from the user account's Remote Control tab take effect. In this case, because you were able to select the Enable Remote Control check box, it was previously disabled. When anyone attempts to gain control of an account with Remote Control disabled, they receive a Terminal Services error stating remote control is not enabled for the user.

D. **Incorrect:** There is no Properties option on the session shortcut menu.

E. **Incorrect:** There is no such option as Disable Remote Control.

70-218.05.03.007

▶ **Correct Answers: A**

A. **Correct:** In the BOOT.INI file, copy the default ARC path and paste it directly below the default. Add the following switch to the end of the copied ARC path: /safeboot:dsrepair /sos. Test this before using it in a remote administration capacity. The detailed procedure can be found in the Microsoft Knowledge Base article Q256588.

B. **Incorrect:** This option does not exist during the installation of Terminal Services.

C. **Incorrect:** There is no such registry value.

D. **Incorrect:** There is no Terminal Server Mode option. The only other option when in administration mode is to switch to application mode.

70-218.05.03.008

▶ **Correct Answers: B and D**

A. **Incorrect:** Because the user is able to print locally, it is not a printer-driver issue. The sharing status does not affect the ability of a Terminal Services client to print to a locally attached printer.

B. **Correct:** The default configuration for Terminal Services is to obtain the connection settings from the user account. On the Environment tab, under Client Devices, select both the Connect Client Printers At Logon and the Default To Main Client Printer check boxes.

C. **Incorrect:** Because the user is able to print to the printer when not connected to the terminal server, it is not a permissions issue.

D. **Correct:** If this check box is not selected, the connection settings are obtained from the terminal server. If both the Connect Client Printers At Logon and the Default To Main Client Printer check boxes are not selected, the client will not have access to its local printer when in a Terminal Services session.

E. **Incorrect:** The ability of a Terminal Services client to print to a locally attached printer is not affected by the Sharing status.

Configure and troubleshoot Network Address Translation (NAT) and Internet Connection Sharing (ICS).

Windows 2000 Server supports two methods by which a **small office/home office (SOHO)** can be given access to the Internet. Both **Network Address Translation (NAT)** and **Internet Connection Sharing (ICS)** allow users from an internal network to gain access to the Internet through the NAT or ICS server. Windows 2000 Professional supports only ICS. A NAT or ICS server requires a network adapter connected to the Internet and another network adapter connected to the internal network. The connection to the Internet is referred to as the external or public interface. The connection to the intranet is referred to as the internal or private interface. The server can take an IP packet on one interface, make changes to the IP packet's address field, and pass it on the other interface.

NAT and ICS both perform network address translation. Because of this capability, only one Internet address or public address is required on the external interface. For outgoing packets, the NAT or ICS server opens the IP packet and changes the source IP address to reflect the IP address of the external (public) interface on the NAT or ICS server. The server keeps a table mapping the ports on which the requests were sent so it can respond to the correct client. NAT and ICS both have the capability to assign internal clients IP addresses. This is termed the **DHCP allocator service**. With both NAT and ICS, the clients must be configured to obtain an IP address from a DHCP server.

There are some important differences between NAT and ICS. NAT can be configured with more than one public and private address, while ICS supports only one. NAT can be configured to assign IP addresses from a configured pool of addresses, while ICS cannot be configured with a different pool than its default, which is 192.168.0.0 with a subnet mask of 255.255.255.0. Although ICS has more limitations than NAT, the configuration of ICS is a simple one-step process. NAT requires more manual configuration.

To answer the questions in this objective, you must understand how NAT and ICS operate. You must also understand the differences between the two, and know when it is appropriate to use one over the other. You must also be familiar with the administrative tools used to configure NAT—the Routing and Remote Access Server Setup Wizard and the configuration of ICS on the Sharing tab of the network connection's properties.

Objective 5.4 Questions

70-218.05.04.001

You have a small office with nine networked Windows 2000 Professional computers and one Windows 2000 Server computer functioning as a workgroup. You will not configure any DHCP or Domain Name System (DNS) servers. You need to provide users with Internet access, but you do not want to configure each computer with a public IP address. Each Windows 2000 Professional computer has been configured as a DHCP client. On your Windows 2000 Server computer, you already configured a high-speed connection to the Internet. How can you configure your environment to provide users with low-cost Internet access with the least administrative overhead?

A. Install and configure Routing and Remote Access on your server to provide NAT.

B. Install and configure Routing and Remote Access on your server to allow routing of all IP traffic.

C. On the Sharing tab for the Internet connection, select the Enable Internet Connection Sharing For This Connection check box.

D. Configure a Microsoft Internet Security and Acceleration server to provide Internet connection services.

70-218.05.04.002

You set up NAT on your Routing and Remote Access server, which has a permanent high-speed connection to the Internet. You have verified that your internal network users are receiving IP addresses. They can connect to the Internet using IP addresses; however, they are not able to connect to any Internet resource by using a unique resource locator. How can you resolve this issue with the least administrative overhead?

A. On the TCP/IP Properties dialog box of the NIC on each client, configure each client computer with the IP addresses of two external public DNS servers.

B. On the TCP/IP Properties dialog box of the NIC on each client, configure each client computer with the IP address of an internal DNS server that is not a forwarder.

C. On the Properties dialog box of the NAT server in the Routing and Remote Access console, click the Name Resolution tab and select the Clients Using Domain Name System check box and the Connect To The Public Network When A Name Needs To Be Resolved check box.

D. On the Properties dialog box of the NAT server in the Routing and Remote Access console, click the Name Resolution tab and select the Clients Using Domain Name System check box only under Resolve IP Addresses For.

70-218.05.04.003

You are the administrator for your corporate network. Your ISP has assigned the public address range of 207.209.68.1 through 207.209.68.254 to your company. Your private IP address range is 10.0.0.1 through 10.255.255.254, which is managed and assigned by a DHCP server. An existing DNS server is configured to resolve all internal and external names. Clients are configured with DNS server information by the DHCP server.

The following requirements must be met for your network:

- You must provide the corporate network Internet access.

- You must allow access from the Internet to an internal Web server with IP address 10.10.10.12.

- Clients will use the existing DHCP server to obtain client IP addresses.

- Clients will use the existing DNS server for name resolution.

You add and configure NAT using Routing and Remote Access. You add and configure an external (public) interface and an internal (private) interface. On the Address Pool tab for the external interface Properties dialog box within the Network Address Translation (NAT) branch of the Routing and Remote Access console, you configure the address pool 207.209.68.1 with the subnet mask 255.255.255.0. You add a reservation configuring a mapping of public address 207.209.68.24 to the private address of your Web server 10.10.10.12. You select the check box Allow Incoming Sessions To This Address for the reservation. On the NAT properties, you click the Address Assignment tab and clear the Automatically Assign IP Addresses By Using DHCP check box. On the Name Resolution tab of NAT, you select the Clients Using Domain Name System (DNS) check box.

Which of the requirements have you met? (Choose all that apply.)

A. You provided the branch office with Internet access.

B. You allowed access from the Internet to an internal Web server with IP address 10.10.10.12.

C. Clients use the DHCP allocator service to obtain client IP addresses.

D. Clients use the existing DNS server for name resolution.

70-218.05.04.004

Which of the following statements are true regarding NAT? (Choose all that apply.)

A. The computer running NAT changes the source IP address on a request received from an internal client to reflect its own IP address instead of the client's IP address before sending it out to the Internet.

B. The client computer determines the destination, changes the packet header, and sends the packet to the computer running NAT.

C. The Web server on the Internet sends the reply directly to the internal client from which the request was initially made.

D. The computer running NAT is configured with an external (private) IP address and one or more internal (public) addresses.

E. The NAT server maintains a table with information regarding the different internal to external (and vice versa) address mappings.

70-218.05.04.005

You are using a DHCP server to assign IP addresses to your Windows 2000 clients. Clients have all been configured to receive an IP address automatically. You have a NAT server that will provide access to the Internet. How can you automatically configure your clients to use the NAT server to connect to the Internet?

A. On the desktop, right-click My Network Places and then click Properties. Right-click Local Area Connection, and then click Properties. Select Internet Protocol (TCP/IP), and then click Properties. In the Default Gateway box, type the internal IP address of the NAT server.

B. On the DHCP server, configure a scope option for the IP address range being used for your clients by selecting option 003 Router with the IP address of the NAT server.

C. On the desktop, right-click My Network Places and then click Properties. Right-click Local Area Connection, and then click Properties. Select Internet Protocol (TCP/IP), and then click Properties. In the Default Gateway box, type the external IP address of the NAT server.

D. On the DHCP server, configure a scope option for the IP address range being used for your clients by selecting option 005 Name Servers with the IP address of the DNS server.

70-218.05.04.006

When configuring a Windows 2000 client to use an ICS server, how are the Internet Protocol (TCP/IP) properties configured and what address range will the client obtain an IP address from?

A. Internet Protocol (TCP/IP) properties are configured to Obtain An IP Address Automatically, and the address range the client will receive an address from is 169.254.0.0–169.254.255.255.

B. Internet Protocol (TCP/IP) properties are configured manually with an IP address from the range of 10.0.0.1–10.0.0.255.

C. Internet Protocol (TCP/IP) properties are configured manually with an IP address from the range of 169.254.0.0–169.254.255.255.

D. Internet Protocol (TCP/IP) properties are configured to Obtain An IP Address Automatically, and the address range the client will receive an address from is 192.168.0.1–192.168.0.254.

70-218.05.04.007

You have a small business network and do not use a DHCP server. Clients are configured to obtain their IP addresses through DHCP. Your ISP has granted you a public IP address, and you will use a modem to connect to the Internet.

You want to achieve the following goals:

- The connection should be dialed automatically when a client sends a request to an Internet Web server.

- You want to grant public access to a Web site hosted on an internal Web server.

- The internal Web server should be able to respond to the specific client that encapsulated the request.

- You do not want to configure a separate DHCP server on the network.

- You have a custom application running on an intranet server using port 888 that you want to make accessible to users over the Internet.

On the Sharing tab of the network adapter properties for the external interface in My Network Places, you enable ICS by selecting the Enable Internet Connection Sharing For This Connection check box and you clear the Enable On Demand Dialing check box. With the Sharing tab still open, you click the Settings button. On the Applications tab of the Internet Connection Sharing Settings dialog box, you click Add and configure the application using TCP port 888 and Incoming Response Ports 1024–1209.

Which goals did you accomplish? (Choose all that apply.)

A. The connection should be dialed automatically when a client sends a request to an Internet Web server.

B. You want to grant public access to a Web site hosted on an internal Web server.

C. The internal Web server should be able to respond to the specific client that encapsulated the request.

D. You do not want to configure a separate DHCP server on the network.

E. You have a custom application running on an intranet server using port 888 that you want to make accessible to users over the Internet.

70-218.05.04.008

You have recently configured ICS to support your small business office. All clients are configured to receive their IP addresses through DHCP. All clients were started at around the same time this morning. Both the clients and the ICS server have all remained online. Clients who could connect successfully yesterday can no longer connect to the Internet or some of the other internal clients. Some clients on the same network have Internet connectivity, but they can access only some of the internal hosts. What is a likely cause of this, and how can you troubleshoot it?

A. The clients who cannot connect are not receiving the correct IP addresses from the ICS server. You verify this using the PING command.

B. You use IPCONFIG to determine that the clients who cannot connect are receiving their IP addresses from a DHCP server other than the ICS server.

C. By using the PING command, you verify that the clients who cannot connect are assigning themselves IP addresses through APIPA.

D. The network cards of the clients who cannot connect failed. You verify this by using the PING command.

70-218.05.04.009

What is the type of connection in which Windows 2000 Server acts as an IP router and forwards all packets from your small office network clients to the hosts on the Internet without any modification of the packet?

A. Translated connection

B. Routed connection

C. VPN connection

D. None of the above

70-218.05.04.010

Which of the following commands would you use to test connectivity to an ICS server from a client on the same internal network?

A. WINIPCFG

B. IPCONFIG 192.168.0.1

C. PING 169.254.1.1

D. PING 192.168.0.1

Objective 5.4 Answers

70-218.05.04.001

▶ **Correct Answers: C**

A. **Incorrect:** Although NAT fulfills the requirement of low-cost Internet access, it does not achieve the objective of least administrative overhead. NAT requires significantly more configuration than ICS.

B. **Incorrect:** Allowing routing of all IP traffic would require that internal clients all have valid public IP addresses. This is also highly insecure because the internal network would be exposed on the Internet.

C. **Correct:** Because the Windows 2000 Professional computers have been configured to receive an address from a DHCP server and there is no other DHCP server on this network, the client computers receive an IP address from the DHCP allocator service on the ICS server. These IP addresses are in the range of 192.168.0.2 to 192.168.0.254. The ICS server configures its own internal interface (the one attached to the internal network) with a static IP address of 192.168.0.1.

D. **Incorrect:** Although a Microsoft Internet Security and Acceleration server can provide access to the Internet, it needs to be purchased separately. It also requires a degree of configuration that does not meet this scenario's requirement for least administrative overhead. Microsoft Internet Security and Acceleration server has many features beyond Internet connection services.

70-218.05.04.002

▶ **Correct Answers: D**

A. **Incorrect:** Although this solution will work, it involves significant administrative overhead. Furthermore, a specific public DNS server might not always be available. Even if several DNS servers are configured, an alternate DNS server will be queried only if the previous DNS server did not contain the information being queried for. If the DNS server is unavailable (offline), it will not query subsequent DNS servers.

B. **Incorrect:** An internal DNS server that is not a forwarder will resolve only internal names. A DNS forwarder is configured to forward the query to an external DNS server. This solution would also involve significant administrative overhead.

C. **Incorrect:** Because this is a permanent high-speed connection, there is no need to select the Connect To The Public Network When A Name Needs To Be Resolved check box. This is used only in the case that the NAT server is using a demand-dial interface that dials a number to connect to the Internet.

D. **Correct:** This is all that is needed. Because clients are already receiving IP addresses, no changes need to be made to the clients.

70-218.05.04.003

▶ **Correct Answers: A and B**

A. **Correct:** By configuring both the external and internal interfaces for NAT, you achieved this requirement.

B. **Correct:** Because you defined the external address pool and subnet mask and configured a reservation mapping an address belonging to this pool to an internal address, a connection will be made to the internal 10.10.10.12 address when a connection is made from the Internet using any address in the pool.

C. **Incorrect:** By clearing the Automatically Assign IP Addresses By Using DHCP check box, you prevent the NAT server's DHCP allocator service from assigning addresses to clients. Clients will obtain their IP address from the existing DHCP server.

D. **Incorrect:** By selecting the Clients Using Domain Name System (DNS) check box, you are configuring the NAT server to provide name resolution for clients, thereby bypassing the existing DNS server.

70-218.05.04.004

▶ **Correct Answers: A and E**

A. **Correct:** The address information in the packet header is changed from an internal address to an external address. The NAT server records a mapping in a table that it uses to track internal-to-external IP addresses for two-way communication.

B. **Incorrect:** The computer running NAT determines the destination, changes the packet header, and sends the packet to the client.

C. **Incorrect:** The Web server on the Internet sends the reply back to the NAT server. The NAT server then parses the mapping table to determine the client to which the packet should be returned.

D. **Incorrect:** The computer running NAT is configured with an internal (private) IP address and one or more external (public) addresses. Using NAT, it is possible to use more than one external IP address. With ICS, the limit is one external IP address.

E. **Correct:** This is the mechanism that allows the NAT server to determine to which specific client a reply from the Internet will be routed.

70-218.05.04.005

▶ **Correct Answers: B**

  A. **Incorrect:** On a client configured to use DHCP for IP address assignment, this option will not be available.

  B. **Correct:** It is possible to use the DHCP server with the option 003 Router to configure the default gateway on clients automatically at the time the IP address is assigned.

  C. **Incorrect:** On a client configured to use DHCP for IP address assignment, this option will not be available. Even if the client were manually configured, the external IP address of the NAT server would be unreachable by the client.

  D. **Incorrect:** This option will not allow clients to access the NAT server. If there is also a DNS server on the network being used for internal and external name resolution, it would be efficient to create a Name Server option so clients obtaining IP addresses from the DHCP server would also be automatically configured with the address of a DNS server.

70-218.05.04.006

▶ **Correct Answers: D**

  A. **Incorrect:** If the client is configured to Obtain An IP Address Automatically and it received an address from the range 169.254.0.0–169.254.255.254, this indicates that the client is not receiving its IP address from the ICS server. This address range is used by APIPA and indicates that the client has auto-configured itself with an IP address. For more efficient troubleshooting, disable APIPA on the client in the registry.

  B. **Incorrect:** The client must be configured to Obtain An IP Address Automatically.

  C. **Incorrect:** The client must be configured to Obtain An IP Address Automatically.

  D. **Correct:** The client must be configured to Obtain An IP Address Automatically. The ICS server will assign the IP address 192.168.0.1 to its own internal network interface. The remaining addresses, 192.168.0.2–169.168.0.254, will be allocated to clients.

70-218.05.04.007

▶ **Correct Answers: D and E**

    A. **Incorrect:** If you select the Enable Internet Connection Sharing For This Connection check box, the Enable On Demand Dialing check box is selected by default. By clearing this box, you disabled on demand dialing.

    B. **Incorrect:** You need to configure this on the Services tab by clicking the Add button and typing the name of the internal Web server, the service port number (80), and TCP. In the IP address, you type the internal IP address of the Web server.

    C. **Incorrect:** Because this was not set up on the Services tab, the internal Web server will have no communication with external clients.

    D. **Correct:** Clients will automatically obtain their IP addresses from the DHCP allocator service of the ICS server.

    E. **Correct:** By adding the application on the Application tab under Settings and configuring it properly, you have facilitated Internet access to the application server.

70-218.05.04.008

▶ **Correct Answers: B**

    A. **Incorrect:** The ICS server will assign addresses only from the range 192.168.0.2–192.168.0.254. The IPCONFIG command is used to verify a client's IP address.

    B. **Correct:** If a separate DHCP server was configured on the network to assign IP addresses in a range that is different from that assigned by ICS, clients receiving their IP address from the DHCP server will not have Internet connectivity. They will be able to connect only to those other hosts that have also received addresses from the DHCP server. Clients who received their IP address from ICS will be able to connect to the Internet, but only to the internal clients who also received their IP address from ICS. IP addresses can be verified by using the IPCONFIG command.

    C. **Incorrect:** Clients assign themselves APIPA addresses only when there is neither an ICS nor a DHCP server present on the network. Because some of the clients are receiving addresses from the ICS server, the ICS server is online. The IPCONFIG command can be used to determine if a client is assigning itself an IP address through APIPA. When the PING command is used alone, only a help screen for the PING command is displayed.

    D. **Incorrect:** Because clients can connect to other certain clients, the network cards are functioning. The PING command can be used to verify connectivity to other hosts.

70-218.05.04.009

▶ **Correct Answers: B**

   A. **Incorrect:** With NAT, internal IP addresses are translated by the NAT server. The NAT server alters IP packets received from internal clients, so the IP packet header contains the public IP address of the external interface on the NAT server instead of the internal client's IP address.

   B. **Correct:** With routed connections, Windows 2000 Server acts as an IP router and forwards all packets to the Internet without altering the IP addresses. Internal clients require public IP addresses to connect with hosts on the Internet.

   C. **Incorrect:** A VPN takes place when two hosts communicate using a public network as the communication backbone. VPN involves the use of encryption technologies to ensure the private transmission of messages.

   D. **Incorrect:** This answer is incorrect for the reasons stated in answer B.

70-218.05.04.010

▶ **Correct Answers: D**

   A. **Incorrect:** WINIPCFG is a Microsoft Windows 95, Windows 98, and Windows Me command that displays IP configuration information within a graphical window.

   B. **Incorrect:** IPCONFIG displays IP configuration and is not used in conjunction with an IP address.

   C. **Incorrect:** PING is the correct command to use, but the IP address assigned to the internal interface is 192.168.0.1 and cannot be changed. The 169.254.0.0–169.254.255.255 range is used by Automatic Private IP Addressing.

   D. **Correct:** Executing PING 192.168.0.1 will test connectivity to the internal interface on the ICS server, which is statically configured to use 192.168.0.1 (and cannot be changed).

Glossary

A

Active Directory The directory service that stores information about objects on a network and makes this information available to users and network administrators. Active Directory gives network users access to permitted resources anywhere on the network using a single logon process.

Active Directory object Any item stored or represented in the Active Directory service. An object can be a user, a group, or even a Group Policy Object. Every object in the Active Directory service must have a definition in the schema, which specifies the attributes associated with it. *See also* attribute; object.

Active Directory Sites and Services An administrative tool for providing information about the physical structure of your network by publishing sites to Active Directory. Active Directory uses this information to determine how to replicate directory information and handle service requests. *See also* Active Directory; Microsoft Management Console (MMC).

Active Directory Users and Computers An administrative tool designed to perform day-to-day Active Directory administration tasks. These tasks include creating, deleting, modifying, moving, and setting permissions on objects stored in the directory. These objects include organizational units, users, contacts, groups, computers, printers, and shared file objects. *See also* Active Directory object; Microsoft Management Console (MMC); permission.

administrative templates In Group Policy, a file (with the .adm extension) that an administrator uses to generate user interface settings. The template file consists of a hierarchy of categories and subcategories that together define how the options are displayed through Group Policy. *See also* Group Policy.

API *See* application programming interface.

APIPA *See* Automatic Private IP Addressing.

application programming interface (API) A set of routines that an application uses to request and carry out lower-level services performed by a computer's operating system.

application server mode A Terminal Services mode that turns Windows 2000 Server into a multiuser computer for thin-client computing. *See also* remote administration mode; Terminal Services.

assigned application An application assigned to users or computers by an administrator using the Software Installation snap-in extension to Group Policy. Assigned applications are always available to users or computers managed by a Group Policy Object (GPO). User-assigned applications appear to be installed on a user's computer. Applications assigned to a computer are installed when the computer is turned on. *See also* published application.

attribute In Active Directory, an attribute describes characteristics of an object and the type of information an object can hold. For each object class, the schema defines what attributes an instance of the class must have and what additional attributes it might have. In a file system, information that indicates whether a file is read-only, hidden, ready for archiving (backing up), compressed, or encrypted, and whether the file contents should be indexed for fast file searching.

Audit Policy The definition of the set of actions that causes an event to be logged in the Event Log. *See also* Event Log.

auditing The process an operating system uses to detect and record security-related events, such as an attempt to create, access, or delete objects such as files and folders.

Automatic Private IP Addressing (APIPA) A feature of Windows 2000 TCP/IP that automatically configures a unique IP address from the range 169.254.0.1 through 169.254.255.254 and a subnet mask of 255.255.0.0 when TCP/IP is configured for dynamic addressing and DHCP is not available. *See also* Dynamic Host Configuration Protocol (DHCP); IP address; Transmission Control Protocol/Internet Protocol (TCP/IP).

B

basic disk   A physical disk that can be accessed by MS-DOS and all Windows-based operating systems. Basic disks can contain up to four primary partitions, or three primary partitions and an extended partition with multiple logical drives. *See also* basic volume; dynamic disk; dynamic volume.

basic volume   A primary partition or logical drive that resides on a basic disk. *See also* basic disk.

Block Inheritance   A flag that blocks inheritance of Group Policy from above in Active Directory. Block Policy Inheritance is set on a domain or organizational unit and, therefore, applies to all GPOs linked at that level or higher in Active Directory that can be overridden. *See also* Group Policy Object (GPO).

C

CDFS   *See* CD-ROM File System.

CD-ROM File System (CDFS)   A 32-bit protected-mode file system that controls access to the contents of CD-ROM drives in Windows 95, Windows 98, Windows Me, Windows NT, and Windows 2000.

CIFS   *See* Common Internet File System.

Common Internet File System (CIFS)   A protocol and a corresponding API used by application programs to request higher level application services. CIFS was formerly known as SMB (Server Message Block).

computer account objects   Objects used to identify a specific computer account in Windows 2000 Server.

D

delegation of administration   In Active Directory, enabling an administrator to compartmentalize administrative functions. The administrator grants rights to a small set of administrators who then have the right to manage users or groups within their responsibility.

demand-dial connection   A connection, typically using a circuit-switched wide area network link, that is initiated when data needs to be forwarded. The demand-dial connection is typically terminated when there is no traffic.

Device Manager   An administrative tool that can be used to manage the devices on your computer.

DHCP   *See* Dynamic Host Configuration Protocol.

DHCP allocator service   A service to assign private IP addresses and a proxy DNS server to perform name resolution services on behalf of all computers in an intranet. ICS includes a DHCP allocator service. *See also* Internet Connection Sharing (ICS).

DHCP Relay Agent   A routing component that transfers messages between DHCP clients and DHCP service located on separate networks. *See also* Dynamic Host Configuration Protocol (DHCP).

DHCP/BOOTP forwarding   A feature of an IP router that allows DHCP/BOOTP packets to be forwarded by the router. *See also* DHCP Relay Agent; IP routing.

DNS   *See* Domain Name System.

domain   In Active Directory, a collection of computers defined by the administrator. These computers share a common directory database, security policies, and security relationships with other domains. In DNS, a domain is any tree or subtree within the DNS namespace. *See also* Active Directory; Domain Name System (DNS).

Domain Name System (DNS)   A hierarchical, distributed database that contains mappings of DNS domain names to various types of data, such as IP addresses. *See also* domain; IP address; Transmission Control Protocol/Internet Protocol (TCP/IP).

Driver Signing   Designates whether drivers and operating system files have been digitally verified by Microsoft to ensure their quality.

dual boot   A computer or device configured with more than one operating system. Users generally select the operating system at startup.

dynamic disk   A physical disk that is managed by Disk Management. Dynamic disks can contain only dynamic volumes (that is, volumes created by using Disk Management). Dynamic disks cannot contain partitions or logical drives, nor can they be accessed by MS-DOS. *See also* basic disk; dynamic volume; partition; volume.

Dynamic Host Configuration Protocol (DHCP)   A TCP/IP service protocol that offers dynamic leased configuration of host IP addresses and distributes other configuration parameters to eligible network clients. *See also* IP address; Transmission Control Protocol/Internet Protocol (TCP/IP).

dynamic volume   A volume that resides on a dynamic disk. Windows supports five types of dynamic volumes: simple, spanned, striped, mirrored, and RAID-5. *See also* basic disk; basic volume; dynamic disk; simple volume; spanned volume, volume.

E

emergency repair disk (ERD)   A disk, created by the Backup utility, that can be used during the Emergency Repair Process to repair your computer if it will not start or if your system files are damaged or erased.

ERD   *See* emergency repair disk.

Event Log   The file in which event-logging entries are recorded. Entries are recorded whenever certain events occur, such as services starting and stopping, or users logging on and off and accessing resources. Typical Event Logs such as system, security, and application logs are viewed in Event Viewer. *See also* Event Viewer.

Event Viewer   An administrative tool for monitoring events on a system. Event Viewer maintains logs about program, security, and system events on a computer, and it can be used to view and manage the Event Logs and monitor Windows 2000 security events. *See also* Event Log.

F

FAT   *See* file allocation table.

FAT12   *See* file allocation table.

FAT16   *See* file allocation table.

FAT32   *See* file allocation table-32.

file allocation table (FAT)   The system used by MS-DOS to organize and manage files. The FAT is a data structure that MS-DOS creates on the disk when the disk is formatted. The FAT is the only file system MS-DOS can use. Several older FAT-related file systems are available, including FAT12 for small disk volumes and FAT16 for small to moderate hard disk volumes. *See also* file allocation table-32 (FAT32); NT file system (NTFS).

file allocation table-32 (FAT32)   A derivative of the FAT file system. FAT32 supports smaller cluster sizes and larger volumes than FAT, which results in more efficient space allocation on FAT32 volumes. *See also* file allocation table (FAT); NT file system (NTFS).

File Transfer Protocol (FTP)   A member of the TCP/IP suite of protocols that is used to copy files between two computers on the Internet. *See also* Transmission Control Protocol/Internet Protocol (TCP/IP).

forward lookup In DNS, a query process in which the friendly DNS domain name of a host computer is searched to find its IP address. In DNS Manager, forward lookup zones are based on DNS domain names and typically hold host address (A) resource records. *See also* reverse lookup.

FQDN *See* fully qualified domain name.

FTP *See* File Transfer Protocol.

fully qualified domain name (FQDN) A DNS domain name that has been stated unambiguously so as to indicate with absolute certainty its location in the domain namespace tree (for example, client1.reskit.com). The FQDN is also known as a full computer name.

G

GPO *See* Group Policy Object.

group A collection of user accounts. By making a user account a member of a group, you give the related user all the rights and permissions granted to the group. *See also* Active Directory Users and Computers; user account.

group object *See* group.

Group Policy An administrator's tool for defining and controlling how programs, network resources, and the operating system operate for users and computers in an organization.

Group Policy Object (GPO) A collection of Group Policy settings. GPOs are essentially the documents created by the Group Policy snap-in, a Windows utility. *See also* Group Policy.

H

Hardware Compatibility List (HCL) A hardware list that Microsoft compiles for a specific product. The Windows HCL, which is posted on the Web, lists the hardware devices and computer systems that are compatible with specific versions of Windows.

hardware profile A set of data that describes the configuration and characteristics of a given piece of computer equipment.

HCL *See* Hardware Compatibility List.

hotfix Software released to address a specific issue such as a newly discovered security threat or performance issue. Because Microsoft releases hotfixes to address a single urgent issue, they do not go through the same rigorous testing as other software. Also known as a patch. *See also* service pack.

HTTP *See* Hypertext Transfer Protocol.

HTTPS *See* Hypertext Transfer Protocol Secure.

Hypertext Transfer Protocol (HTTP) The protocol used to transfer information on the Web.

Hypertext Transfer Protocol Secure (HTTPS) A protocol for transmitting individual messages securely over the Web. SSL complements HTTPS. *See also* Secure Sockets Layer (SSL).

I

ICS *See* Internet Connection Sharing.

input/output (I/O) The complementary tasks of transferring data from one location to another so that a process or thread can work with it.

Internet Connection Sharing (ICS) A Windows 2000 feature that enables users to connect a home network or small office network to the Internet.

Internet Information Services (IIS) Software services that support Web site creation, configuration, and management, along with other Internet functions. IIS includes NNTP, FTP, and SMTP. *See also* File Transfer Protocol (FTP); Network News Transfer Protocol (NNTP); Simple Mail Transport Protocol (SMTP).

Internet Protocol (IP) A routable protocol in the TCP/IP protocol suite that is responsible for IP addressing, routing, and the fragmentation and reassembly of IP packets. *See also* Transmission Control Protocol/Internet Protocol (TCP/IP).

Internet Protocol Security (IPSec) A set of industry-standard, cryptography-based protection services and protocols. IPSec protects all protocols in the TCP/IP protocol suite and Internet communications using L2TP. *See also* Layer 2 Tunneling Protocol (L2TP); protocol; Transmission Control Protocol/Internet Protocol (TCP/IP).

interrupt request (IRQ) A signal sent by a device to get the attention of the processor when the device is ready to accept or send information.

I/O *See* input/output.

IP *See* Internet Protocol.

IP address A 32-bit address used to identify a node on an IP internetwork. Each node on the IP internetwork must be assigned a unique IP address, which is made up of the network ID, plus a unique host ID. *See also* Dynamic Host Configuration Protocol (DHCP).

IP routing The process of forwarding a packet based on the destination IP address. Routing occurs at a sending TCP/IP host and at an IP router.

IPSec *See* Internet Protocol Security.

IRQ *See* interrupt request.

L

L2TP *See* Layer 2 Tunneling Protocol.

LAN *See* local area network.

Last Known Good Configuration A hardware configuration available by pressing F8 during startup. If the current hardware settings prevent the computer from starting, the Last Known Good Configuration enables you to start the computer and examine the configuration.

Layer 2 Tunneling Protocol (L2TP) An industry standard Internet tunneling protocol. Unlike Point-to-Point Tunneling Protocol (PPTP), L2TP does not require Internet Protocol (IP) connectivity between the client workstation and the server. L2TP requires only that the tunnel medium provide packet-oriented, point-to-point connectivity.

LGPO *See* Local Group Policy Object.

local area network (LAN) A communications network connecting a group of computers, printers, and other devices located within a relatively limited area (for example, a building). A LAN allows any connected device to interact with any other on the network. *See also* wide area network (WAN).

Local Group Policy Object (LGPO) A set of system configurations that exist on individual systems, regardless of whether that system participates in an Active Directory. Settings defined within an LGPO can be overridden by a policy defined at the level of the Active Directory.

M

Microsoft Management Console (MMC) A framework for hosting administrative tools, called consoles. A console might contain tools, folders or other containers, Web pages, and other administrative items.

Microsoft Systems Management Server *See* Systems Management Server.

Microsoft Windows Installer Service *See* Windows Installer Service.

mixed mode The default mode setting for domains on Windows 2000 domain controllers. Mixed mode allows Windows 2000 domain controllers and Windows NT backup domain controllers to coexist in a domain. Mixed mode does not support the universal and nested group enhancements of Windows 2000. You can change the domain mode setting to Windows 2000 native mode after all Windows NT domain controllers are either removed from the domain or upgraded to Windows 2000. *See also* native mode.

MMC   *See* Microsoft Management Console.

multimaster replication   A system of replication in which all replicas of a given directory partition are writable, allowing updates to be applied to any replica. Active Directory uses a multimaster replication system, and replicates the changes from a given replica to all other replicas automatically and transparently. *See also* replication.

N

name resolution   The process of translating a name into some object or information that the name represents.

NAT   *See* Network Address Translation.

native mode   The condition in which all domain controllers within a domain are Windows 2000 domain controllers and an administrator has enabled native mode operation (through Active Directory Users and Computers).

NetBIOS   *See* network basic input/output system.

NetBIOS over TCP/IP (NetBT)   A feature that provides the NetBIOS programming interface over TCP/IP. It is used for monitoring routed servers that use NetBIOS name resolution.

NetBT   *See* NetBIOS over TCP/IP.

Network Address Translation (NAT)   A protocol that allows a network with private addresses to access information on the Internet through an IP translation process. With NAT, you can configure a home network or small office network to share a single connection to the Internet.

network basic input/output system (NetBIOS)   An API that can be used by programs on a local area network (LAN). NetBIOS provides a uniform set of commands for requesting lower level network services. *See also* application programming interface (API); local area network (LAN).

Network News Transfer Protocol (NNTP)   A member of the TCP/IP suite of protocols, used to distribute network news messages to NNTP servers and clients, or newsreaders, on the Internet. *See also* protocol; Transmission Control Protocol/Internet Protocol (TCP/IP).

No Override   A Group Policy flag that prevents GPOs linked at a lower level of Active Directory from overriding a policy. *See also* Group Policy Object (GPO).

NT file system (NTFS)   An advanced file system that provides performance, security, reliability, and advanced features that are not found in any version of FAT. *See also* file allocation table (FAT); file allocation table-32 (FAT32).

NTFS   *See* NT file system.

O

object   An entity, such as a file, folder, shared folder, printer, or Active Directory object, described by a distinct, named set of attributes. *See also* attribute.

object class   The object class is the formal definition of a specific kind of object that can be stored in the directory. An object class is a distinct, named set of attributes that represents something concrete, such as a user, a printer, or an application. The attributes hold data describing the thing that is identified by the directory object. Attributes of a user might include the user's first name, last name, and e-mail address.

Open Shortest Path First (OSPF)   A routing protocol used in medium-sized and large-sized networks. This protocol is more complex than RIP, but it allows better control and is more efficient in propagating routing information. *See also* Routing Information Protocol (RIP).

organizational unit (OU) An Active Directory container object used within domains. An OU is a logical container into which users, groups, computers, and other OUs are placed. *See also* Active Directory; Group Policy Object (GPO).

OSPF *See* Open Shortest Path First.

OU *See* organizational unit.

P

parallel installation A method of troubleshooting a computer by installing a second copy of the operating system into a different folder or partition. This enables you to select either installation at startup.

partition A portion of a physical disk that functions as though it were a physically separate disk. After you create a partition, you must format it and assign it a drive letter before you can store data on it. *See also* basic disk; basic volume; dynamic volume.

Performance Logs and Alerts A component of the Windows 2000 Performance tool that enables you to configure logs to record performance data and set system alerts to notify you when a specified counter value is above or below a defined threshold.

Performance tool A Windows 2000 utility for monitoring network performance that can display statistics, such as the number of packets sent and received, server-processor utilization, and the amount of data going into and out of the server.

permission A rule associated with an object to regulate which users can gain access to the object and in what manner. Permissions are granted or denied by the object's owner. *See also* object; privilege; user rights.

Plug and Play (PnP) A set of specifications developed by Intel that allows a computer to automatically detect and configure a device and install the appropriate device drivers.

PnP *See* Plug and Play.

Point-to-Point Tunneling Protocol (PPTP) Networking technology that supports multiprotocol VPNs, enabling remote users to access corporate networks securely across the Internet or other networks by dialing into an Internet service provider (ISP) or by connecting directly to the Internet. *See also* virtual private network (VPN).

PPTP *See* Point-to-Point Tunneling Protocol.

privilege A user's right to perform a specific task, usually one that affects an entire computer system rather than a particular object. Privileges are assigned by administrators to individual users or groups of users as part of the security settings for the computer. *See also* permission; user rights.

protocol A set of rules and conventions for sending information over a network. These rules govern the content, format, timing, sequencing, and error control of messages exchanged among network devices.

published application An application that is available to users managed by a Group Policy Object (GPO). Each user decides whether to install the published application by using Add/Remove Programs in Control Panel. *See also* assigned application.

R

Recovery Console A command-line interface that provides a limited set of administrative commands that are useful for repairing a computer.

remote access policy A set of conditions and connection parameters that define the characteristics of the incoming connection and the set of constraints imposed on it. Remote access policies determine whether a specific connection attempt is authorized to be accepted.

remote access server A Windows 2000 Server–based computer running the Routing and Remote Access service and configured to provide remote access.

Remote Access Service (RAS) Part of the Routing and Remote Access service, RAS provides dialup and VPN connectivity to clients and other servers.

remote administration mode A Terminal Services mode that allows remote administrative connections to a computer. This mode installs only the remote access components of Terminal Services rather than the higher overhead application sharing components found in application server mode. *See also* application server mode; Terminal Services.

replication The process of copying data from a data store or file system to multiple computers that store the same data for the purpose of synchronizing the data. In Windows 2000, replication of the directory service occurs through Active Directory replication.

replication topology In Active Directory replication, the set of connections that domain controllers use to replicate information among themselves, both within sites and between sites. The site topology is defined by site link objects. The connection topology is defined by connection objects.

reverse lookup A query in which the IP address is used to determine the DNS name for the computer. *See also* forward lookup.

RIP *See* Routing Information Protocol.

router A network device that helps LANs and WANs achieve interoperability and connectivity and that can link LANs that have different network topologies. Hardware routers are dedicated devices that provide IP routing, while software routers are generally a component of an operating system. *See also* IP routing.

Routing and Remote Access The feature in Windows 2000 that provides multiprotocol routing, dial-up remote access, and VPN remote access. *See also* virtual private network (VPN).

Routing Information Protocol (RIP) An industry standard distance vector routing protocol used in small- to medium-sized IP and Internetwork Packet Exchange (IPX) internetworks.

S

Safe Mode A method of starting Windows using basic files and drivers only. Safe Mode is available by pressing the F8 key when prompted during startup.

SAM *See* Security Accounts Manager.

SECEDIT.EXE A command-line tool that performs many of the same operations as the Security Configuration and Analysis snap-in. SECEDIT.EXE also provides some capabilities that are not available in the graphical user interface, such as performing a batch analysis. *See also* Security Configuration and Analysis.

Secure Sockets Layer (SSL) An open standard for establishing a secure communications channel to prevent the interception of critical information, such as credit card numbers. *See also* Hypertext Transfer Protocol Secure (HTTPS).

Security Accounts Manager (SAM) A protected subsystem that manages user and group account information. In Windows 2000, workstation security accounts are stored by SAM in the local computer registry, and domain controller security accounts are stored in Active Directory.

Security Configuration and Analysis An MMC snap-in for analyzing and configuring local system security.

security principal An account-holder, such as a user, computer, or service. Each security principal within a Windows 2000 domain is identified by a unique security ID (SID). When a security principal logs on to a computer running Windows 2000, the Local Security Authority (LSA) authenticates the security principal's account name and password.

security template A set of security settings that are applied to a GPO in Active Directory or a local computer. *See also* Group Policy Object (GPO).

Security Templates snap-in An MMC snap-in used for viewing, defining, or modifying security templates. *See also* Microsoft Management Console (MMC); security templates.

service pack A software upgrade to an existing software distribution that contains updated files consisting of enhancements and hotfixes. *See also* hotfix.

Simple Mail Transport Protocol (SMTP) A member of the TCP/IP suite of protocols that governs the exchange of electronic mail between message transfer agents. *See also* protocol; Transmission Control Protocol/Internet Protocol (TCP/IP).

simple volume A dynamic volume made up of disk space from a single dynamic disk. A simple volume can consist of a single region on a disk or multiple regions of the same disk that are linked together. *See also* dynamic disk; dynamic volume; spanned volume; volume.

slipstreaming The process of creating a distribution share of the Windows 2000 operating system files and applying a service pack.

small office/home office (SOHO) An office with a few computers that can be considered a small business or part of a larger network.

SMS *See* Systems Management Server.

SMTP *See* Simple Mail Transport Protocol.

SOHO *See* small office/home office.

spanned volume A dynamic volume consisting of disk space on more than one physical disk. *See also* dynamic disk; dynamic volume; striped volume; volume.

SSL *See* Secure Sockets Layer.

Startup and Recovery A Windows 2000 troubleshooting and configuration tool used for computers with dual boot configurations to indicate the default startup operating system. Also configures the actions the computer performs if the system stops unexpectedly because of a severe error.

striped volume A dynamic volume that stores data in stripes on two or more physical disks. Data in a striped volume is allocated alternately and evenly (in stripes) across the disks. *See also* dynamic disk; dynamic volume; spanned volume; volume.

System Monitor A tool that supports detailed monitoring of the use of operating system resources. System Monitor is hosted, along with Performance Logs and Alerts, in the Performance console. *See also* Performance tool.

Systems Management Server (SMS) A Microsoft product for centrally deploying and managing software in an organization.

T

Task Manager A Windows utility that offers an immediate overview of operating system activity and performance.

TCP/IP *See* Transmission Control Protocol/Internet Protocol.

template accounts A user account that is created with settings, such as group membership, that are common for many users. When a new user must be created with these common settings, this user is copied. *See also* user account.

Terminal Services A Windows 2000 service that enables all client application execution, data processing, and data storage to occur on the server. Terminal Services provides remote access to a server desktop through terminal emulation software.

Transmission Control Protocol/Internet Protocol (TCP/IP) A set of networking protocols widely used on the Internet that provides communications across interconnected networks of computers with diverse hardware architectures and various operating systems. *See also* Internet Protocol (IP); protocol.

U

UDF *See* Universal Disk Format.

UNC *See* Universal Naming Convention.

Uniform Resource Locator (URL) An address that uniquely identifies a location on the Internet.

Universal Disk Format (UDF) A file system defined by the Optical Storage Technology Association (OSTA) that is the successor to the CD-ROM File System (CDFS). UDF is targeted for removable disk media like DVD, CD-ROM, and magneto optical (MO) discs.

Universal Naming Convention (UNC) A convention for naming files and other resources beginning with two backslashes (\), indicating that the resource exists on a network computer. UNC names conform to the \\SERVERNAME\SHARENAME syntax, where SERVERNAME is the server's name and SHARENAME is the name of the shared resource.

URL *See* Uniform Resource Locator.

user account A record that consists of all the information that defines a user to Windows 2000. This includes the user name and password required for the user to log on, the groups in which the user account has membership, and the rights and permissions the user has for using the computer and network and accessing their resources. *See also* Active Directory Users and Computers; group account.

user object *See* user account.

user rights Tasks a user is permitted to perform on a computer system or domain. There are two types of user rights: privileges and logon rights. Both types are assigned by administrators to individual users or groups as part of the security settings for the computer. *See also* permission; privilege.

V

virtual directory A directory name, used in an address, which corresponds to a physical directory on a server running IIS. *See also* Internet Information Services (IIS).

virtual private network (VPN) The extension of a private network that encompasses encapsulated, encrypted, and authenticated links across shared or public networks. VPN connections can provide remote access and routed connections to private networks over the Internet.

virtual server In a server cluster, a set of resources, including a Network Name resource and an IP address resource, that is contained by a resource group. In a Web server environment, a virtual server is a single computer that hosts multiple Web sites appearing as multiple servers.

volume An area of storage on a hard disk. A volume is formatted by using a file system, such as FAT or NTFS, and has a drive letter assigned to it. *See also* file allocation table (FAT); NT file system (NTFS); simple volume; spanned volume; striped volume.

VPN *See* virtual private network.

W

WAN *See* wide area network.

wide area network (WAN) A communications network connecting geographically separated computers, printers, and other devices. A WAN allows any connected device to interact with any other on the network. *See also* local area network (LAN).

Windows Installer Service A service that allows the operating system to manage the installation process. Windows Installer uses the information contained within a package file to install the application.

Windows Internet Name Service (WINS) A software service that dynamically maps IP addresses to computer names (NetBIOS names). This allows users to access resources by name instead of requiring them to use IP addresses that are difficult to recognize and remember. WINS servers support clients running Windows NT 4 and earlier versions of Microsoft operating systems. *See also* Domain Name System (DNS); IP address; network basic input/output system (NetBIOS).

Windows Update A Microsoft-owned Web site from which Windows users can install or update device drivers. By using an ActiveX control, Windows Update compares the available drivers with those on the user's system and offers to install new or updated versions.

WINS *See* Windows Internet Name Service.

Index

A

B

C

U

V

W

Z

Wood Angle Square

Angle squares are used to align or test right angles in woodworking and other activities. Squares consist of two arms that are at right angles, or 90°, to each other. Miter squares have 45° angles. A combination square is shaped so that it can check both inside and outside 90° and 45° angles; it usually includes a small bubble level for quickly checking level and plumb positions as well. Bevels or bevel protractors are used to measure other angles; in these devices, the angle of the square is adjustable.*

At Microsoft Press, we use tools to illustrate our books for software developers and IT professionals. Tools are an elegant symbol of human inventiveness and a powerful metaphor for how people can extend their capabilities, precision, and reach. From basic calipers and pliers to digital micrometers and lasers, our stylized illustrations of tools give each book a visual identity and each book series a personality. With tools and knowledge, there are no limits to creativity and innovation. Our tag line says it all: *The tools you need to put technology to work.*

*__Microsoft® Encarta® Reference Library 2002__. © 1993–2001 Microsoft Corporation. All rights reserved.

The manuscript for this book was prepared and galleyed using Microsoft Word 2000. Pages were composed by nSight, Inc., using Adobe FrameMaker+SGML 6.0, with text in Times Roman and display type in Helvetica. Composed pages were delivered to the printer as electronic prepress files.

Cover Designer: Methodologie, Inc.

nSight, Inc.
Project Manager: Kristen Ford
Technical Editor: Thomas Keegan
Manuscript Editor: Bernadette Murphy Bentley
Desktop Publisher: Donald Cowan
Indexer: Rebecca Plunkett
Proofreaders: Renee Cote, Jacqueline Fearer, Rebecca Merz

MCSE Training Kits
Learn by doing. Learn for the job.

Master the skills tested by the Microsoft Certified Systems Engineer (MCSE) exams—and, more critically, by the job—with official MCSE TRAINING KITS. These book-and-CD self-study kits take you inside Microsoft technologies, teaching you everything you need to know to plan, deploy, and support business-critical systems. Best of all, you drive the instruction—working through the lessons and skill-building exercises on your own time, at your own pace. It's learning you can really put to work!

MCSE Training Kit: Microsoft® Windows® 2000 Core Requirements
ISBN 0-7356-1130-0
Four kits in one!

MCSE Training Kit: Microsoft Windows 2000 Server
ISBN 1-57231-903-8

MCSE Training Kit: Microsoft Windows 2000 Professional
ISBN 1-57231-901-1

MCSE Training Kit: Microsoft Windows 2000 Network Infrastructure Administration
ISBN 1-57231-904-6

MCSE Training Kit: Microsoft Windows 2000 Active Directory™ Services
ISBN 0-7356-0999-3

MCSE Training Kit: Microsoft Windows 2000 Accelerated
ISBN 0-7356-1249-8

MCSE Training Kit: Designing Microsoft Windows 2000 Network Security
ISBN 0-7356-1134-3

MCSE Training Kit: Designing a Microsoft Windows 2000 Network Infrastructure
ISBN 0-7356-1133-5

MCSE Training Kit: Designing a Microsoft Windows 2000 Directory Services Infrastructure
ISBN 0-7356-1132-7

MCSE Training Kit: Microsoft Exchange 2000 Server Implementation and Administration
ISBN 0-7356-1028-2

MCSE Training Kit: Microsoft SQL Server™ 2000 System Administration
ISBN 0-7356-1247-1

MCSE Training Kit: Microsoft SQL Server 2000 Database Design and Implementation
ISBN 0-7356-1248-X

Core Requirements Kit:		**All Others:**
U.S.A.	$199.99	U.S.A. $59.99
Canada	$289.99	Canada $86.99 or $92.99

(see **mspress.microsoft.com/certification** *for details)*

Accelerated Kit:
U.S.A. $89.99
Canada $129.99

Learn
the latest development
tools and technologies
step by step
at your own pace !

Teach yourself how to use the latest development tools and technologies with the Microsoft Press® STEP BY STEP programming series of books. Choose your own best starting point with these self-paced guides to learn what you need to know, when you need to know it. Easy-to-follow lessons with real-world scenarios and examples show you exactly how to maximize the power of programming languages such as Microsoft Visual Basic .NET, Visual C# .NET, Visual C++ .NET and technologies such as ADO.NET, ASP.NET, XML, and OOP. Numerous screenshots and CD-ROMs full of practice files help you master programming procedures the fast, easy way.

MICROSOFT LICENSE AGREEMENT

Book Companion CD

IMPORTANT—READ CAREFULLY: This Microsoft End-User License Agreement ("EULA") is a legal agreement between you (either an individual or an entity) and Microsoft Corporation for the Microsoft product identified above, which includes computer software and may include associated media, printed materials, and "online" or electronic documentation ("SOFTWARE PRODUCT"). Any component included within the SOFTWARE PRODUCT that is accompanied by a separate End-User License Agreement shall be governed by such agreement and not the terms set forth below. By installing, copying, or otherwise using the SOFTWARE PRODUCT, you agree to be bound by the terms of this EULA. If you do not agree to the terms of this EULA, you are not authorized to install, copy, or otherwise use the SOFTWARE PRODUCT; you may, however, return the SOFTWARE PRODUCT, along with all printed materials and other items that form a part of the Microsoft product that includes the SOFTWARE PRODUCT, to the place you obtained them for a full refund.

SOFTWARE PRODUCT LICENSE

The SOFTWARE PRODUCT is protected by United States copyright laws and international copyright treaties, as well as other intellectual property laws and treaties. The SOFTWARE PRODUCT is licensed, not sold.

1. **GRANT OF LICENSE.** This EULA grants you the following rights:

   a. **Software Product.** You may install and use one copy of the SOFTWARE PRODUCT on a single computer. The primary user of the computer on which the SOFTWARE PRODUCT is installed may make a second copy for his or her exclusive use on a portable computer.

   b. **Storage/Network Use.** You may also store or install a copy of the SOFTWARE PRODUCT on a storage device, such as a network server, used only to install or run the SOFTWARE PRODUCT on your other computers over an internal network; however, you must acquire and dedicate a license for each separate computer on which the SOFTWARE PRODUCT is installed or run from the storage device. A license for the SOFTWARE PRODUCT may not be shared or used concurrently on different computers.

   c. **License Pak.** If you have acquired this EULA in a Microsoft License Pak, you may make the number of additional copies of the computer software portion of the SOFTWARE PRODUCT authorized on the printed copy of this EULA, and you may use each copy in the manner specified above. You are also entitled to make a corresponding number of secondary copies for portable computer use as specified above.

   d. **Sample Code.** Solely with respect to portions, if any, of the SOFTWARE PRODUCT that are identified within the SOFTWARE PRODUCT as sample code (the "SAMPLE CODE"):

      i. **Use and Modification.** Microsoft grants you the right to use and modify the source code version of the SAMPLE CODE, *provided* you comply with subsection (d)(iii) below. You may not distribute the SAMPLE CODE, or any modified version of the SAMPLE CODE, in source code form.

      ii. **Redistributable Files.** Provided you comply with subsection (d)(iii) below, Microsoft grants you a nonexclusive, royalty-free right to reproduce and distribute the object code version of the SAMPLE CODE and of any modified SAMPLE CODE, other than SAMPLE CODE, or any modified version thereof, designated as not redistributable in the Readme file that forms a part of the SOFTWARE PRODUCT (the "Non-Redistributable Sample Code"). All SAMPLE CODE other than the Non-Redistributable Sample Code is collectively referred to as the "REDISTRIBUTABLES."

      iii. **Redistribution Requirements.** If you redistribute the REDISTRIBUTABLES, you agree to: (i) distribute the REDISTRIBUTABLES in object code form only in conjunction with and as a part of your software application product; (ii) not use Microsoft's name, logo, or trademarks to market your software application product; (iii) include a valid copyright notice on your software application product; (iv) indemnify, hold harmless, and defend Microsoft from and against any claims or lawsuits, including attorney's fees, that arise or result from the use or distribution of your software application product; and (v) not permit further distribution of the REDISTRIBUTABLES by your end user. Contact Microsoft for the applicable royalties due and other licensing terms for all other uses and/or distribution of the REDISTRIBUTABLES.

2. **DESCRIPTION OF OTHER RIGHTS AND LIMITATIONS.**

   - **Limitations on Reverse Engineering, Decompilation, and Disassembly.** You may not reverse engineer, decompile, or disassemble the SOFTWARE PRODUCT, except and only to the extent that such activity is expressly permitted by applicable law notwithstanding this limitation.

   - **Separation of Components.** The SOFTWARE PRODUCT is licensed as a single product. Its component parts may not be separated for use on more than one computer.

   - **Rental.** You may not rent, lease, or lend the SOFTWARE PRODUCT.

- **Support Services.** Microsoft may, but is not obligated to, provide you with support services related to the SOFTWARE PRODUCT ("Support Services"). Use of Support Services is governed by the Microsoft policies and programs described in the user manual, in "online" documentation, and/or in other Microsoft-provided materials. Any supplemental software code provided to you as part of the Support Services shall be considered part of the SOFTWARE PRODUCT and subject to the terms and conditions of this EULA. With respect to technical information you provide to Microsoft as part of the Support Services, Microsoft may use such information for its business purposes, including for product support and development. Microsoft will not utilize such technical information in a form that personally identifies you.

- **Software Transfer.** You may permanently transfer all of your rights under this EULA, provided you retain no copies, you transfer all of the SOFTWARE PRODUCT (including all component parts, the media and printed materials, any upgrades, this EULA, and, if applicable, the Certificate of Authenticity), **and** the recipient agrees to the terms of this EULA.

- **Termination.** Without prejudice to any other rights, Microsoft may terminate this EULA if you fail to comply with the terms and conditions of this EULA. In such event, you must destroy all copies of the SOFTWARE PRODUCT and all of its component parts.

3. **COPYRIGHT.** All title and copyrights in and to the SOFTWARE PRODUCT (including but not limited to any images, photographs, animations, video, audio, music, text, SAMPLE CODE, REDISTRIBUTABLES, and "applets" incorporated into the SOFTWARE PRODUCT) and any copies of the SOFTWARE PRODUCT are owned by Microsoft or its suppliers. The SOFT-WARE PRODUCT is protected by copyright laws and international treaty provisions. Therefore, you must treat the SOFTWARE PRODUCT like any other copyrighted material **except** that you may install the SOFTWARE PRODUCT on a single computer provided you keep the original solely for backup or archival purposes. You may not copy the printed materials accompanying the SOFTWARE PRODUCT.

4. **U.S. GOVERNMENT RESTRICTED RIGHTS.** The SOFTWARE PRODUCT and documentation are provided with RESTRICTED RIGHTS. Use, duplication, or disclosure by the Government is subject to restrictions as set forth in subparagraph (c)(1)(ii) of the Rights in Technical Data and Computer Software clause at DFARS 252.227-7013 or subparagraphs (c)(1) and (2) of the Commercial Computer Software—Restricted Rights at 48 CFR 52.227-19, as applicable. Manufacturer is Microsoft Corporation/One Microsoft Way/Redmond, WA 98052-6399.

5. **EXPORT RESTRICTIONS.** You agree that you will not export or re-export the SOFTWARE PRODUCT, any part thereof, or any process or service that is the direct product of the SOFTWARE PRODUCT (the foregoing collectively referred to as the "Restricted Components"), to any country, person, entity, or end user subject to U.S. export restrictions. You specifically agree not to export or re-export any of the Restricted Components (i) to any country to which the U.S. has embargoed or restricted the export of goods or services, which currently include, but are not necessarily limited to, Cuba, Iran, Iraq, Libya, North Korea, Sudan, and Syria, or to any national of any such country, wherever located, who intends to transmit or transport the Restricted Components back to such country; (ii) to any end user who you know or have reason to know will utilize the Restricted Components in the design, development, or production of nuclear, chemical, or biological weapons; or (iii) to any end user who has been prohibited from participating in U.S. export transactions by any federal agency of the U.S. government. You warrant and represent that neither the BXA nor any other U.S. federal agency has suspended, revoked, or denied your export privileges.

DISCLAIMER OF WARRANTY

NO WARRANTIES OR CONDITIONS. MICROSOFT EXPRESSLY DISCLAIMS ANY WARRANTY OR CONDITION FOR THE SOFTWARE PRODUCT. THE SOFTWARE PRODUCT AND ANY RELATED DOCUMENTATION ARE PROVIDED "AS IS" WITHOUT WARRANTY OR CONDITION OF ANY KIND, EITHER EXPRESS OR IMPLIED, INCLUDING, WITHOUT LIMITA-TION, THE IMPLIED WARRANTIES OF MERCHANTABILITY, FITNESS FOR A PARTICULAR PURPOSE, OR NONINFRINGEMENT. THE ENTIRE RISK ARISING OUT OF USE OR PERFORMANCE OF THE SOFTWARE PRODUCT REMAINS WITH YOU.

LIMITATION OF LIABILITY. TO THE MAXIMUM EXTENT PERMITTED BY APPLICABLE LAW, IN NO EVENT SHALL MICROSOFT OR ITS SUPPLIERS BE LIABLE FOR ANY SPECIAL, INCIDENTAL, INDIRECT, OR CONSEQUENTIAL DAM-AGES WHATSOEVER (INCLUDING, WITHOUT LIMITATION, DAMAGES FOR LOSS OF BUSINESS PROFITS, BUSINESS INTERRUPTION, LOSS OF BUSINESS INFORMATION, OR ANY OTHER PECUNIARY LOSS) ARISING OUT OF THE USE OF OR INABILITY TO USE THE SOFTWARE PRODUCT OR THE PROVISION OF OR FAILURE TO PROVIDE SUPPORT SERVICES, EVEN IF MICROSOFT HAS BEEN ADVISED OF THE POSSIBILITY OF SUCH DAMAGES. IN ANY CASE, MICROSOFT'S ENTIRE LIABILITY UNDER ANY PROVISION OF THIS EULA SHALL BE LIMITED TO THE GREATER OF THE AMOUNT ACTUALLY PAID BY YOU FOR THE SOFTWARE PRODUCT OR US$5.00; PROVIDED, HOWEVER, IF YOU HAVE ENTERED INTO A MICROSOFT SUPPORT SERVICES AGREEMENT, MICROSOFT'S ENTIRE LIABILITY REGARDING SUPPORT SERVICES SHALL BE GOVERNED BY THE TERMS OF THAT AGREEMENT. BECAUSE SOME STATES AND JURISDICTIONS DO NOT ALLOW THE EXCLUSION OR LIMITATION OF LIABILITY, THE ABOVE LIMITATION MAY NOT APPLY TO YOU.

MISCELLANEOUS

This EULA is governed by the laws of the State of Washington USA, except and only to the extent that applicable law mandates governing law of a different jurisdiction.

Should you have any questions concerning this EULA, or if you desire to contact Microsoft for any reason, please contact the Microsoft subsidiary serving your country, or write: Microsoft Sales Information Center/One Microsoft Way/Redmond, WA 98052-6399.

- -

Proof of Purchase

Use this page as proof of purchase if participating in a promotion or rebate offer on
this title. Proof of purchase must be used in conjunction with other proof(s) of
payment such as your dated sales receipt—see offer details.

MCSA Managing a Microsoft® Windows® 2000 Network Environment Readiness Review; Exam 70-218

0-7356-1636-1

CUSTOMER NAME

Microsoft Press, PO Box 97017, Redmond, WA 98073-9830

System Requirements

To use the Readiness Review companion CD, you need a computer equipped with the following minimum configuration:

- Microsoft Windows 95 or Microsoft Windows NT 4 with Service Pack 3 or later, or Microsoft Windows 98, Microsoft Windows Me, Microsoft Windows 2000, or Microsoft Windows XP

  - Multimedia PC with a 75-MHz Pentium or higher processor

  - 16 MB RAM for Windows 95 or Windows 98, or

  - 32 MB RAM for Windows Me or Windows NT, or

  - 64 MB RAM for Windows 2000 or Windows XP

  - Super VGA display with at least 256 colors

  - Microsoft Mouse or compatible pointing device and keyboard

- Microsoft Internet Explorer 5.01 or higher (additional 13 MB minimum of hard disk space to install Internet Explorer 6.0 from this CD-ROM)

- 17 MB of available hard drive space for installation

- A double-speed CD-ROM drive or better